A Natural History of Legal Argument

A Natural History of Legal Argument

Etiology, Elements, and Effects

Geordie Duckler

BLOOMSBURY ACADEMIC
NEW YORK • LONDON • OXFORD • NEW DELHI • SYDNEY

BLOOMSBURY ACADEMIC
Bloomsbury Publishing Inc, 1359 Broadway, 12th Floor, New York, NY 10018, USA
Bloomsbury Publishing Plc, 50 Bedford Square, London, WC1B 3DP, UK
Bloomsbury Publishing Ireland, 29 Earlsfort Terrace, Dublin 2, D02 AY28, Ireland

First published in the United States of America 2026

Cover image: Hollyer, Samuel, Engraver, and W. H Beard. *"Flaw in the title" / painted by William H. Beard; engraved by Samuel Hollyer*, ca. 1871. New York: Published by Louis R. Menger, 22 Dey Street. Photograph. https://www.loc.gov/item/2004669643/.

Library of Congress Cataloging-in-Publication Data
Names: Duckler, Geordie, 1959- author
Title: A natural history of legal argument : etiology, elements, and effects / Geordie Duckler.
Description: New York : Bloomsbury Publishing, Inc, 2026. |
Includes bibliographical references and index.
Identifiers: LCCN 2025032992 (print) | LCCN 2025032993 (ebook) | ISBN 9781666954111 hardback | ISBN 9781666954135 paperback | ISBN 9781978748866 | ISBN 9798765192917 pdf | ISBN 9798765192924 epub
Subjects: LCSH: Forensic orations —History | Law —Methodology | Law —Philosophy | Semantics (Law)
Classification: LCC K213 .D833 2026 (print) | LCC K213 (ebook) | DDC 347/.075 —dc23/eng/20250728
LC record available at https://lccn.loc.gov/2025032992
LC ebook record available at https://lccn.loc.gov/2025032993

ISBN: HB: 9781666954111
ePDF: 9798765192917
eBook: 9798765192924

Typeset by Deanta Global Publishing Services, Chennai, India

Contents

Introduction

This is a book about Lawyers and their Arguments, and the capitals placed on both words are deliberate. It is not a book about "lawyers" in that word's lowercase and technical dress, such as those works reciting stories about, and offering descriptions and criticisms on, the universe of people who practice law, those O.G. "influencers" who tangle with, tangle others within, and are themselves tangled up by, webs and webs of rules. Biographical and historical works on lawyers as people tend to tack toward the personal and anecdotal "war story" along a path which I wish to steer clear of. Neither is it a book about "arguments" in that word's lowercase and derogatory sense, such as those litanies of emotion-drenched, cried-and-shouted, exchanges of anger and entreaty overheard in classroom, bedroom, and boardroom, those all-too-often intractable bickerings, snide retorts, and proclamations of adamant certitude which all people (regardless of their occupation or marital relationship) universally tend to tangle and wrap themselves up in as well.

My selected twin topics of Lawyers and Arguments in turn naturally imply that their intersection is going to be all about the law, but the Law analyzed in this book is also presented with a large "L." My design is to skirt the nitpicking outlines and lists proffered to educate others about what is allowed or disallowed as to rules of lawful conduct and legal responsibility. Faithful to its goal of eschewing the lowercase, this is not one of those practical works on the "tips and tricks" of advocacy by which legal practitioners might learn to use and abuse legal rules, or a recitation of the various lawyerly techniques by which such people engage in such pursuits.[1]

My attention is distanced from the "who" and the "how" and aims instead for the "why." I seek to offer the reader a front row seat in a real-world courtroom to ponder something larger of interest than "just lawyers," "just arguments," or "just law," in the more pedestrian and utilitarian respects noted above. I want instead to analyze and talk about *why* all those concepts exist as concepts in conjunction at all, to try and expose the beating heart of *why* it is that unusual people in an unusual setting have been talking in such an unusual way for so long—and what their doing so means at the most fundamental of levels.

I aim to identify how such behavior is at one and the same time (a) *specifically directed* by individuals in personal campaigns as they march toward achieving goals of self-interest and client-interest (yet ones distinct from simply "winning" a case or developing a better technical repertoire), and (b) *is an activity that embodies no organization or direction whatsoever* by large social groups which have no "goals" at all, yet whose combined efforts end up constructing what we recognize as Law as a result.

Yes, the participants are "lawyers" and yes, the various sounds heard emanating from their throats certainly reflect the act of people "arguing the law," but it is far more than, far less about, and floats light years away from, the heat, discomfort, and narrowness of a spat, a public yelling match which just happens to be laced with specific references to specific legal principles and authorities. What abstract forces pressure the participants in such a unique environment to have to express themselves so oddly, and yet what spacious license they are given to be so unusually personal, peculiar, natural, and artificial all at one and the same time as they do so, will comprise three of the four key themes I wish to explore in this book.

As Lawyers and Arguments and Law embrace the first three themes, then my fourth theme involves a quite particular *topic* of discussion for such people so engaged, and that is the topic of Animals—those multitudes of furred, feathered, and scaled products of evolution by natural selection which we find underfoot, overhead, by our sides, and surrounding us at every turn. In that sense, this is an exploration about Law and Argument and Animals conducted from the vantage point of an Attorney, specifically a lawyer who has had a hand in helming the relatively nascent specialty field of animal law. Close to four decades of engaging exclusively in an animal law practice have led to my handling over 3,000 animal law cases in over thirty states in which whatever the cognizable dispute has been, it has arisen from, or had at its source the presence of, some animal—from secreted raccoon to secretive ratite, from infected camel to inventive cat. From the vantage point of being a trial lawyer over that period, including in having stood in front of more than 100 jury panels, I have come to notice a delicate confluence of the Animal, the Lawyer, the Law, and the Argument at the trials held in those cases, the significance of which appears to me to deserve a deep explanation, at least one deeper than is being presently offered by the war story or case study.

The quartet of themes—the looping together of Lawyers, Argument, Law, and Animals—is redolent to me of the lawyer's catchphrase "on all fours." "On all fours" is a peculiar boast which many lawyers will front to a judge in claiming that the facts and law of a case citation are—miraculously!—identical to the facts and law in the very case at hand.[2] The layperson should know straight off that, as a likelihood, the chance that two unrelated cases are truly "on all fours," that is, that the operative events and rules in an officially published appellate opinion are the *exact* same events subject to the *exact* same rules as those in one's own pending lawsuit, is pretty much nonexistent in the real world. The phrase, in essence, is simply a handy fiction, an industry-unique exaggeration leveraged for dramatic effect. Nevertheless, lawyers—being inveterate exaggerators by trade—are not shy about invoking the phrase to try to attain the large reward for its acceptance: winning the pending point. Were two cases to in fact *be* on all fours, the doctrine of legal precedent then strongly favors (if not outright mandates) application of the cited proposition as nearly inescapable legal authority which the fact finder in the case at hand must then be pressed to dutifully apply to grant the movant their motion or petition.

I unholster the phrase throughout this work because not only do I have all four topics to intertwine and not only is the pun apt given that most of the animals in animal law cases are tetrapods,[3] but mostly because it readily matches the fourth and remaining theme in this book: the creative correlation of facts with which one is stuck in the mundane world with the creative construction of scenarios which one is allowed to propose in an imagined world. If they do nothing else, there is no question that lawyers create, lawyers construct, lawyers imagine, lawyers hypothesize, and lawyers propose—and of special note is that they do all those things most frequently with two special goals in mind, both of which involve correlation.

As to those peculiar goals, the first is to propose to a group of strangers that there is an important conceptual relation between two seemingly distinct spheres of common experience, that is, that one pattern in the world is "on all fours" with another pattern, and that accepting the relation which the lawyer describes will provide a valuable insight to the listener by virtue of the correspondence being demonstrated. The second goal is to manipulate the strangers' minds toward subconsciously utilizing the projected links (via a form of actual "mind control" which science fiction authors can only wistfully dream about) to cast a vote and then write down the result of that vote on a piece of paper.

Specifically, with this goal the "on all fours" alignment offered aims to surreptitiously massage the listener's mind into justifying their act of selecting how to vote and choosing what box to mark on a form. The first goal involves stories. The second goal involves control. The lawyer needs both stories and methods of control in order to obtain that vote and mark, to earn a decision favorable to the lawyer's client.

Stories and control are the basic elements of many games. The special game being played by the lawyer here has serious social effects and financial consequences for all involved, lawyer, client, and stranger alike. It is a game of mental conduct taking place in an almost exclusively verbal realm. The constituent gameboard and gamepiece elements are in the form of expressions, words, and phrases; at times, the players may be confronted with rather fantastic arrangements of linguistic novelties, including complex configurations fashioned to appear simple, as well as basic ones erected to appear sophisticated. The most outlandish aspect of this peculiar game's process is that the "on all fours" offering relies on constructs and utterances which have hefty restrictions attached to their construction and utterance, restrictions far more substantial than those imposed on any architectural drawing or building code.

The verbal structures which get built, and the restrictive scaffolding used to brace those structures, are what enable the participating concepts around the margins to be placed on all fours. Yet none of this is that foreign to the human experience in general. Visually and verbally aligning disparate concepts with each other is a basic human activity, a type of creative endeavor engaged in by everyone from birth on. Children do it to render the unfamiliar familiar. Adults do it to render the insignificant significant. Matching unique things to see if they might "fit" with other unique things is an evolutionary adaptation essential to all organisms piloting around the perils and promises of complex environments.[4]

Thus, we are entirely unsurprised that animals can be (literally) "on all fours," that facts from reported opinions and facts in active cases can be (figuratively) "on all fours" with each other, and thus that a lawyer's speech acts and arguments may be (conceptually) "on all fours" with the salient issues in a dispute as well. Familiarity with forming alignments in numerous aspects of social life lead the way to us recognizing how they work in law specifically. In a sense, the lawyer's two goals are not that foreign at all from basic goals all of us seek to attain outside of law.

Posed from a trial lawyer's perspective, this work is the culmination of my wish to explain those goals in greater detail, to set down some thoughts on the creative alignments made possible for correlating stories, control, animals, cases, and arguments in the complicated ways that I have seen those elements tangle and disentangle across the years, across the bar, and across the bench. I believe that their inventive joining in law, the type of gameplaying I have done for thirty-eight years, is a direct function of the activity of "manipulation," and a discrete goal of this work is to divest that word of its pejorative connotations when used in law and about lawyers and their special goals.

To that end, I have arranged this book into four sections, each delving into the origin, art, tasks, and goals of manipulation by the trial lawyer as they argue to juries in their trials. Like any worker in any field, all lawyers rely on tools to achieve objectives; the tools I address and use here happen to be the peculiar mesh of words which trial lawyers' brains employ, and the objectives sighted upon happen to be the peculiar outcome of those tools' exertion. Like many authors, my writing style is referential to my topic; thus, the reader is advised that as each section examines some correlation, the explanation is likely to be infested with metaphors.

For instance, if we want to grasp what is meant by the "goals of manipulation," we might imagine the words which a trial lawyer's brain might select, the order in which those words might be arranged, and the oratory format chosen for their offering, to mimic a form of archery, to form a rash of arrows aimed at trying to strike distant marks called "judgments," and as those marks have been planted by others at uncertain locations and as the field has relatively undefined borders, so we consider that shooting style must be highly creative and the arrows themselves must be uniquely wiggly and evasive enough to best the strange challenge which "an arrow hitting the target" in this scene poses.

Certainly, the correlation may not be tight: in this somewhat awkward metaphor the archer is apparently the lawyer, but there is considerable uncertainty about what the quiver, bow, and arrows themselves "are": perhaps they are thoughts, spoken words, legal writings, mental decisions, formal arguments, or some untidy combination thereof. Yet the overall imagery ostensibly assists, not hampers, the recipient as they ponder how to resolve an unfamiliar intellectual problem. In a sense, metaphors offer stories to listeners to help them understand foreign concepts. Metaphors also impose control on listeners and help authors channel the range and timing of that understanding. Lawyers, being social agents driven hard by the need to use stories and the need to control listeners, are therefore of course going to use metaphors to the best effect they can.

My chapters also consider the specific *recipients* of words' utterances—clients, judges, the public, and juries—in hoping to glean the importance of exactly how and when those words get delivered. Each chapter additionally takes into account the structural and conceptual impediments around which the words must careen as they fly like arrows to pierce the judgment target. In my argument about what Argument altogether is, I hope to earn the reader's appreciation for the astonishing effectiveness and plasticity (lexical as well as moral) with which a trial lawyer's specific speech acts in the form of carefully aimed arrows can have, must have, as a massive community of lawyer-archers frenetically notch, point, and release their missiles toward an ever-shifting arena of moving targets.

Chapter 1 discusses the trial lawyer's manipulation of *language* in order to advance the client's personal interests in getting to those judgments. The power of locution and elocution have an important place in the employment of a participant's power in numerous walks of life and is of particular significance in a field such as litigation where not just words overall, not just a single phrase, but even *the specific manner of enunciation of a single word*, can potentially be dispositive to an important and likely intractable result.[5]

Chapter 2 discusses the trial lawyer's manipulation of *people* in order to advance the client's personal interests in getting to the ultimate award. Its emotionally disparaging implications aside, the phenomenon of manipulation has historically had value as a very necessary human activity; one of those places it has both express and tacit social approval is where a systemic or institutional directive enables it to operate to benefit the participants overall. Law, and especially that subset of legal practice involving jury trials, has taken pains to set down intricate rules by which some citizens, in their role as trial lawyers, are given leeway to interfere and impinge on the impressions and decision of other citizens in formalized social settings such as courtrooms. Those directives are to be recognized and appreciated as a form of permissible and even necessary manipulation and are characterized specifically in the form of oral argument about the facts and law presented in civil and criminal court cases, and particularly those that involve trial by jury.

Chapter 3 discusses the trial lawyer's manipulation of *objects* in order to advance the client's personal interests and this chapter focuses tightly on animals as the objects of interest. The objectification of animals has its own philosophical justifications[6] and a system such as law which incorporates hosts of rules regulating animal behavior is a system that also sanctions using them as conduits to get people to act or cease from acting in certain important respects. The conceptual border between a "leash law" commanding that a dog be physically restrained, and a "rule of evidence" commanding that a decisionmaker cannot be told about the physical restraint of a dog, is on a metaphysically thin dividing line—and its fragility and import is addressed in this penultimate section.

Finally, Chapter 4 grapples with where all that manipulation tends to lead society to, and it does so through the exercise of a metaphor adopted from cell biology. Scientific knowledge is not just a wealth of data and propositions about the observable universe, but is also a wealth of conceptual mechanisms engineered for developing the act of learning itself—as the epistemology of science is just as valuable as its methodology, so I have sought to harvest the scientific concept of how cells operate, grow, and evolve to proffer to the reader as a model for how argument operates, grows, and evolves into Argument. As with all metaphors, disjunction and separation between the compared processes can be glaring at places, but I am hopeful that detailing it nevertheless garners some insight for the reader into the "point" of argument as they mull over what the "point" of cell evolution might happen to be.

This book is dedicated, as my first book was, to my beautiful and charming wife Lori who sadly never read the first one and who may choose to similarly pass on contemplating the ideas this work offers, but, to paraphrase Joseph Heller in "Catch-22," I am never without misery and never without hope.

Notes

1 See, e.g., Morrow, David R., and Anthony Weston. *A workbook for arguments: A complete course in critical thinking*. Hackett Publishing, 2019.
2 See, e.g., In Matter of Abu-Ali, 73489, 1998 WL 827592, at 5 (Ohio Ct App Nov 25, 1998) (distinguishing a previous opinion from being "on-all-fours" with the instant opinion on the somewhat finicky basis that "a karate chop to the throat is less intrusive than a punch in the stomach").
3 Well, apart from the nicely dressed bipedal simians on the book's cover.
4 See, e.g., Sherratt, Thomas N. "The optimal sampling strategy for unfamiliar prey." *Evolution* 65, no. 7 (2011): 2014–25.
5 See generally, Williams, Glanville. "Language and the Law-I." *Law Quarterly Review* 61 (1945): 71.
6 Duckler, Geordie. *Juris zoology: A dissection of animals as legal objects*. Rowman & Littlefield, 2022.

1

The Manipulation of Language to Advance Personal Interests

In which a bestiary of trial lawyers' elocutionary acts (the stylized delivery of their utterances) and illocutionary acts (the communicative effects of their utterances once delivered) is set forth in detail, a descriptive compendium of strange "play behaviors" engaged in by such lawyers, behaviors which are hopefully made explainable (or less strange anyway) by appreciating (a) the myriad sets of demands imposed on the lawyers which hem them within behaviorally restrictive cages, and (b) the myriad opportunities given the lawyers while confined inside such cages to at least get to fool around with all sorts of linguistic playthings pliable enough to use to promote their clients' causes (along with their own) and to have those causes eventually championed by a judge or jury.

Style in Law

The practice of law includes the expression of style, but that expression is notoriously ineffable.[1] Certainly, in literary and cinematic renditions a lawyer's style is often presented as being synonymous merely with their physical presentation.[2] That idea, though facile, is not completely wrongheaded: an observation about the "style" which a lawyer places on display to others is, unremarkably, knotted within a tangled ball of outward visually noteworthy characteristics about the lawyer as a person, including intimate details of their face, hair, dress, conversational tone, general attitude in public and private, and their specific way of speaking or writing. As in other vocations, in law external traits certainly may correlate with internal ones, including by overriding them. Plenty of billboards and television ads confirm that the aspect of an attractive face, for instance, will be frequently viewed as favorable enough by audiences to excuse flaws in the message which that face happens to be delivering, while books on tape and college lecture halls remind us that transmission of an attractive message may still suffer reception poorly when conveyed with a tic or via an irritating nasal drone. Appearance and presentation do not correlate *exactly*, of course, and appalling or mundane as the participant themselves may be the content may still pass through perfectly fine to the receiver. Nevertheless, wild or tame, the combination of the external and internal effects at least press together in some appreciable fashion to generate individualized emotional responses in each observer in turn.[3] And, of course, there is nothing peculiar about law alone that has observers consider and adjudge outward appearances and perceived personalities to reflect that the related expressions do or do not have value—attentive students of human conduct have been engaging in that assessment shortcut for millennia:

> In the apprehension of the savage and the barbarian the limits of his person do not coincide with the limits which modern biological science would recognize. His individuality is conceived to cover, somewhat vaguely and uncertainly, a pretty wide fringe of facts and objects that pertain to him more or less immediately. To our sense of the matter these items lie outside the limits of his person, and to many of them we would conceive him to stand in an economic rather than in an organic relation. This quasi-personal fringe of facts and objects commonly comprises the man's shadow; the reflection of his image in water or any similar surface; his name; his peculiar tattoo marks; his totem, if he has one; his glance; his breath, especially when it is visible; the print of his hand and foot; the sound of his voice; any image or representation of his person; any excretions or exhalations from his person; parings of his nails; cuttings of his hair; his ornaments and amulets; clothing that is in daily use, especially what has been shaped to his person, and more particularly if there is wrought into it any totemic or other design peculiar to him; his weapons, especially his favorite weapons and those which he habitually carries. Beyond these there is a great number of other, remoter things which may or may not be included in the quasi-personal fringe.[4]

Be it coarse, savage, and barbarian, or be it refined, enlightened, and erudite, an individual lawyer's "style" in attending to the law is nevertheless something deeper even than just the aggregate of sense data about the person's own physical and verbal presentations of legal topics, that is, how their insistences and proclamations work with or against their clothing accessories and hairdos. Outside of the law, the phrase "I guess that's just their style" is mostly excusing type language, the tacit acknowledgment that someone has subbed in an external affect for what could be better expressed or replaced by a more solid facet of their internal character. "Style" is amorphous enough to cloud, as well as clear, perceptions of who one is or what one is trying to express.[5] In summoning forth the specter of a trial lawyer's style in argument, I want to tamp down the disdain in that type of phraseology and appreciate its insight instead.

When we think about lawyers engaging in their profession, a set of good questions to ask include "Why *is* that their style?" and "Why *that* style instead of another?" and "Why is the style they have chosen even significant to others interacting with them?" In raising those types of questions, I will be imploring the reader to consider the value imbued in the selective process itself, to counter the frivolity of "it's *just* style" with the gravity of "it's *that* style," and specifically in the context of litigation practices; to fold thoughts about what trial lawyers are and what their jobs entail into how a peculiar presentation style may be key to not just those jobs being well executed and effective, but to Law itself trudging forward in time as a social force.

Surely, adopting styles of speech and dress and conduct is goal-oriented behavior engaged in by individuals which can disclose some intensely personal choices they make during their private lives and public workdays. When lawyers in particular make such choices, however, it is an activity that is intimately bound to *what they are required to do in order to pursue law*, which for trial lawyers is argue to strangers in order to convince them to make certain decisions about other strangers. In contrast to management-style, or salesperson-style, or doctor-style, as we ponder lawyer-style, an appreciation can be developed that visual and aural appearance in presentation is not merely a façade awkwardly tracking or masking the core individuality of the presenter, but is instead a mandate, an institutional requirement of the highest order. In law, style doesn't just *tip* to substance, style *is* substance. I get it that such a claim sounds facile and distasteful at first blush, but a few analogies will help us with that appreciation along the way, including some discrete proposals that superficial aspects of phenomena in some areas of inquiry often closely match, that is, possibly are "on all fours with," material aspects of the same phenomena. For example, I will note later on in this work some parallels of this idea in certain scientific disciplines; every paleontologist is familiar with the notion that what is being observed in the specimen's phenotype aren't just mere scratches in the surface of what is likely a far richer genotype hidden below but are integral ingredients reflective of the genotype itself.[6]

Additionally, trial lawyer style is unique in part because of who the recipients of their messages are and because of what the messages themselves distinctly consist of. The recipients are unusual groups of people termed "fact finders," and execution of their core purpose is dependent on their assessment of the unique manner in which the trial lawyer publicly "presents" themselves. In trial circumstances in particular, that assessment is welded to a peculiar consideration of elocution, particularly how the trial lawyer *delivers argument*.[7] That brings up the topic of the superficiality and materiality of their unique messages, and the connections between the former and latter. Really, "presentation through argument" is the level at which we as a society even start to become interested in lawyers as generic social constructs at all. Just as we assess personality more fundamentally in acknowledging that an actor, politician, or salesperson's beautiful hair, fine facial features, melodic voice, and/or impeccable apparel may be the superficial overlays to radically more telling components of their real person, so too our assessments of lawyers *qua* lawyers is made valuable only when we come to recognize that they need to use their unique and purportedly superficial tool, argument, to effectuate their core and purportedly material purposes of advocacy and counsel and interest protection.

It sorely misjudges the full role of "Lawyer" to place emphasis primarily on how they are people who merely talk for others in a specialized language; their true "lawyerly" acts are at a level well above the linguistic and grammatical, at a level beyond even just the creative *use* of language and grammar—their acts critically include the illocutionary variety as well, that is, the performances and directions intimately associated with making the utterances.[8] Think, for a moment, of what distinctions can be drawn between one who *states* to another "you will get off the steps," *requests* that "you will get off the steps," *orders* that "you will get off the steps," and *questions* if "you will get off the steps." Clearly more is at stake than simply that the same phrase is being articulated in each instance; the *import* of the phrase is a function of what other words are used before and after it, what peculiar tone and demeanor may attend it, what body language effects accompany it, in short, what style is imbued in both selecting it and then vocalizing it.[9] All that is the lawyer's illocution. As Professor James Boyd White put it, law is an art "carried on in a language of art."[10]

While a rote definition of a lawyer embraces the dry concept of one who is a licensed professional entrusted with the task of advising and representing others in legal matters, without violating that concept we can start to incorporate the cognizance of style as a foundational element and better redefine a trial lawyer to be "an illocutionary device manufactured by social forces to enable one individual from a group to persuade the balance of the group to accept a theory about the world so that the group can then impose commands on the rest of the world based on their acceptance of the theory." In that reconstruction, the group is in the form of juries, the theory is in the form of legal argument about a case, and the commands are in the form of judgments. The basic roles of professional advising, counseling, and generally representing are not disserved in such a definition, they are just reoriented to give sense to why status distinctions among citizens allow a community to use both specialized individuals and small groups to better regulate large group conduct.

While we will explore the categories and sources of "laws" in far more detail below, with that definition of "lawyer" at hand as something far more than "spokesperson" alone, we can consider "law" in turn to be the particular set of empirically discoverable resources made available by a specific culture to be used by those necessary illocutionary devices in order to do their persuading and thus to regulate the larger scale social conduct. Unwieldy, certainly, but at least that definition of laws refocuses attention from simply being dull as dishwater words running down a printed page as propounded by an even duller local legislative body (e.g., the "leash law" being a numbered code section requiring dog owners to physically restrain their dogs) to being large group understandings, technical and nontechnical, exploring all the ways we have found valuable as a self-governing community to be able to convince ourselves in our different roles to adhere to and impart value to critically important social compacts.

To function, self-governing societies require cohesion.[11] It is self-explanatory that cohering into a group is a project which will fail if the group doesn't mutually put work into then staying together. Among the bonds that keep self-governing groups connected are bonds formed through members convincing other members of the benefits of cohesion, and one key benefit is that the group enjoys some sort of workable system of dispute resolution so that members don't destroy each other or disintegrate into separate antagonistic cohorts.[12] Self-governing social groups simply cannot survive without developing effective judicial subsystems, and those systems are by necessity and definition ones requiring and relying upon self-persuasion.

To be truly effective, the self-persuasion must be in the most compelling form available, and for American social structure that form has a complexity and sophistication all its own which borrows heavily from theater. As the device delivering the persuasive power of the working theory of dispute resolution to the group, the lawyer is thus recast as an actor on a stage in the form of one who announces to their audience propositions made on behalf of another who happens to be sitting behind or near the stage but who is not actually at its center. The announcements are designed to advance the other's position in a personal dispute but those cohesive forces make it so that there is more at stake in the dynamic than simply personal interests alone.

This is a process that has been transpiring over generations of dispute resolvers, and repetition is inevitable. Just as there have been innumerable individual "cases" over our nation's history, so too there have been innumerable individual theories floated by individual devices, that is, actors, about those cases,[13] but, unsurprisingly, those theories tend to repeat given that the operable facts of many, many civil and criminal cases tend to eventually be recurrences of each other over time. Our self-persuasion has a long history in which, as the conduct to be regulated recurs over and over with each affected cohort in dispute, so too does the encapsulation of those disputes.

The reason that any layperson inherently knows, without the need for an academic explication of particular names, dates, and places, what a "car crash" case is, what a "slip and fall" case is, or what an "eviction" case is, arises out of shared core components stemming from that history. Disputed events which require resolution transcend the niceties of individual's names and incident dates. The happenstance of two vehicles colliding after a driver's thoughtless behavior behind the wheel, of a person banging their hip after unknowingly stepping onto a slick substance inside some business establishment, of an apartment building's resident and the building's owner posturing at odds with each other over utility payments, all these are regular features and byproducts of long-standing and necessary social interactions that fueled the need for law in the first place.

As one then envisions those scenarios, in addition to images of drivers and shoppers and residents, correlative images of lawyers and courtrooms inevitably pop up as well. It isn't hard to see that the core aspects of what the lawyers are saying in those environments must follow their own duplicate routes each time the event arises and in spite of the particularities to be discerned about the current participants. An agent of the group's self-persuasion efforts, the lawyer is simultaneously both confined and liberated by the recurring events of the past in finding and then interpreting laws which likely dictate a group-acceptable disposition of those events at present and into the future.

In our newly minted vision of lawyers as socially necessary dispute resolution devices intrinsic to self-governing systems, we can also appreciate that not only must their operation be housed in conceptual enclosures designed exclusively for resolving the differences, courts and trials, but that successful resolutions require participation by a host of others in representative capacities as they act within those enclosures. There is simply no room for *everyone* to get involved in solving the conflict at hand, so the group must appoint surrogates to craft economical routes to good solutions. Judges are representatives, as are juries, referees, arbitrators, mediators, evaluators, and facilitators, but the most transparent of representative players in the resolution process are lawyers.

As a trial lawyer talks then, not one, but several people are in fact talking all at once. Trial lawyers can "present" themselves as if they were another person; they can present themselves as if they were a child, or a married couple, or a small neighborhood, or a business; they can present themselves as a very large group of people, including an entire political body or a category of class members spread across a wide swath of the entire country; or they can even present as the anonymous, an amorphous *thing* somehow possessing independent legal interests such as a particular sum of money which hasn't quite identified any specific entity, member, or group as even connected to it.[14] Yet in doing all of those things, trial lawyers of course facially remain one sole individual, an actual person engaged in the representation efforts. With that one person's words alone, the intimate identity of, the very existence of, individuals or groups are both masked and unmasked at one and the same time.[15]

In that sense, the expression of style for a trial lawyer is demanded to be a maelstrom of theatrical events swirling around the important acts of masking and unmasking: the donning of a carefully selected and socially approved disguise, the recitation of carefully selected and socially approved dialogue in service of that disguise, and the use of that disguise and of a cleverly written script to express a societally necessary manner of public influence to obtain favor.[16] The trial lawyer is themselves and yet not themselves since they are both the stand-in for others while physically and privately not being those actual others in any non-legal respect. Their style in advancing legal matters thus utilizes a curiously constructed cloak of fashion worn by an actor tasked with inducing and manipulating listeners to agree with them for the personal and social rewards sought by two others: the trial lawyer as the agent with their client as the principal. The use of veils and disguises—including that of sincerity—is integral to how that reward is sought for both themselves and for the masters whom they represent.[17]

Now if talking alone were the be-all and end-all of that masking and unmasking, then trial lawyers would be no more or less than any other actors strutting about on a stage, albeit ones whose costumes don't vary much in their ornament and where the backdrops are routinely the same uninspired sets of "scene: interior office building, mid-afternoon." We need to be careful to recognize that the manipulation at work is not just a mastery of using language to communicate; most evolutionary biologists note that all communication is a procedure by which one organism manipulates another's behavior and certainly that manner of manipulation is at play with lawyers no differently than with starlings or cuckoos.[18] Lawyering, especially in trial work, is much more than communicating and much more than acting and much more than speaking lines trying to communicate something to an audience. The key distinction we will come back to again and again in this work is that with lawyers in particular there is the *antithesis* of real communication occurring, that is, there is a constant and frantic *suppression* of information, and that the restrictions occur in large part because there is far more than one stage, one script, one audience, and one set of players in the mix.

With trials, there are stages hidden well behind the physical stage on which the lawyer presently poses and there are actors whom the audience never sees or hears yet whose voices have manufactured key portions of the scene at hand. Because a dispute which others have is getting resolved by society as a group, the play being put on is not the play that the audience is watching. In a metaphorical sense, the audience tasked with resolving the dispute is necessarily being fooled at a deep level as to what the actual information is that is supposed to be communicated to make a resolution occur. Trial lawyering is the overt in service of the covert, and it involves a universe of utterances, including outright deceptions, where style is not just an incidental mechanism by which alternatingly correct and incorrect information is delivered to another, but is a motivating force in and of itself, that is, a crucial basis to explain why any information is even being delivered to the other at all.

The Pride, Prejudice, and Predecessor of Style as a Tool of Persuasion

Tritely then: the trial lawyer persuades. To get to the genotype of capital "L" Lawyers, however, we need to appreciate that persuasion—as a function of legal style being expressed through alternative forms of legal argument—has a very distinctive pedigree. It is a direct descendant of the art of oratory which itself is a close relative of the art of human verbal expression in general.[19] Orators from Cicero forward, like trial lawyers, always plead their causes.[20] Orators, only tangentially like trial lawyers, frequently have an agenda while on task of *educating* as well as persuading; they mean to teach the listener some sort of lesson that the listener is presumed to be unaware of in either scope or significance.[21] And orators, like trial lawyers, cannot completely escape the past: as they formulate their talks they constantly find themselves bumping into predecessors and historically repeated themes with each newly initiated project. It is easily recognized that a speaker at a funeral, at a political rally, at a wedding reception, or at a charitable or memorial event, notes with a wry gulp that many others have been there long before them, armed with slightly different messages and hampered by slightly more engaged or more antagonistic audiences, but chained in part to the recurring themes and staid repetitions of those who have gone before nonetheless.

Many attempts have been made to display the full rainbow of available styles of expression both verbal for the orator and written for the author to do all those things under all those constrictions, and a real appreciation of the entire spectrum of choices is too large a project for this work.[22] In terms of the discrete plethora of styles available to anyone who wishes to argue from a premise to a conclusion in convincing another of the propriety of a local or universal theme, however, my first outrageous proposal (as an inveterate exaggerator myself) is that ideas from a few past authors may be "on all fours" with my thesis. To secure it, I will claim that one of my objectives is strictly informed by (and will acknowledge that this work owes a substantial intellectual and academic debt to) a specific "evolutionary lineage" of four overtly and covertly connected writings from the past.

The four ancestors begin (in reverse chronological order) with Philip Ording's 2019 book *99 Variations on a Proof*,[23] a mathematical fantasy in which a single algebraic equation is re-demonstrated by the author to be "true" via arguments through use of a fantastic hodge-podge of alternative arithmetic styles. Ording's work, interweaving the detailed techniques of math calculations with the broad strands of scientific creativity, is pure argument through and through. It posits that in between one premise and one conclusion a kaleidoscope of directions exist in getting from the former to the latter. Ording's "dispute" was about a mathematical equation, and his "resolution" of that dispute was to argue that acceptable proofs, solutions, to the equation could be located nearly anywhere and everywhere one bothered to look. His book is a superb illustration of how trial lawyers earn their audience's conviction through example. In turn, Ording clearly derived his many-world interpretive themes from at least two literary and philosophical predecessors a bit further down the historical line.

The first, a more indirect predecessor, was Ralph Gun Hoy Siu's 1971 *The Portable Dragon*,[24] a Westernized elucidation of the 3,000-year-old classic Chinese work, the *I Ching*. Siu offered a modern re-telling of the sixty-four different "human situations in which a person might find himself" via short historical and literary quotations followed by extensive commentary on the collective significance of each respective quotation. Siu lauded the *I Ching* as "a comprehensive description of human sentiments and motivations [and] a valuable synopsis for meditations on human relationships," and his (then) contemporary presentation of each universal situation embodied two goals.

One of Siu's goals was to encourage readers to glean life lessons from an admixture of numbered set pieces of abstraction and reality about how human minds and aspirations work in tandem and in conflict. A second goal was, as Ording's work also sought, to adjust the reader's mental behavior by convincing them to learn from what others had done before them—an eloquent demand in argumentative form that the reader alter their present-day conduct in light of what the past conduct of others had taught the author as a life lesson.

In a more literary fashion, Siu also convinced by example, but he was not alone in that effort. The second, more direct, predecessor to Ording was Raymond Queneau in his 1947 work *Exercises in Style*,[25] an essayist's inventive re-telling of an exceedingly abbreviated story about a man on a bus. Queneau's exploration of forms is a masterclass in the deformation of an ordinary source event into something extraordinary. Each one winding its way from a small premise to a small conclusion, all of his numbered retellings bent the contours of a mundane interaction between two people into a complicated scaffold of explanatory (and increasingly artificial and bizarre) literary techniques. Although it is hard to discern at first reading, all of his techniques are also essentially arguments reasoning to a conclusion; Queneau strived toward accomplishing a goal similar to Siu's in generally illustrating the more fascinating aspects of the human condition but did so in reverse from Siu's interpretations of the *I Ching*: rather than take numerous examples of different human experiences and condense them into a demand for universal truths, Queneau took a single humdrum transportation-related event and through creative literary devices exploded it into a broad form argument for the embracement of artistic individuality. Queneau would have been comfortably at home in a courtroom.

Ording, Siu, and Queneau's works, as creative as they are, nevertheless have their own derivative aspects, as all rhetoric does. It is hardly speculation to say that each had to have been influenced or informed at some basic level by Ralph Boas and Frank Smithie's 1938 prank academic article "A Contribution to Mathematical Theory of Big Game Hunting" (published by the pair under the punning pseudonym "H.W.O. Petard"),[26] the most eccentric "re-envisioning of the spectrum of human experience" of the lot. At heart, Boas and Smithie conducted a meandering application of various alternative math- and physics-based explanations on how to best accomplish the imagined task of capturing an imaginary lion.

In the same breath that Boas and Smithie's piece helps absolutely no one actually capture a lion[27], their article is of considerable help to those who wish not just to argue but to understand argument as a broad concept entangling reader and author together in a jointly created fantasy, and thus is a writing which is truly more "lawyerly" than most legal treatises. Each proposed version of the lion's capture is an arrow of discourse that two scientists have fashioned, notched, and then sent flying, all in order to convince a mostly academic audience that matters of scientific substance cannot be disconnected from matters of scientific style. The message at the marrow of Boas and Smithie's piece is that who the inquirer is, and what the inquirer does, materially affects what is being inquired upon. Every orator in general pines to be even half as innovative in such an effort and few trial lawyers achieve even half as sublime an effect.

Boas and Smithie's article's influence is inversely proportional to its length—its two short pages, though written in a gentle and humorous vein, was one of the first writings to explore the universal value of cross-disciplinary approaches to teasing out the explanatory power of human creativity.[28] It is in that sense a scholar's proposal, an analysis of the Renaissance-based idea that adherents to a certain philosophy need not be confined to their own disciplines in seeking useful results, that is, that hunters can be and often are scientists, that physicists can be and often are naturalists, and that the goals of one field of study can be and often are influenced and achieved by mechanisms employed in an entirely different field. Boas and Smithie's article is thus an engraved invitation to trial lawyers to be things other than trial lawyers in their efforts to capture big game.

And of course, although Boas and Smithie are clearly ancestral to their three descendants, the skeptic notes that even *their* concept did not spontaneously arise like Athena from Zeus' brow without its own predecessor germ line. The closest literary author who was (at least partially) precedential to all of the above would likely be James Joyce in his 1934 work *Ulysses* where, in Chapter 14, Joyce cavalierly narrated part of his tale via a progression of historically advancing styles, starting with early folk language, to Old and Middle English, to the King James Bible, to Shakespeare, to Dickens, and then finally to early twentieth-century Dublin slang.[29] We can draw our line of ancestors even farther past Joyce given that his excerpt really makes no effort to argue or convince down along a line of reasoning, but operates mostly to use style as a device alone and thus to entertain and nothing more. Those arguers and convincers who came before Joyce span the centuries, and generations of style-infused persuaders include a long stretch of dialogues, monologues, proclamations and remonstrations in which we can pick out even the distant strains of Socrates' and Aristotle's voices in the din.

As a blend of all those works enlisting "the argued expression of the value of substance through the lens of alternative styles," a lawyer's argument at trial is the culmination of a socially approved summons to use representative power to track or reform any or all words which have come before: the opening and closing statements which the trial lawyer makes to the jury embrace, not shy from, derivative aspects and the best ones deliberately conflate aspects of each predecessor's work in turn. Just as each numbered section of Ording's book (99 examples) and Queneau's book (12 examples) describe a diverse way in which either "legal" evidence from a mathematical proof or "factual" evidence from a narrative could be re-demonstrated as proof of a proposition, so too trial lawyer arguments frequently identify distinct frames by which the practitioner may re-demonstrate their version of a factual event as legally significant and as justification for a resulting outcome—and may use ancestral voices to do so.

Similarly, just as Siu illustrated sixty-four "situations" of human characteristics and relationships as a creative method by which personalities may be interpreted through their stylistic expression, so too trial lawyers as representatives are granted the liberty to conceive of diverse ways in which people and legal situations may correlate and overlap, ways to have messages transmitted and received between themselves and their audiences elucidating the human side of the dispute resolution process.[30] Shoehorning recognized packets of "human nature" into legally recognized categories in order to illustrate legal issues directed toward conflict resolution targets is a stylistic task assigned to all trial lawyers.

Finally, just as Boas and Smithie compressed the goal of lion taming within the as-loose-as-it-is-tight framework of twenty-one distinct, increasingly ridiculous but empirically justifiable "cages" of proof, lawyers too in trial arguments are granted substantial leeway to compress a goal of truth taming into the comparable confines of distinct jurisprudential "holding pens" of as-loose-as-they-are-tight evidentiary rules and requirements. While all trial lawyers are regularly restricted in their deliveries to the fact finder, acknowledging those restrictions is a boon, not a curse. Part of the sophistication of how persuasion works in self-regulated communities such as courtrooms is through the regulators pointing out their admiration and approval for their own bars and cages, how they are in fact truly *glad* for, not antagonistic to, the imprisonment, the existence of all those pesty, prohibitory chains and locks. Lion taming as an art comes in a variety of constructs; whips and cages are not always used, but when they are, the animals at both ends of the whip and both inside and outside of the cage have to *appreciate* the stings of restraint for the point of the project to really take hold.

The Vanquishing of Truth Using Authority

One commonality apparent to all the legal, literary, and scientific authors as they chew on the application of rules to others is a need to stick close to a core concern of law: what is "true" and what is not. The tripartite concepts of truth in disguise, relative truths, and evidentiary boundary lines between truths each lie at the heart of a trial lawyer manipulating language to reach a desired end. The most basic claim to know something requires at least stating some discrete fact and then being able to justify that it is indeed a fact:

> If I know that the Battle of Hastings occurred in 1066, that krypton is a colorless inert gas with an atomic number of 36 and atomic weight of 83.80, or that a

> snowstorm is raging in the immediate vicinity, then my knowledge is about these facts, entities, or events. The statement is what we usually designate as true or false depending on whether what it represents, the fact or state of affairs, is in accordance with this representation or not, while the fact or state of affairs is neither true nor false, but either is or is not the case. Thus, claiming to know something places on the individual a certain obligation to be able to articulate and justify what is being claimed, a type of knowledge that is usually referred to as sentential or propositional.[31]

One way to justify (and convince another to accept or recognize) that a piece of knowledge is a truth (or a truism at least) is by one's "appeal to authority"—a speaker claiming that what is said is a true proposition because some noteworthy historical, highly reputable, expert, and/or traditionally authoritative figure at one time also said it, that few since have effectively challenged it, and that the vast majority of recipients have accepted it.[32] The doctrines of judicial opinion precedent and of *stare decisis* owe a strong legal and intellectual debt to the principle of appeal to authority, and the weight of past precedents is one rooted in both logic and public policy;[33] it is the kind of weight which makes it supremely difficult to budge the professional listener (read, jurors and jurists) off their perch of having to accept some line of argument as genuine truth. Many listeners accept many speakers to be sincere in their utterances purely as a function of "well, that has always been so, and everyone of course knows it is so."

Progressive political slogans notwithstanding, law yields to stasis far more than it embraces change, so trial lawyers can frequently do well in beseeching the wisdom of predecessors as irrefutable commands. An appeal to precedent is in part employment of what might be called scare tactics; as Ording himself noted, "A proof by authority becomes a proof by intimidation."[34] In that equation, what is "scary" is the threat of change: as any evolutionary biologist will tell you, just about every organism's most cautious and conservative route for selecting future action is to default to actions that worked in the past, not to steer clear of them and try something brand new. Neither judges nor juries are exempt from acting out of a generalized fear of the novel.

The ever-present imprimatur of past authority thus helps as well as hampers trial lawyers. Which it is, help or hamper, becomes contingent on both who the authority is and on just how "past" is the proffered pronouncement. Was it one issued from a co-equal judge, a colleague right down the hall? Was it one from a court of last resort, or from a foreign jurisdiction? Was it by a decision made last month on a topical issue or by a decision made one hundred years ago on a classic problem? All those considerations affect appeals to authority. Selecting sources and arguing that those selected carry more authoritative weight than others is all in a day's work for the trial lawyer. To use authority to manipulate, especially where fear of the novel is omnipresent, requires being cagey with one's sources and being cryptic with one's references. As Ording and those who preceded him remind us, convincing others by various proofs includes harnessing creativity to simply create authority for some proof where none may have existed before.

One "enhancement" of (read, way to escape having to locate or embrace) a past authority is the practice of *layering* of purportedly authentic proofs within other proofs, in the trial lawyer's case this being often in the format of stories nestled within stories, an oratorial technique as old as Scheherazade herself and an excellent way for either an orator or author to massage their unique fiction into an argument for the audience's further acceptance of a set of already acceptable public "facts."[35] Layering can create hoary precedent out of nothing more than older yet similar sounding stories.

Consider, as a good literary example, Herman Melville's expert layering trick of persuasion in chapter 9 of his opus *Moby-Dick*.[36] There, Melville the orator executes one of the most intricate and subtle layers in all of literature as a ploy to persuade the reader that what they are presently reading must be a true recitation of crucial past events. At the very lowest layer, Jonah is merely telling a story to some sailors about himself. Above that, it is clear that Father Mapple is telling a story to a congregation about Jonah telling that story. Ishmael, the novel's narrator, perches above both in telling a story to Melville, the author, about Father Mapple telling his story. The last layer (or at least what seems like the last) is a recognition that Melville is telling a story to the reader of the book about Ishmael telling his story to Melville and the other layers gain an authority of having already been accepted down the line.[37]

As the reader of this work comes to realize that I am telling this story to them about Melville telling his story to his readers in order to convince this reader of my recitation's authenticity and authority, the reader is confronted with two choices: accept my rendering whole cloth and move on, or stop reading for a moment and go pick up a copy of *Moby-Dick* to independently check for themselves if what I have described is genuine. It is not laziness that makes most refrain from doing the latter, it is the very human trait of tending to be impressed with an author telling a listener that they are authoritative that does so. There is great creative argumentative power in a speaker nesting recited versions of truth within the confines of what seems like other recited versions of others' truths which have already been accepted by fiat. Questionable recitations of events can be made less questionable by pointing out how others have endorsed them in their initial or re-telling—an appeal to authority by association as opposed to directly attained knowledge or expertise.[38]

The Speaker's Manner and Mannerisms in Presenting

Buoyed by present innovation or weighted down by inescapable past authority, in the frothy realm between Melville and Ording lies an enormous ocean of arguers all employing language tricks to convince, a sparse few better, so many far worse. Nevertheless, quality aside, think for a moment about the awesome power any speaker has to use language and its paraphernalia to control the influences available over their audience. Tricks such as layering to reveal twice- and thrice-told truths are the mere surface of the depths of technique available. The oldest of the arts, the exercise of oratory, requires no special equipment other than fluency of speech and some degree of self-confidence in presenting in front of others. Nevertheless, readiness in speech, confidence, and a basic command of normal language skills alone is hardly going to sum up automatically to amount to *effective* argument, as most college students and job interviewees will attest. Like their once-removed cousins and close family relations, telemarketers and filmmakers, trial lawyers will readily acknowledge that the most effective oratory in particular is that which relies on the physical as well as on the conceptual.

One, the physical and postural stances which a speaker takes, and the body language with which their words are delivered in argument to an audience, undeniably have their own communicative content.[39] Positioning while talking runs the entire gamut from cold and distant (as often occurs with frightened trial lawyers shielding themselves behind a podium, lectern, or whiteboard), to intimate and intrusive (as can be suggested by those bold souls who noisily drag up the counsel table chair to plunk themselves down right beside the jury member at the very edge of the box), and all stops in between: aggressive and confrontational feet apart stances, or passive and contrite hands clasped behind one stances, distracting pacing and pocket fumbling movements, and impersonal and removed tossed-over-the-shoulder deliveries. Even freezing still and not moving at all is its own display of postural emphasis; as the philosopher Walter Ong puts it, "Spoken words are always modifications of a total, existential situation, which always engages the body. . . . In oral verbalization, particularly public verbalization, absolute motionlessness is itself a powerful gesture."[40]

Two, the tone of voice and inflections which the orator uses, along with personalized manners of pronunciation through which the words are delivered in an argument, can be and are content-laden.[41] Sounds alone—be they the soothing rhythms and stressed syllables of the motivational conference speaker or the sneering insult and exhorted breathlessness of the stand-up comic—are not merely affective in their express content but aurally convey an implied substantive message as well. As the indistinct murmurs of a theater crowd before the curtain rises portend, the majority of verbal sounds people make create patterns of oblique meaning even if individual words themselves cannot be distinguished at all, and listeners are attuned to draw some usable connotation out of all patterns and rhythms that are heard, whether it is discernible as language or not.[42] The content marches along or behind the sounds—and the actual words being used during the author's eventual reveal may thereby smoothly jive with or entirely disconnect from those aural impressions.

When compatible, sound and statement gain a heightened significance in combination, even if tonally improvisational and bombastic, as often happens with the stand up's chattering-enhanced monologue, or even if nuanced and flowery, as conveyed (more rarely) through the hypnotic ebb and hum of the romantic poet's moony lilt. In those cases, perhaps the argument works because the subsurface sounds have already worked. When incompatible, background sound and the disjointed statements trailing behind threaten to, and can easily, dissolve or destroy the intended communication, for instance as breathless claims of confidence are accompanied by the constant nervous shaking of a sheath of handheld papers. In those cases, perhaps the most carefully prepared argument fails simply as a result of one modest yet sufficiently annoying bit of interference emanating as a semantic signal beeping persistently from behind the speaker's overt message.

Lawyers ignore the semantic complexity of pure sound at their peril. Because even supposedly "neutral," that is, calmly stated matter-of-fact, enunciation conveys subliminal information, it is at their hazard that any speaker is oblivious to their own particular tonal delivery; the smallest of rising and falling aural patterns create dissonances in the listener sufficient to correspondingly raise and lower anticipation and expectation.[43] It is not mere happenstance that "silver-tongued" is more complimentary than back-handed given that social science research shows that listeners are more easily persuaded to act by a pleasant-sounding voice than by an unpleasant one.[44] Droning is concerningly off-putting, as are coughs, hoarseness, or uncomfortably lengthy pauses, all of which subconsciously suggest a speaker's ill health and a possibly corresponding positional weakness. The sound of a person's voice always provides *some* information about the person and often projects new data in isolation from or antagonistic to the message content which the voice hoped to convey. A steadily lowering and softening tone can make one appear concealing, disarming, or conspiratorial, while the subtly raised inflection at the end of a sentence or the rapid burst of a clenched fist-punctuated staccato delivery can suggest contempt, disrespect, or a boastful assurance. With appropriate cynicism, the trial lawyer comes to learn that compelling rhetoric is often a careful mix of a lot of superficially suggestive (yet content-empty) sounds combined lyrically with a few more deeply embedded (yet still content-empty) reasons:

> For in speaking the language of the law the lawyer must always be ready to try to change it: to add or to drop a distinction, to admit a new voice, to claim a new source of authority, and so on. One's performance is in this sense always argumentative, not only about the result one seeks to obtain but also about the version of the legal discourse that one uses – that one creates – in one's speech and writing. . . .The legal speaker always acts upon the language that he or she uses; in this sense legal rhetoric is always argumentatively constitutive of the language it employs.[45]

Three, of course, are then the specific words selected to be used by the orator in the substantive part of an argument's delivery. Available options span the cosmos of what words have to offer: among that universe's sparkling constellations sit word and sentence choices forming the vaguest of prepositional abstractions, the sharpest of colloquial references, the most calculated of rhetorical devices, the long stacks of intellectual sounding adjectives or short bursts of folksy sayings, the flaunting of pop culture jingles and sound bite recitations, the most derivative of sophomoric allusions, the most monosyllabic of basic noun and verb pairings, or the most downright straightforward or misleading of definitional phrases.

Combined with the pauses, facial expressions, and "unspoken words" carefully or carelessly hidden between and behind the actually spoken words in an argument, the overall effect of truly fastidious word choice can be the most impressive part of the persuasive effort. Influential power may span a range from being pandering and conciliatory, as in "you *must* acknowledge that . . . ," to pedantic and contrived, as in "I think that we all know what it means when . . . ," to hyperbolic, inflammatory, and overly dramatic, as in every (inexperienced) trial lawyer's "how dare they say that!" By its nature, it is hard to see *any* oratory as truly sincere, given how prepared and professorial it is as a form of normal human communication; to be compelling in the right sense means that a trial lawyer's argumentative oratory has to be word-sensitive to a fault in using the heaviest of pedagogical artifices to suggest that what is being heard is really just the lightest of natural human conversations.

Four, the order and arrangement of the parts of an argument itself have import. Political speechwriters are well aware that what type of organization an orator chooses their words to march in, that is, what sentence structure might precede or follow each sentence in turn and the tightness or looseness of a talk's organizational frame, imparts a message which enriches the words used in those sentences.[46] Arrangements during trials can often be demagogical, following a classically Socratic system where a flow of rhetorical questions are followed up by a matching flow of answers as if the speaker were interviewing and then educating themselves. Structures chosen can also be metaphorical and interpretative, as when the paragraphs continually divert off the topic at hand to discuss parallels and models of the chosen topic. Sentence arrangements may "build up" by starting with small points or illustrative minor truisms and then piling on larger and larger universals to a crescendo of proclamations of what must be "The Real Truth." Some speakers find persuasive value in the itchy cleverness of internally folded structures, talking back to themselves (or interrupting themselves) and then applauding or criticizing themselves for what they themselves just said a minute prior, a manner that can quickly become precarious should self-reference tumble into a form of "lip service" which no one is really listening to. A few of Quineau's and Ording's styles provide implicit warnings about the dangers of too involved self-reference.

When the speaker wishes to appeal to baser instincts through an argument, quantification in the form of the countdown is a powerful tool: sentences can be numbered and arranged in an imposing descending list of terrible horrors to start as merely suggestive, and then tramp toward the denunciating, mercenary, frightening, or outright insulting as far down as one dares to sink; the end is as definite as it is dreadful. When the speaker wishes to appeal to a higher conscience through an argument on the other hand, sentences can be arranged in a similar quasi-arithmetical fashion to advance up a limitless slope, to line up and then scale a quantified increase of marvelous wonders, assertions which start as rhetorical questions interspersed with comma-ridden dependent phrases, and which then raise in aspiration to be period-free, open-ended, run-on sentences where the allegorical, spiritual, enlightening, or celebratory verbiage of each subsequent statement eventually overpowers all structure entirely in an attempt to mimic the speaker's aspirations of the message being Boundless and Without End . . .

Five, the largest *themes* which the words in *toto* in an argument may all ultimately be directed toward can work to trigger socially inclusive, global feelings in the recipients. One method of theme engagement is where the speaker deliberately means the entire project to be all-inclusive, that is, those reactionary, political, or erudite speeches where from start to finish it is constantly all about "We the people" and "Our society" and "What everybody wants" as global proposals for the listener to join with a desirable and cohesive social unit. Alternatively, the speaker may arrange the thematic framework to be *exclusive*, that is, those talks focused narrowly about "that man sitting right there" or "Smith" or "Jones" acting alone as if no one else and nothing else in the world has mattered or should matter.

When either of those types of structures work well in argument, the ultimate message becomes founded on an underlying taxonomy in which the listener grasps their own peculiar place as one that makes categorical sense in light of a dynamic which includes them, the subject, and the speaker as joint venturers. At trial, a large theme that hits home garners the grand prize of the genuine head nod, that supremely desirable gesture which a juror may make (if sincerity can be discerned at all) indicating that they have at last accepted the straightforward and economic message of "*this* is what happened" or "*this* is what it all means." If a message has earned their personal conviction, it is because they have invested their own personality in a foreign outcome, have placed themselves personally inside of a strange tale about strangers being told by another stranger.

Ofttimes, it seems somewhat self-apparent that the speaker who is the more self-effacing, topically relevant, humorous, and gently encouraging one in the room is the one ultimately most beneficially received by their audience. Similarly, it can seem self-apparent that the speech which is laced most tightly with the most rational of data points and leads to the most rational of conclusions is the one that has its message ultimately adopted as well. In both instances, it feels like logical consistency in reasoning, quickness in wit, and what has been called, archaically, "personal magnetism," that is, that mystical command some have over the sentiments of others, all should have their presence and their positive impacts.

While the idealist nods sagely at these seemingly obvious conclusions, the trial lawyer as an experienced cynic shakes their head: audiences, they note, must be tailored to a complex suite of personalized goals, and not just to superficially appealing presentations alone. Even when arguments go poorly, when the vacuous, awkward, jargonistic, dogmatic, pretentious, disconnected, frivolous, or baroque announcer of the message flails, or mumbles, or chooses an ill-suited theme, or steps in an improper direction along a poorly worked out path, still success can arise anyway as a function of personal goals which the audience already embraced long before the opening salvo even issued.

Yes, from odd sounds to poor word choice to ill-suited theme choice, what one emits in argument may well have the regrettable consequence of the speaker being simply ignorable and ignored at the conclusion. Do not forget, however, that in jury trials the speaker and recipients form a dynamic pairing, and there is input on both sides of the equation which is integral to the success of the overall project, that is, the favorable decision. Control is never just in the hands of the speaker alone, regardless of what the Hollywood scriptwriter or military commander may insist must be the clear case.

Rules, Rules, and More Rules

In acknowledging that dynamic, that mutualistic and opportunistic dialogue among nonequals, the trial lawyer must stay as focused as a laser on their objective, must employ all that language and all that style, layered or not, to its directed end. The trial lawyer has to manipulate their special language to convince and obtain that great prize, a decision or judgment in the client's favor (which, by the way, doesn't necessarily have to come by way of a verdict, although it often does). Favorable decisions, including as judgments, form the very point of why those in dispute are even litigants in the first place, to resolve in their favor and interest and against the favor and interest of a competitor. Apart from exceptional circumstances where a *pro se* manages to snag one themselves without professional assistance, the only real way for any party to get the favorable decision is through a lawyer's words alone.

Decisions are created by judges. At least in the American adversarial system, however, judges can't and don't independently issue decisions, orders, and judgments, simply because they personally feel that a dispute needs to be formally determined; they do so only because a lawyer speaking on behalf of a litigant has finally proposed one form of order or judgment to them to formally choose from and to then issue (or two or more lawyers have proposed competing versions of orders or judgment forms for the jurist to select from)—and this occurring only after a fight has both formally been started and then formally and finally been prepped for resolution.[47] Judgment and order issuance is a function of lawyer requests via lawyer arguments made pre- and mid- and post-trial, not of unfettered judicial power exercised in spite of or before any trial has occurred or any lawyer has spoken.[48]

To get to those prizes, uncountable problems with the trial lawyer's argument project, of course, abound: in the same instant that the power of rules is bestowed on them to use to argue with, the trial lawyer is then beset by those very same rules to also have to *limit* their argument as well. Restriction and restraint for the trial lawyer comes in the form of rules as written (legislative) and spoken (judicial) commandments to only say certain specific things and to not say other specific things, all at the risk of rebuke and sanction—yet "all statements that can possibly be imagined," not "a limited set of statements," are at the heart of what trial lawyers truly desire to explicate to the crowd. Rules frustrate that desire, a frustration which is a function of just how many rules there are; it is difficult to describe the sheer number and vast scope of all the rules which the trial lawyer must find, then interpret, then manage, then process, then adhere to, then cleverly wiggle out from under, and then even more cleverly parse or restate, as they engage in *all* their lawyerly tasks of representing and persuading, not simply just in their trial arguments alone.

The most basic rules are those which apply to all writers and speakers: the academic, semi-subjective, and only roughly standardized rules of grammar and syntax. Technically, these are impotent in that any lawyer at any level of law practice can ignore these rules outright since they form no law in the official sense of having socially mandated obligations and penalties which are publicly enforceable. Nonetheless, oratory admonishes that the trial lawyer disdains such rules at their hazard; most audiences may forgive a stumbled delivery or an inapt metaphor, but few will forget or absolve a plainly grammatically faulty sentence. Grammar and syntax can subtly signal intelligence and proficiency, and the persuasion of most audiences relies on their underlying acceptance that the speaker doesn't just know what topic they are talking about but also knows how to follow educational and community established linguistic protocols in the first place, whatever the topic may be.[49]

Next are the rules of professional responsibility and ethics with which all lawyers specifically are encumbered within their governmentally regulated vocation and profession. Professional responsibility rules don't directly impact trial argument in their application but certainly do indirectly in their violation—an advocate disclosing privileged matters, creating conflicts of interest by demanding relief on behalf of connected parties, or outright lying straight to the tribunal, all comprise seriously proscribed aspects of a trial lawyer's language, including to a jury.[50] The impact is tangential since language which treads on ethical boundaries and even language which implies or reveals ethical transgressions is not explicitly disallowed as language in argument—it can be employed. Yet the knowledge by both speaker and listener that the trial lawyer will likely be paying a disciplinary price later for doing so casts a heavy pall over its efficacy as argument and thus its untrammeled use to persuade.

Then come what are called "the local rules," those peculiar formats, forms, and regionally circumscribed practice guides arising out of proclamations made by the councils and boards of the particular provincial jurisdiction which the trial lawyer may be in front of on any given date. Local rules as enacted have a sideways effect on the practice of litigation: they don't so much require explanation for exactly what the practitioner is saying as much as they require adherence to forms, formats, and trivialities in order for the practitioner to be able to say it at all.

If there are "traps for the unwary" in litigation practice—and every trial lawyer as well as jurist will tell you that there certainly are[51]—then here is where most of the spikes are buried. Missing an innocuous-looking step quietly demanded by some local practice regulation requiring, say, that notice to the court be provided by date-stamped mailing of a printed form before 5:00 p.m. on the third Friday of the month before any argument will be received by the judge on the next Monday morning, is one of the more particularly vicious and unforgiving ones in that once sprung, the trap is nearly impossible to disengage. Freeing oneself from local rule snares is usually fruitless and imploring local (read, hometown) *largesse* is mostly of no avail.

Considerably more elaborate still are those thick rules adorning the heavy volumes which compose the city ordinances, county codes, administrative regulations, state and federal statutes, and state and federal constitutions (aka "codified law"), legislative writings which govern all areas of legal practice, from forum selection to the limitation of remedies to proclamations of basic rights and all stops in between. As with local rules, codified law manifests the benefit of being explicitly stated in print and the detriment of that print being ever-changing. Every legislative session serves up a revised version of what had been enacted the session before, and merely keeping track of each new iteration is itself a Sisyphean chore. Even in stasis, ordinances and statutes can be imposing pieces of formalized legal instruction, ones packed full of summaries, articles, preambles, sections, subsections, and subsubsections; ones peppered throughout with intricate definitions, exceptions, exemptions, and exclusions sufficient to concern a chess grandmaster; and ones worded so obtusely that a third and fourth reading of the text only tends to make the points raised *more*, not less, bewildering to the reader.

As the layperson hears the trial lawyer recite alphabetized subsection headings, numbered paragraphs, and arithmetical sounding phrases, they are hearing the clicks and clacks of a unique type of Morse code. The messages being transmitted are argumentatively necessary, to be sure, just not ones meant for *their* ears. Codified law is a species of authority typed out over telegraph wires strung exclusively between lawyers themselves. Codified law is a species of authority where the rapid keystrokes sound like incoherent noise only because the selected recipient is presumed to be so especially versed in law that they can privately translate the clattering sounds' true significance. Codified law is a Goldberg-esque communication contraption that defies lay intuitions about legal meaning, that decimates folk law beliefs about applicable rules, that expands the already broad information gap between lawyer and non-lawyer, and that shuttles data from courtroom to courtroom through a channel of words disguised as complex parenthetical outlines. Learning to talk in legislative code language to a colleague and to a judicial audience is mandated before one can really talk well in persuasion code language to the non-lawyer audience such as the jury.

Critically, *within* every set of state and federal statutes lies a vital section called the evidence code. That behemoth's predictably numbered sections rarely vary from jurisdiction to jurisdiction and—being based on a model code of evidentiary rules—limns the exact same topics of evidentiary allowance and disallowance in each and every courtroom across the country. One can know absolutely nothing about New Jersey state law for instance, yet nevertheless be quite secure in an educated guess that the New Jersey evidence code almost certainly prohibits hearsay, almost certainly lists numerous hearsay exceptions for when the declarant is, as well is not, available, and almost certainly parades more than a few additional exceptions to those exceptions.[52] The evidence code brooks no laxity and ultimately cares not in what state or county jurisdiction the trial lawyer happens to be standing: as long as one is in a courtroom anywhere, one better know the full list of those exceptions to the exceptions to hearsay when the declarant is unavailable. A steep price is paid for evidentiary noncompliance, adherence to local rules be damned, since whether a jury is even allowed to see an exhibit or listen to a witness is vitally dependent on evidentiary admissibility of the same.

If law practice was like going out for a drive, then for all the coasting, driving, steering, honking, parking, shifting, idling, and speeding the trial lawyer does in the back-and-forth of their exchanges with the judge on the bench, with the witnesses on the stand, and with the jury in the box, the evidence code is the premiere traffic light—and, the legal scholar warns, one that is far more often illuminated red (or at least changing to yellow briefly on its way to red), flashing green only once every other rule of the road has been religiously followed.

All the Law That's Fit to Print

And then there is that colossus called "case law," also known as reported law, judge-made law, or, most collectively, the common law. For any dispute among litigants, in any jurisdiction in any court, in which the judge handling the dispute makes a written ruling on the issues, and the ruling is then officially published in a case reporter, it is by that process that the body of case law initiates and then consequently swells by a respective fraction. In our traffic analogy above, case law is a feature of the vehicular landscape that creates nearly uncontrolled driver/pedestrian/traffic cop chaos: a relentlessly advancing-yet-reversing, confusingly parked, ever-turning-but-rarely-yielding fleet of transport vehicles clogging every arterial and intersection, each vehicle packed full of trial level and appellate level opinions and their accompanying dissents, and each then being recklessly launched into the already crowded roadway by unimpressed judicial clerks sitting at dispatch centers as overworked judges in loading docks fill bays with the resolution of others' legal queries, queries which themselves arrive (without let up, yet each demanding to be resolved) from individual cars driven and parked each day in front of them by lawyers, and ones which need to be constantly unloaded and moved so that others arriving can take their spot.[53]

These written opinions are a crucial form of rules and laws comprising not just books, but volumes, editions, series, bookshelves, whole libraries, and entire buildings creakily stuffed to the top floor full of tomes called reporters. Out of the reporters' pages spill the wit, wisdom, waste, and weariness of hundreds of thousands of jurists who have had to draft, edit, and publish a written decision in a contested matter by which they set down their rationales and explanations in a formally structured writing. The layperson knows but a miniscule smattering of these, at the most perhaps a few misquoted phrases from the tattered remnants of old colossi such as Roe v. Wade or Brown v. Board of Education. The trial lawyer, in contrast, has a head absolutely stuffed full of them—or better have anyway. Only that day's current docket, that judge's off-the-cuff query, signals the trial lawyer that another case cite better be yanked out of the memory store to be presented for consideration.

And situationally useful propositions from hastily recalled cases are not easy to employ even once they are accessed, since reported cases run a huge range as to informational content. Many judicial decisions are economically constructed short sentences or simple paragraphs and nothing more. Numerous others, however, bloat into quasi-novels or devolve into philosophical proclamations and diatribes on topics far beyond the singular dispute presented with the truly useful bits buried deep below in throwaway comments and footnotes.[54]

It is a small surprise to anyone to hear that judicial decisions in the form of reported cases are expressions of considerable power: they can dictate the amount and distribution of people's and communities' resources, and they can dictate the course and termination of people's and communities' very lives. Reported decisions can put a hard stop to one fight with a pen stroke or egg on another by calling out a litigant's artifice or absurdity.[55] Reported decisions can mimic the intensity of the participants or insert a sense of decorum, they can try to subsume emotions or inflame them, they can make sense and nonsense of individual people and of all society in the same breath.[56] Judges, aka "ordinary and imperfect people in robes," in issuing their rulings, orders, dissents, and judgments, and in thereby contributing to the latest published reporter, are at one and the same time the creators and the servants of dispute resolution rules no differently than the trial lawyers and the combating parties to whom their energy is pointedly directed.

Case in Point

The resulting printed out follies and masterpieces are not just for the participants to be bound by, but are for the public to be informed by and for the trial lawyers to be closely attentive to, given that the latter's entire profession is sharply inhibited by the ebb and flow of such law. Reporters themselves engender the art and practice of case citation, the complicated references trial lawyers must make to Jones v. Smith using volume, page, line, court, and date identifiers, and from which the doctrine of *stare decisis*, of legal and judicial precedent, arises.[57] Every trial lawyer's own currently litigated case may live or die due to the citation to, the miscitation of, the correct or incorrect application of, a precedential case from a case reporter—or due to the slight distinction of the same from their own. Whether the precedent is directly on all fours or is the faintest of allusions, it is citation, citation, citation, and citation that is the call which the trial lawyer must heed and yield to in providing authority for why a motion must be granted, an evidence rule applied, or a decision finally reached to the client's benefit *en route* to accessing that judgment.[58]

As trial lawyers ply their tools (including the law sucked out of the thousands of hopefully applicable cases in case reporters) to manipulate the people called jurors, their tools ply them, and those tools are crafted by those other people we have been referring to as judges. Judges decide, and by deciding, impose their control of the law simultaneously with that which the legislator levies. As language use drives trial lawyer actions, so too is it a defining force for judges: judges are the ultimate linguists *par excellence*, scholars of various levels of intelligence mostly agonizing over the parsing and dissection of words and phrases, the Louis Pasteurs of the legal laboratory squinting hard through the microscopes of dictionaries and macro lenses of legislative records to better pin down the wriggling organism in dispute as it is scrutinized under the glass.[59]

As their opinions are compiled in the case reporters, judges more than anyone else appreciate that confusingly arranged and oddly organized location from which each judge everywhere—the most timid municipal referee to the most volatile presiding justice of the largest appellate panel of heavyweights—can get their own personal say in, smart or dumb as each proclamation may be. And it is crucial to the final message of this book that the reader gleans that no overweening editor applauds the gems or removes the detritus; that no publisher exists to select to promote or forego that day's edition; that all judicial opinions are printed and disseminated as if all were and are equally noteworthy and valuable. While that last premise is highly unsupportable given what we know of the fallibility of people, judges and nonjudges alike, its existence is key to an important insight: the realization that the common law grows and grows inexorably.

The start and the finish of the common law's development and trajectory is "the case." Cases are disputes turned into words and their authors are lawyers. Judicial opinions in case reporters are resolutions of those cases and their authors are also lawyers. The targeted readership of reporters is more lawyers. The more lawyers, the more cases, and the more cases, the more opinions, and the more opinions, the more law for the more lawyers to get embroiled in. Nothing in such a system offers respite; we can thus add in to our road chaos metaphor above the crushing observation that not only do none of the vehicles involved apparently have working brakes but that none of the vehicles, be they classic cruisers or zippy sports cars, ever get taken off the road.

While case reporters are compiled by date, a calendar is literally zero help to the researching trial lawyer as to where to find the truly applicable opinion to their case, and a glance at the topics by which judicial opinions are purportedly "arranged" in reporters tips to the bizarre organizational schemes offered. Headnotes to them supposedly encapsulate specific propositions of law but those propositions bleed into or stray far afield from other supposedly like-minded propositions which may well even be placed under the very same headnote. Legal search engines and computer databases do what they can to differentiate sense from nonsense in those propositions and some categorizations make broad sense such as "Search and Seizure" and "Assault" while others, such as "Time" or "Sunday" can befuddle even the most astute researcher or practitioner. Older reported cases often have no headnotes at all and the newest reported cases may concoct far too many for what the few words of the opinion actually warrant.

A cladist or taxonomist examining the state and federal reporters would quickly abandon all hope of identifying the working elements of the "classification scheme" actually being employed by the publishers of case reporters, but luckily for the cladists they do not need to participate or weigh in on the agonizing prospect of locating the latest word on a legal topic or securing the residence of a precedential judgment. Finding the law is anything but, indeed the antithesis of, a scientific activity.

Without any editor, the case reporter comprises the bevy of both careful judicial thought as well as careless judicial thoughtlessness, and the fact that the valuable is mixed in thoroughly with the valueless means that the trial lawyer has extensive leeway in picking and choosing authority from their offerings to suit that moment's argumentative need. More is more for the trial lawyer scouring case law for support; with enough effort and enough opinions, every proposition can eventually be located—and distinguished. And these days, there is more than enough to work with: reported trial opinions started out as a small set of relatively slim, archaic, and provincial rulings back in the early 1600s, but their explosion over the ensuing 400 plus years has not just given strength to the trial lawyer needing material for that day's motion, it has extended an influence into every nook and cranny of social life sufficient to render many opinions into a form of literature as well. They have flourished into being the new great American novels; like their fictional counterparts, the ratio of benefit to detriment of what is offered inside of them is a proportion which oscillates with each new judge appointed and each new court session held.[60]

Again, it cannot be overemphasized that among the largest boons and burdens which the body of common law has created is that there is no reduction in its yawning growth—there are only *more* reported cases every day, not less. The miniscule culling that is conducted occurs when an opinion is reversed or modified but, one, that event is done by way of issuance of a *new* opinion so the body of work in general grows regardless, and, two, there is always certain to be some lawyer somewhere who still finds it useful or technically appropriate to cite to a portion of a reversed, distinguished, or modified decision anyway—perhaps as an illuminating cultural aside, or as confirmation of judicial mistakes overall, or even as the propping open of a small semi-closed window through which the next reversing or modifying opinion might wiggle with its revised alterations affecting the current body of law.

Statutes can at least be formally abrogated and lose all legal import; the common law is different, it inflates exponentially, and true abrogation as an entire body of authority is simply not an option. It is metaphysically fascinating that the common law cannot be curtailed even by itself—a proposition issued in a case which says "this proposition cannot be overruled" or that "the doctrine of *stare decisis* will no longer apply" are themselves appealable rulings for a review court to ponder and—via the doctrine of *stare decisis*—likely reverse and be published thereby.[61]

Supplement all that law with the most labyrinthine set of rules, the myriad hornbooks, treatises, *amicus* briefs, and law review articles published regularly commenting on each aspect of the above authorities, and one can appreciate the problem with a layperson cavalierly throwing about the word "law" in either its lowercase or capitalized version as "a thing a lawyer is supposed to know": it is a designator whose internal ingredients are nearly too voluminous and wide-ranging to even describe, much less capture and use within a hierarchy of particular and generalized categories—and the trial lawyer is beset and besieged by all. Partaking in the daily task of "learning the law" in order to be sufficiently attendant to getting the answer for a particular question raised by a client's legal problem, is an experience that summons forth author Amy Leach's dazzling depiction of one facing near hopelessness: "it feels like being tossed endless apples while trying to retain a total of zero apples."[62]

What truly does the foregoing litany of "types of law" have to do with argument or with Argument? What is the interesting connection, the helpful correlation, between laundry listing all the written formats by which law regulates lawyers with considering all the presentation formats by which lawyers regulate juries? To me it is that law is both free expression and a severe constraint on free expression at one and the exact same time. At heart, lawyers are not free at all to "express" themselves unfettered; indeed, they are one of the most constrained groups of speakers who exist in our society. But the shackles of rules tightly binding lawyer throats powerfully affect lawyer minds—and are what enable them to develop an ability to mind control others, to engage in the true mind control of society writ small and writ large.

So, persuasion is infected by style, and style is infected by presentation, and presentation (for a lawyer anyway) is infected by all that expanding and constricting law. Casual conversation isn't so infected (or really regulated by any means at all), even by the implied rules of politeness or social decorum that we think hold sway, whatever those rules might comprise today or tomorrow. Trial "conversation," in sharp contrast, is refereed by every rule one can think of and even some that a trial lawyer may have unfortunately forgotten about or not even known about in the heat of that moment's discussion. "But not in *my* courtroom!" the rural county judge bellows at the peak of an unfortunate exchange, and, by the mere utterance of those words, all of a sudden a brand new and apparently unwritten and unspoken rule now rears its head to join the fray.

A Provable Feast

What the trial lawyer must contend with in their legal conversations, which the layperson can shrug off at will in their casual ones, is the concept of "proof." Jurisprudential pressure on the trial lawyer to "prove it" is constant. We can perhaps envision the pressure better as a physical restriction in literal space: that is, during a case, each lawyer must stay within a corral, the fencing of which is mostly (but not entirely) constructed of the evidence code.

It is an enclosure whose boundaries are somewhat flexible, and which can constrict and expand upon requests for the boundary line to be shifted by an adversary. Every shift event starts by a lawyer being triggered by some words having been spoken by someone: words in examination eliciting a response by a witness, words uttered by a witness themselves, or words by an opponent offering to formally admit some piece of evidence. Upon the utterance being heard, a request to shift part of the corral border is stated as an *objection*, and after a brief colloquy with the judge takes place, a decision to *sustain* the objection draws in the fence line while a decision to *overrule* it broadens the usable space. The flexibility of the corral's boards is a construction material feature that is dependent on two evidence code principles: *burdens* (i.e., concerning which lawyer is tasked with convincing the judge and how much convincing needs to be done) and *weight* (i.e., concerning how impressive or unimpressive the evidence is to the judge). Board flexibility can also be affected by non-evidence-code factors such as whether a jury happens to be present or absent at the moment the words issue, historical interactions between the same participants regarding the same or similar words, admissibility problems raised by the words which the evidence code does not address, and simply the judge's level of patience at the time regardless of the words being scrutinized.

Nonetheless, the fencing is never dismantled entirely, and no lawyer ever gets to leave the corral, regardless of what side they are on, what stage a case may be at, or what issues are present to be decided. To be able to partake in part of a courtroom conversation or pursue a case at all, the lawyer must remain in the enclosure. In this metaphor, then, proving a fact or position requires that the lawyer exhibit control in two major respects: voluntarily staying within the defined space, and voluntarily complying with the judge's rulings regarding the scope of the barrier. The pressure to know the parameters of the space involved is substantial. The pressure to comply with changes in those parameters is substantial. The pressure to memorize and recognize the benefits and consequences of offering and objecting, while simultaneously noting how doing so is going to likely then transform the parameters, is substantial. It isn't just control that is required of a lawyer "proving a point"; it is specialized legal knowledge of codes, and extensive litigation experience with motions, and access to folk wisdom type intuition, and reliance on some old fashioned gambling instincts as well.

Superficially, it is the players *other* than the lawyer who seem to be in charge of the whole "proof" operation. The corral seems to have been constructed by legislators and its maintenance seems to be under the auspices of the judge alone; proof thus seems like it operates rather mechanically via the judge's (albeit discretionary) consideration of objections, application of burdens, and assignments of weight pursuant to established standards which have been previously dictated by lawmakers. From a distance, the corral therefore appears to be a robust lawyer-free structure as to which the legislative and judicial branches seem to definitely be the builders, keepers, and ones in charge.[63]

Closer inspection of the apparatus, however, discloses that supposition to be misleading. Recall above where I noted the fencing to be "not entirely" constructed of the evidence code. That is because it is really far more a construction product of persuasion and presentation erected by generations of trial lawyers. When we think about proof more globally, we must accept that (a) how the judge and jury even learn of what is to be proved at all as opposed to what does not have to be proved is through the trial lawyers (it is their pleadings which "frame the issues," remember). We must accept that (b) how the judge and jury are provided choices about the burdens available is through the trial lawyers (it is their motion practice and manner of examination of witnesses which create the facts for burdens to even apply to, remember). We must accept that (c) how the judge and jury are led to their decisions about whether a burden has been overcome or not is through the trial lawyers as well (it is their arguments which convince the judge or jury to decide if enough proof has been submitted, remember). Not only is the corral actually run by its residents, but in observing just how elastic its construction and maintenance truly is, it becomes revealed that the purportedly objective rigidity penning in the residents as they are charged with "proving that something is true" is not solid like wooden fencing at all but is a spongy and permeable substance prone to malformation by its users.

Proof, in short, is as much a function of the looseness of persuasion by lawyers as it is a function of the strictness of code or rule commanded by judges or mediated by legislators. The laity has a misguided sense of what proof in lawsuits is really all about. To that same end, it is also a layperson misconception to believe that lawyer persuasion in deriving their proofs requires audience comprehension of the proof—that the listener who comes to understand a proven point is then lined up to ultimately embrace the point as justified by proof. In the oddity that is a jury trial, such is not necessarily so at all. Bowing under the weight of all the rules described above, the trial lawyer notes that comprehension by the fact finder (a) is costly in terms of time, time which the trial lawyer definitely does not have much of in order to do their job, and (b) threatens to interfere with emotion-driven decisions, decisions which the trial lawyer can manipulate far easier than rational ones. The lawyer's control of proof includes the lawyer's control of comprehension of that proof.

The manipulation of proof is mandated for a case to progress. Imagine the trial lawyer in closing reading out loud to the jury every single word on every page of a multi-page exhibit that also sits in front of each of them projected on a screen or held by each of them in a printed format. Although better comprehension can perhaps be obtained in doing so versus relying on them to read it for themselves back in the jury room, the project is an absolute catastrophe in its execution. Reading in such a manner angers the intelligent, bores the stupid, irritates the bench, disserves the client, and derails the significance of all else that has come before it. The linguistic device of starting a recitation but then interrupting it with the phrase "blah, blah, blah" is a trope pointing out that overattention to the small stuff can vitiate comprehension of the larger picture.

The euphemism, paraphrase, and editorial condensation are not just convenient tactics by which a lawyer as reader gains some economy of time and effort, they are also invaluable means by which a trial lawyer may be able to recast the objective into the subjective, may earn a chance to transform what is written for all persons into what is peculiarly important for one person alone. Complete comprehension jeopardizes that fevered quest which trial lawyers are always on: to create biased convictions inside other's minds.

Proof cannot escape manipulation. Additionally, proof cannot, never will be, objectively measured. To think so is to be fooled by how "proving things" works in a system where truth is relative and where the presentment of law and fact is heavily filtered by the exclusion of information and the exploitation of style. In that vein, falling for the "straight talker," the lawyer who is going to "cut right to it," who is simply going to "tell it like it is," is falling for one of the biggest fake-outs of all, one promising the premier illusion of a good proof. For one thing, the person "telling it like it really is" is still a lawyer, with a client, an agenda, in close control of issues and procedures, and armed with an excess of influence devices to utilize in service of all the above. For another thing, for someone to *really* do so would require that the speaker essentially spout pure nonsense; one straight talker explaining a day at the seashore for instance, would have to replace the most socially acceptable shorthand way of talking with the most awkward of technical, neurological, and experiential descriptors:

> These people do not sit on the beach and listen to the steady roar of the pounding surf. They sit on the beach and listen to the aperiodic atmospheric compression waves produced as the coherent energy of the ocean waves is audibly redistributed in the chaotic turbulence of the shallows. . . . They do not observe the western sky redden as the Sun sets. They observe the wavelength distribution of incoming solar radiation shift towards the longer wavelengths. . . . They do not feel common objects grow cooler with the onset of darkness, nor observe the dew forming on every surface. They feel the molecular KE of common aggregates dwindle with the new uncompensated radiation of their energy starwards, and they observe the accretion of reassociated atmospheric H^2O molecules as their KE is lost to the now more quiescent aggregates with which they collide. . . . They do not warm themselves next to the fire and gaze at the flickering flames. They absorb some EM energy in the 10^{-5}/m range emitted by the highly exothermic oxidation reaction, and observe the turbulences in the thermally incandescent river of molecules forced upwards by the denser atmosphere surrounding.[64]

In short, a genuine "straight-talker" would sound like an alien, and be just about as attractive and convincing. Actually "telling it like it is" in fact involves the exact *opposite* technique: it is the very height of "telling it like it *isn't*," a special type of highly stylized, cleverly arranged, end-run around quasi-technical recitation which, by necessity, employs the convenience and mandatory usage of shortening, substitution, consolidation, retooling, and revamping of every noun phrase, adjective, and verb. It almost goes without saying that proofs are strewn skewered like discarded shish-ka-bobs from last week's barbeque along the backyard path of such a recitation.

Openings, Their Mythos and Real Purpose

The special part of the trial lawyer's "conversation"—that strange artifice in all its layering, in light of all chosen styles, and as the words inside the words slice through various truths yet cower under siege by all those fierce rules—which I seek to visit and revisit throughout the rest of this work is that mode of persuasion presented at two crucial junctures in a jury trial: the opening statement and the closing argument.

Ostensibly, the official and mundane purpose of an opening statement is to briefly state the nature of the party's claim or defense, what the party expects to prove, and the relief sought.[65] In general, the opening statement seems like a critically important portion of any case since it does at least comprise the trial lawyer as advocate's first opportunity to really talk about why everyone is there. Trial lawyers are sometimes eager to personalize their client (though not always, depending on the particular client), to detail the helpful evidence and deflate the unhelpful, maybe even to convey a party's majestic theme of righteousness or reasonable reward. This first opportunity to "persuade" the jury in those respects is a special pledge of allegiance which merits some careful preparation and some thoughtful execution. In their best iterations, openings are the bright and cheery alarm clocks of the courtroom waking everybody up to the promise of a full and productive day ahead with a clear end in sight; at the worst they are the equivalent of the substitute homeroom teacher at the generic high school, a dullard reading dutifully from an even duller notebook about today's sad lesson plan.[66]

Consider for a moment the dramatic scene in the movie courtroom when the advocate rises to issue the opening statement. Through *voir dire*, there has already been a lengthy period of questioning of the prospective jurors about their personal likes and dislikes, their private and public experiences, and their individual attitudes. The jurors have already been introduced to the parties and their representatives, have already been told by the judge about the seriousness of their task, and have already taken an oath to swear to decide the case impartially. They should be, it seems, now ready to hear from the opposing lawyers and the witnesses and begin their role as decision-makers.

Hardly. A reality check from the social sciences tells us that they have already been pretty adept decision-makers from long before. From the first moment that they stepped into the courthouse itself and saw other people around them, well before noticing the specific parties and nicely suited individuals in this courtroom, prospective jurors have already been consciously and unconsciously forming all kinds of impressions about others based simply on appearance, body language, demeanor, tone, stance, and interaction.

From before receiving their summonses and before the first incantations in the *voir dire* process, the disparate members of the jury pool have already cultivated biases and sharp impressions about lawsuits in general and about this suit's representatives' and litigants' personalities, have already made off-the-cuff predictions about the final winners and losers, and have already developed intensely personal and quite partial feelings and opinions about each of the parties based simply on mere trifles: on the spelling of names alone, on the triviality of how anyone may be perched on their chair or dressed, on someone's smallest tics and mannerisms, and on how faces and bodies of all present look in aspect.[67] Jurors, being people, by necessity have a "theory of mind," the uniquely human trait combining inductive reasoning, empathy, and a sense of what to expect in a given situation, to produce the ability to reason in a complicated way about what other people know, what other people believe, and what other people want, well before the other person even looks their way or utters a single syllable.[68]

It is a fact of life then that opinions about the merits of a dispute are developed well before any trial lawyer ever first opens their mouth. Operational theories of mind combined with human nature dictate that no juror can or will stay neutral about any disputed issues any longer than they absolutely must. From the very beginning, jurors are intuitively deciding whom they can trust and whom they cannot trust, who is probably in the right and who is almost certainly in the wrong. Those initial impressions quickly harden into fixed judgments, judgments that are extremely difficult to soften and nearly impossible to drastically change, although some minor change is, with luck and skill, potentially available to affect. The axiom that a juror's first impressions "harden like cement" is the threshold reality for trial lawyers to overcome—or embrace. Conventional wisdom among practitioners is that as many as eighty percent of jurors align themselves with one side or the other before the opening statement, and just do not shift their loyalty thereafter regardless of what they eventually hear and see.[69]

Part of this is because sociological studies have shown that jurors engage from the start in "story construction" and will draft and approve in their heads their own multiple and personally appealing storylines as to who is who, what is truly going on, and why people are doing the things that they are doing.[70] Those private story constructions occur before, during, and after trial, and selecting among different versions of stories to choose the one that seems to fit best with their world view, their own background and upbringing, and what is being shown to them, is a classic human behavior.

As more information is provided, some of the storylines change and the selection among the options changes too. The information that is being provided of course is not only what comes out of the participants' mouths, but nearly *everything* that may be in front of eyes and ears: from the way that the judge may cast a glance, the neatness or disorderliness of how papers and files are arranged on counsel table, and the very orientation of the parties as they are seated or move about the room, all of those elements have already been subconsciously folded into and solidified over some sort of evolving storyline that each juror will eventually accept, reject, or modify.

The trial lawyer does not have substantial control over most of those elements, of course, so pretending that their words in opening are the quintessential components is to ignore that numerous other equally compelling elements are swirling about; in short, the high emotional and aesthetic impact of trial paraphernalia might as easily supplant or undo a lawyer's words as support them. Truly, expectations about what openings offer should be deflated, not inflated.

The Art of Fighting by Not Fighting

It is true that the psychological principle of primacy suggests that the opening statement's position at the beginning of the trial is of some importance, that it does color each juror's impression of the facts, and that it can influence how jurors view the information they learn later in the trial.[71] It is also true that such an opportunity to color and to influence is made available to the trial lawyer at their option and it is correspondingly true that many trial lawyers are quite passionate about the belief that engaging in opening, deflated expectations notwithstanding, must be seized and exploited to its full potential.

But that is simply one belief among several, and there are plenty of experienced trial lawyers who recognize that presenting an opening has a serious negative side. It is a practice which contains some real danger at *later* trial stages, including the danger of giving jurors a new reason to vote against a party which they did not ever have before and which the speaker now gave them and has only themselves to blame for handing out. Reserving (not waiving) the opening, or, at the very least, selecting an extremely abbreviated and truncated opening, at least comports with the effective trial lawyer thinking a lot more globally— that is, about the entire case and every part of it being geared toward the desired end, not just about the entertaining or dramatic public aspect of the trial where the jury is formally present, but also the pickier and more convoluted aspects where the jury is only informally present, or not present at all, or where a step hinges on technical application of a law or rule through motion disregarding the jury's involvement altogether.

The effective trial lawyer keeps in mind that while the jury is important, they are not the "be all and end all" of each case and that many cases can be and are won on a type of motion that discards the jury as entirely unnecessary, or by taking advantage of a specific procedural rule or of the opposing side's missteps or omissions before the jury even gets to decide. If there is an essential element to the other side's case that the trial lawyer is aware is missing or will not be noticed unless the other is reminded, then opening morphs unfortunately into a hazard, a conceptual pit fallen into by pointing out things not just to the jury, but to the judge and to the other opposing counsel as well that they should *not* have been made cognizant of or as to which it would have helped to subtly place aside and take advantage of later via motion. Openings promise "tell alls"—yet very, very few trial lawyers really want to *actually* tell all, and partaking in opening opens up prospects of telling too much or at the very least disappointing the expectant with not telling nearly enough of the right thing.

The cult of the trial lawyer in our country tends to heighten the thrill and appeal of a courtroom lawyer talking and talking and talking as if every rasp and whisper issuing from their throat must be vitally important to capture.[72] Many trial lawyers themselves buy into that delusion and many act as if every chance they get to talk must be strenuously seized, leveraged, and exhausted. None of that is true, it is all part of the mythos, and frequently the more effective trial lawyer (especially the defense lawyer at trial who has to likely be tacking against the prevailing wind) developing the most productive strategy available is the trial lawyer who has selected to *not* talk—or at least to talk quite a bit less and then to exploit rules between the constructed gaps of silence to alter the talk that is occurring.

Preparing to Trounce

All right, for the moment let's pretend that a primary objective during opening is at least to make an attempt to try to psychologically gain the allegiance of the jurors. To accomplish that difficult objective, every trial lawyer has on their wish list aspirations to introduce a theme, to humanize their client, to have the jury identify with their side of the dispute, to defuse the other side's strengths, to expose the other side's weaknesses and omissions, and to develop any rapport with the jury one possibly can, including by outright pandering to their most distasteful biases and sympathies. It is a long list, no question.

But there is a time to do all that, and literally none of that can in fact be done in opening. Nearly every item on the wish list recited above requires that (a) there be some evidence to argue for or against, (b) that there be some law to base argument on, and (c) there be some option to note connections or disconnections between the evidence and the law sufficient to actively persuade a listener into a firm position. Yet opening is far in advance of every one of those criteria, and it is for that reason among others that a critical restriction in the opening statement is the "rule against argument," a material limit on what can be mentioned and how it can be stated.[73]

The rule precludes the trial lawyer from "arguing" anything during opening at all. Yes, it is ill-defined and poorly understood, and yes, application of the rule against argument varies from jurisdiction to jurisdiction and even from judge to judge within jurisdictions, but what *is* uniform across the board is that its violation is bad. Given that all lawyers argue to some degree or another, avoiding doing so in opening is as dicey as it is necessary, and the uncertainty of that rule's application and the opportunity for objection causes many trial lawyers great anxiety and visually appreciable tension in making openings. To make a direct impression on the jury but also to avoid "arguing" to them means that the trial lawyer needs to be almost religiously cautious about what words are used. The resulting admonition? Step lightly and engage in the most subtle of pretense.

Caution and fakery, though, are not what movie and TV show scriptwriters have their actor trial lawyers acclaim since those attributes are clearly antagonistic to admiration for the protagonist and the high drama of nobility to which such entertainments cater—yet caution is imperative and pretense must not be ignored as a valuable means of informational control. Acceding to the "rule against argument" requires use of a more soft-spoken approach conjoined with healthy doses of what is called the predictive phrase—the words that signal that a trial lawyer is merely "predicting the future" not "arguing for a result." The difference is subtle but not that subtle; think of one's mother saying to them as a child "You are going to hurt someone if you continue to do that." Tone and inflection alone, not to mention history and common sense about the language used by irritated mothers, tells the listener quickly that the sentence is not simply a disinterested prediction by an indifferent bystander but is something far more reproving, instructive, and judgmental by someone with a very pointed agenda. To that end, smart word choice for the opener becomes an unyielding assignment, a treacherous path where active verbs are probably preferrable to pejorative modifiers, where descriptors are hopefully lined up that enhance the importance of an event but where one does not resort to adjectives that enhance the importance or the disregard of a person, and where past tense, not present tense, is the serious order of the day.

The rule against argument forecloses one in opening from doing anything about explaining laws or rules, procedural or otherwise, to the jury panel so as even slight steps are taken toward mentioning the "rule which will be at focus in this case" or suggesting a condensed layperson version of the statute governing the dispute, the opportunity for having the jury embrace an opening salvo of themes and ideals is squandered. Instead, alienation from the jury is risked by the sustaining of an objection, verbal admonishment by the court, and the judge reciting a cautionary or curative instruction to the jury to disregard what was just said.[74] The last thing any lawyer wants in any trial is to have the people who are supposed to be paying close attention to them to be told by the clear authority figure in the room, the judge, to actively forget about them instead.

Caution and pretense are what actors work to have installed in their brains to access when necessary—and good lawyers should try to be good actors. As a special type of actor, however, lawyers are constantly in the throes of an existential directive to maintain their secret identity. Stuffed into the pockets of the weighty robes that trial lawyers stomp around in on stage in the courtroom theater are sheaths of underlined marginalia and scrawled side notes strenuously and cautiously reminding them *what they are not*. Remember, reads the private script, you are *not* the litigant and your own money, your own life, your own liberty, is *not* at stake here, it is merely another's which will actually be impacted by the outcome. Remember, the private notes emphasize, you *aren't* the community writ large, you are the individual writ small; don't try to help everyone or solve all problems, focus only on the singular. Most importantly, the yellow highlighted text screams, you are *not* one of the witnesses in the case itself and what you personally feel or believe as an individual is of zero consequence and of zero value to accomplishing your mission.

This last reminder is the most strident: above all, the trial lawyer cannot, should not, insert themselves personally into the case in any manner, as much as the opportunity for them to do so may arise over and over throughout the case and trial's course. It is natural to want to personally lend support to, and even perhaps privately identify with, the person standing next to one, especially one who has spent considerable time with them privately in preparation and who is paying them to stand up publicly for them, but for all the sympathetic feelings or struggling consciences with which trial lawyers are either blessed or cursed, the one word they really cannot and must not use in any argument is the word "I." At all costs, the real ego must stand down.

Fake egos are of course perfectly fine to launch forth, and much of theater is getting the audience to believe strongly in the main character's pride, approval, and personal investment in what is transpiring. Still, only the audiences should be falling for that ploy, not the actors themselves. True personal distancing includes refraining from expressing a personal feeling for another's credibility or reliability, an activity that in law is not just useless but highly objectionable, comprising a distasteful phenomenon called "vouching," which is both unpermitted by case law[75] and is counter to how people tend to, psychologically anyway, weigh the credibility of others as witnesses. Particularly in the trial setting, the more someone tells another to really trust or believe someone, especially one who is a stranger, the far more likely it is that they actively won't—or are at least will be made much more skeptical about doing so.[76]

Trial lawyers are also not anything more than, or above being, mere persons. Trial lawyers may well be authority figures to many, and there is an indefinite power and reputation that society cavalierly grants them and which they sometimes can leverage by the existence of the vocational position alone, e.g., by simply writing "attorney at law" or "Esq." after their names. It is a social influence which can be exaggerated or minimized as the case or opportunity may allow, including as others look to them to intuitively know and exhort "all laws," and to handily impart specialized directives to others about life, liberty, money, housing, work, and family upon inquiry; as Henry David Thoreau mockingly put it, "the lawyer had only to weave arguments, and, by some magic, wealth and standing followed . . . "[77]

At the same time, trial lawyers are of course no different than any other individual citizen saddled with their own failings, knowledge deficiencies, job problems, basic human needs, inherent prejudices, and wished-for-but-frustratingly-impeded goals. Like it or not, these must be tamped down, hidden. Even bored or annoyed jurors are attentive to distasteful human character traits being bandied about as if they were strengths, including affects of handicap or vulnerability, attitudes of unique superiority, private disrespect being made public, the expression of perceived slights, or generic peevishness toward those in the room at large. It is counterintuitive but accurate to note that politeness and casual self-effacement and humility, even if not genuine, will get trial lawyers much further along the path of a jury listening to and then selecting their manipulated storyline as the appealing one, than will boast, or assertions of social or positional power, or claims of having the expert or special knowledge which a specialized law degree suggests (but clearly does not always provide).

Are lawyers anything really special in that regard? Well, lawyer egos first germinate in the soil of legislative grants of power. They are then nurtured in the gardens of specialized educational institutions, thrive in the breezes and rainfall of judicial attention, and blossom or blister in the sunlight of public forums. An ego's growth or decline is also influenced by minerals and toxins embedded in the local environment along the way, ground-level factors which, for lawyers, include techniques other lawyers use as well as techniques which the lawyer themselves employ. Lawyers by necessity listen to themselves speak. The more intensely they do so, the greater the risk that they may become consumed by their own persuasions, start to fall for the Truths that their chosen style that day has manufactured to deliver to others.

Style choices, in short, can augment the existential threat to the author's very identity, which we worried about earlier. Maybe, the lawyer starts to think, that authoritative sounding voice in their heads truly embodies a genuine Authority? Maybe, the lawyer starts to wonder, that handsome and convincing presence standing in front of those enthralled spectators truly represents actual Knowledge? Developmental deformities in lawyer egos occur where the practitioner forgets that it had only been just a style all along, and real trouble arises swiftly where outside of the courtroom one starts to substitute avocation for a vocation, where one inside of the courtroom starts to propose a dangerous existential trade off of oneself in exchange for all selves.

Jurors can act as corrective supplements to foster healthy routes of development in that environment. Jurors tend to help curtail lawyer egos. Really, to that end, it behooves the trial lawyer to identify with the juror probably far more than the juror needs to identify with the trial lawyer. This is not an easy task for the trial lawyer, however. A bit like lawyers, jurors begin as anonymous citizens, identified by number more than name, who are forced to be somewhere they'd rather not be. They are forced to reveal some aspects of their identity, including about their names, addresses, work, relationships, domestic lives, feelings, and opinions, and they don't particularly like doing any of that and suspect rightly that others in power are partly to blame for them having to do so. If trial lawyers don't particularly care one way or another about each juror personally, it is nevertheless true in spades that jurors don't particularly like trial lawyers generally. And as jurors regulate lawyer egos, good trial lawyers should take careful note of why.

One reason is that from the lay perspective of legal actions and procedures, jurors most readily employ their own "folk law," that informal, personalized, orally transmitted, body of true and false information gleaned from family, school, work, and entertainment sources which describe obligations, prohibitions, rewards, and punishments which laypeople generally believe apply to conduct among all social groups.[78] Jurors are unsettled then when the "law" they are instructed to apply diverges from the folk law which they are almost positive comprises the proper rules to use. In gripping tightly to what they feel is more customary, that with which they are familiar from childhood and which they prefer (especially since it has served them well in casual exchanges with others), jurors will privately "play lawyer" by silently disagreeing with the know-it-all disagreeable lawyer and disdainfully inserting their own rules in place, rules which they are adamant must more appropriately control a good outcome. The trial lawyer who does not think like a juror and who ignores folk law is one all too swiftly overturned by its inexorable force.

Another reason is that jurors are trying desperately to employ their *own* caution and engage in their *own* pretenses. Among the harshest realities learned by trial lawyers from sufficiently lengthy experiences—that is, after engaging in multitudes of jury trials, participating in multitudes of arguments, and hearing multitudes of verdicts being delivered in a variety of different courtrooms—is the awful truth that the body language, expressions, and gestures of jurors are utterly unreliable indicators of anything, most especially allegiance to a side. The wizened and chastened trial lawyer eventually comes to get it that a lot of people just like to shake their heads or smile for no real reason, and that a lot more just look pissed all the time or frown, also for no discernable reason. Faces don't often, or even *ever*, flag the thoughts and decisions that the owners of the faces have made and are presently making.

In fact, the impenetrability of faces is a mere part of the larger problem which is that *nothing* either material or observable about jurors workably links to gleaning their mental processes. Contrary to what many "expert" jury psychologists espouse, a juror's marital or relationship status, their choice of clothing brand, their first and last names, and their demographic factors are all ultimately content-empty signals, highly unreliable indicators of any specific fidelity a juror might have to any specific cause. The necessary result for the trial lawyer, especially in opening, is that since "reading" jurors' actual minds is an unavailable stratagem, then inhabiting the best role for the panel and "playing juror" themselves to show the panel what their mental processes *should* be becomes a paramount trial lawyer activity.

Closings, Their Mythos and Real Purpose

So, let's take a page from the book of "discontinuity style" and jump ahead for a moment to the end to learn something about our previous topic by looking at its counterpart. Closing is opening's close blood relative. In the television series or movie, closing argument is the auspicious final act, the culmination of all the preceding drama in the form of a one-person, one-shot display of supreme grandiosity, a repackaging and reproduction of those who have spoken throughout the trial into a single ferocious speech, one where the trial lawyer steps forth and, through the majesty of oratorical skill, somehow uses pure persona and rhetoric to win the case. Or at least that's the common perception from fiction and entertainment mediums where teams of scriptwriters have all the time and help they might need to envision, craft, and rewrite a beautiful, moving elegy for an accomplished actor to memorize and then carefully announce to an enthralled paying audience.

In reality, a real-world closing is tremendously different and in several material respects, including in who crafts it, how much time there is to do so, who the audience truly is as it is being delivered, and what an effective one really looks like in action. Just about the only thing that dramatic versions have right is its potential: closing is the third and final chance that the trial lawyer gets to talk directly to the jury (first is *voir dire* and second is opening) and is the one and only opportunity to pull evidence and law together into some sort of compelling and persuasive whole, if at all possible.

There *is* drama in closing, necessarily so, including eloquent turns of phrase and earnest and impassioned appeals to the jury members apart and together to each find some resonance with a good result, even, perhaps, with a reasonably parallel outcome found in cultural and literary references. Drama, of course, has its limits: significantly distinct from media renderings of closings, and the tipping point where doing too much threatens to inflame too much, real-world closings trespass on legal restrictions when they raise fervent calls for "justice" to be delivered, a fairly solid no-no in nearly every courtroom and case such calls have been attempted in.[79]

We can note that there is a definite constitutional right to closing in criminal cases and which exists regardless of whether a jury is involved or not[80], but that precept is more of an open question in civil cases.[81] In many jurisdictions, argument to the civil jury is much more in tight control of the trial judge and it can be sharply curtailed, indiscriminately limited in scope, or taken away altogether depending on a trial judge's discretion. Argument by a litigant's counsel in those forums is simply not considered to be that essential a component of due process so the trial lawyer should not just assume that it of course will occur—yes, traditionally it seems to accompany just about every jury trial as a given, but technically it doesn't have to, including in the ideal respect that the layperson imagines the combatants' respective "pit bulls" emphatically finishing out the trial with competing fiery speeches as some sort of rock-solid principle of all litigation.

Once allowed, there really is no passing on or "waiving" closing in a way that would still comport with ethical obligations to be an effective and zealous advocate—it really must be conducted. Yet it is a sad fact of the real world that as they stand to deliver, the trial lawyer (a) has no scriptwriters assisting them, (b) has had no chance to truly memorize anything worthwhile of any real length, (c) may have waited too long or missed an earlier opportunity to have the necessary parts in place to do a closing argument well, (d) may have misjudged their intended audience entirely as to effect, and/or (e) may have not grasped the devastating lesson that closing is not really even the device by which one effectively "wins or loses" the case anyway, since that mystical event may have already occurred before closing even starts, and often through no impact by the trial lawyer at all.

Egos interfere with argument. As is true even well outside the courtroom, many lawyers in general are filled to the brim with self-importance and many frequently give themselves a lot of credit, sometimes far too much credit, as to their role of the "primary influencer" in client interactions as well as within a case specifically. Sociological studies show that many, if not most, jurors will have already reached either tentative or unshakable conclusions at some point earlier in the trial, including when they first walk into the courtroom and before they begin *voir dire* as we have seen.[82] Preconceived beliefs, be they blight or not, will resolutely stain the attempt to affect later beliefs.

Trial lawyers do not easily, but must eventually, come to some sort of grip with the harsh reality of the *low* impact that they actually have in trial, as opposed to what either they wish or anticipate they have landed versus where the ultimate basis for the jury's decision actually stems from. Trial lawyers with big egos whose heads are filled with self-importance and who like mostly to listen to themselves announce things to the world at large usually make for terrible trial practitioners, including because that sort of self-selective and self-directed listening is absolutely disastrous to what is needed to be heard to best exploit in a closing—which are the key words and phrases uttered by all the *others*, not by them.

Of all the hindrances to deal with at closing, the time crunch is the most serious. Trial lawyers learn very quickly that there is rarely any time given them between the last witness on the stand and the time to close and it is an eye-opening experience for the neophyte to realize quite soundly that not even five minutes tops is available before one is expected to immediately stand and start pontificating about all that has gone before over the last several hours or days, and to do so in hot and heavy detail and with emphasis and grand conviction. What is there to be done in the panic that severe time limitations create? The answer: read. The illusion is that closing reflects a practiced dramaturgical skill; the reality is that it actually reflects a practiced literary skill: that of taking and referring to good notes. Drafting a comprehensive closing is impossible in the short span allowed, but *constructing* a closing outline in that span from what has already been drafted, that is., the notations scribbled during trial, can be accomplished. Doing that is an exercise in the high art of paraphrasing, the impromptu actor's trick of taking three days of testimony and ten pages of notes and collapsing it all into ten words or short phrases to glance at for a moment and then use the most compelling points within to issue thirty minutes of forceful conviction from.

To consolidate the massive bulk of others' unending words during testimony into a few choice phrases, a record of what was spoken by those witnesses over the three days is mandatory—and the trial lawyer themselves is the only choice available to step in as "testimony recorder." Relentless and expansive note-taking during trial is imperative since *there is no other transcript to refer to*; unless one has carefully heard and then written down all or at least most of the words uttered by opposing counsel, by the judge, by a lay witness, party, or an expert, then there is no independent accessible source to refer to by which to recite those crucially important words right back to the jury when the time comes.

Note-taking is the original progenitor cell from which all argument divides, grows, blossoms, and fruits—or is starved and withers. As a helpful or deadly response to direct, cross, or recross-examination arises via a witness's words, the besieged trial lawyer must mark it down in some manner (usually a panicked shorthand), ascribe whatever asterisk or underline or highlight to it to remind them to perhaps use it in argument if *apropos* of a material issue in the case, and then later quickly scramble through those notes in the precious few moments before standing to compose all into a striking set of convincing propositions mostly composed of the language which others have selected.

Part of the necessary pretense here is that the trial lawyer did the note-taking and the recall perfectly even if they actually didn't; jurors aren't given any trial transcript either, and while jurors are regularly given paper and pen to write down their own notes, and while some few jurors may well be proficient note-takers, they are not lawyers, and they are definitely not *the lawyers in this case* so they don't have a good head at all for materiality, that is, for which specific words to have noted and which to have ignored based on what is factually and legally at issue.

The lawyer therefore swings into action in a new role: the indispensable secretary. Complimenting themselves out loud for being such careful note-takers during testimony can enable closing advocates to substitute in a little pretense for accuracy should the jury look down at their own pads and only see blank paper, but like every self-promoting office assistant knows doing so carries risk. Any pretense at recalling exact statements better have some objective support since there actually *is* a court record in each trial which will eventually later get transcribed and which can enable sharp-eyed opponents (and appellate lawyers) to locate and point out blatant falsehoods, thus overturning all the hard work (and misquoted excerpts) that had come before.

Appreciating the idea that note-taking during trial is mandatory to success at the end of trial is one thing; accomplishing such a task, however, is something else. The trial lawyer definitely doesn't have the grand luxury which the jurors have of simply being able to sit and listen for the alarm bell of a key word being spoken. The trial lawyer is laden with pressing demands to do what seems cognitively impossible: jot every important word down right as the word is uttered, at the very same time that they are also carefully (a) thinking about what just occurred and what next step is coming up in the trial process, (b) conducting the examination of a witness or listening to the opponent's examination in order to raise objection if necessary, (c) considering if an objection needs to be made or motion raised about the statement just made, and (d) attending to what someone else just said at the same time to see if it is significant or not.

It is a deep-level type of mental processing going on in parallel with the more subtle distractions of having a client by one side, opponent to another, and critical audiences in front and behind. The threat of being preoccupied just at the wrong moment, or to have failed to take the note at all, is rife throughout every trial, short or long. Attention requires focus, and focus requires actively ignoring interruptions posed on all sides, those stemming from the client at counsel table, the visitors in the gallery, the clerk shuffling papers, the clock ticking above the courtroom door, and the opposing counsel and judge offering their reactions to what is transpiring as the witness speaks.

The notes ultimately taken are not *just* a record for the convenience of the lawyer. They also serve as a template for selecting an appropriate style, the blueprints necessary for the lawyer as architect to refer to in constructing on-all-fours type constructs which might be pleasing to a captive audience waiting to be swayed. Actively ignoring others' insignificant interferences and attending to others' significant expressions demands the very individual use of discretion about what is significant personally to the trial lawyer in the case. Significance in every case has to be relative to that case. What is worthwhile to pay attention to is situationally dependent on the lawyer's peculiar goals for that day, on the client's peculiar instructions from the week before, on the particular relationship with the judge from earlier that same month, on the topical news stories from that year, and on the specific cultural touchstones from that decade.

The core point here is not so much that trial work requires note-taking, it is that note-taking is a premium control device directed toward enabling the taker to build comparisons out of relationships forged over time—and thereby effectively influence the jury in light of what has been learned as it might particularly affect them. The close attention which a lawyer pays to words used by others during a trial has a specific reward attached: it founds the construction of influence by giving them a supply of concepts for use in correlation.

The Unspoken and Spoken in Concert

Should one believe that a single word spoken in argument can tip the jury to the correct result, then it is a near guarantee that the word was not one created whole cloth from the trial lawyer's teeming imagination, but instead was lifted from a scramble of hastily transcribed marginalia jotted down on the side of an exhibit at a key point in the proceedings. The magic is in *which* word is the one chosen to recite.

Linguists will tell you that words in isolation convey very few semantic features and that what is essential to true discourse are propositions, those strings of words revealing relationships such as actions and properties.[83] Trial lawyers will tell you, however, that within a single term can nevertheless rest an inferred suite of propositions and that the term alone can have powerful semantic force. The preconditions to eliciting meaning include that the jury has previously heard it used by a witness in a specific context during the course of the trial, and that it is then repeated to them at the appropriate moment at the end of a trial by the advocate in conjunction with a suggested link to a specific thematic concept or emotional state. Length is not the bellwether of impact—the abrupt can serve persuasive purposes just as well as the protracted, and a conflagration of desired reactions can be sparked from the recitation of a key word alone *if it is the right one* and if it can be salvaged and then recollected from the waves of accessory testimonial data in which it was earlier engulfed.

Composed substantially of emotional terminology, closing at least has a core emotional purpose. Appellate opinions are not remiss from proclaiming publicly what every trial judge and every experienced trial lawyer knows is not true at all: that closing argument "must not be used to inflame the minds and passions of the jurors so that their verdict reflects an emotional response rather than the logical analysis of the evidence in light of the applicable law."[84] It may be vaguely discouraged, but "inflaming" is not a bad descriptor for the type of activity that closing intimates needs to be ultimately accomplished. Certainly, for any jurors already committed to the advocate's proposal, fortuitously or otherwise, closing is ceremonial and merely needs be endured. For the uncertain, it affords an opportunity for the trial lawyer to generate *some* sort of flame, of emotional heat, at the very least to simply warm up that portion of a chilly audience and earnestly resolve any lingering questions they might have sufficient to hopefully stop their shivering and solidify their tentative commitment to the client's cause.

As to the fully antagonistic portion of the panel, the trial lawyer must be aware that the objective is really not to sway them as separate individuals (a highly unlikely result) but to do one's best to usurp individual autonomy, to get the resistant to engage in "groupthink," that is., capitulate and cave to any pressure being exerted on them to go along with what the larger group feels is imperative. This is not an impossible task: much has been studied about the phenomenon of "peer pressure," according to which a person's preferences are changed in response to the preferences of a "peer group."[85] There is nothing modern about the phenomenon nor any restriction or mandate about the number of participants—people in all sizes of groups coalescing to act as one mental unit is an occurrence that stretches back through antiquity and has included entire nations:

> Men, it has been well said, think in herds; it will be seen that they go mad in herds, while they only recover their senses slowly, and one by one. . . . We find that whole communities suddenly fix their mind upon one object, and go mad in its pursuit; that millions of people become simultaneously impressed with one delusion, and run after it, till their attention is caught by some new folly more captivating than the first.[86]

Passion or no, the problem of course is that since a trial lawyer can't have a real dialogue with the jurors, then they really don't know what it is that the jurors are genuinely questioning or concerned about—the lawyer doesn't have access to any empirical data on their thoughts and feelings empowering them to ameliorate (or intensify) decisional pressures. The trial lawyer therefore must take on that previously acknowledged role in the play—pretending that they themselves are now a juror and then projecting outward by imagining what would have alerted, puzzled, or concerned them the most during the case as it unfolds if they were to have stepped outside themselves and listened to themselves speak.

A trial lawyer is a person then who talks to themselves—first quickly within their own head as they jot down notes, and then more measuredly out loud to others. Their professional role obligates them to do so craftily, without anyone thinking that they are insane or getting it that they are even talking to themselves. One's internal monologue working through puzzles and eventually composing the core of one's transformed external monologue is a stage trick, and a psychological reality, and a necessary ingredient to constructing rational as well as irrational analyses[87]—and thus a vehicle for argument. In short, well beyond merely taking on the representative role, a new level of pretense is now required. With argument at trial specifically, at least three important pieces of information have to be first conveyed from the trial lawyer to themselves and have to be taken to heart before they can consequently be expressed.

One, a trial lawyer in closing talks to themselves and tells themselves out loud that this dispute is not their dispute and that it is the dispute of two completely different entities, a plaintiff and a defendant who have brought their private tiff into a public forum and one as to which a representative is paid to present it and which strangers are forced to consider it and decide something about it. It is at once disquieting as it is crucial for the trial lawyer in argument to do two things simultaneously: privately to themselves adopt the core concession that it is supremely unwise to get personally involved, while publicly to the jury make it seem supremely important to seize a core opportunity they have been afforded to get personally involved. The two voices clash but both must be heeded.

Two, a trial lawyer in closing talks to themselves and tells themselves out loud that this pool of strangers in front of them in the box are both alone and together at the same time. No single juror is thematically distinct from any other. At the same time, no group of jurors are a cohesive indivisible unit who are all joined together "at the hip" to decide something only as a group—they aren't, they are a set of individuals with individual minds and thoughts tasked with each voting their own conscience and their own convictions about what was heard and presented.[88] The trial lawyer has to find some avenue of reconciliation between appreciating that jurors are each independent decision-makers and appreciating that they still can be converted by majority rule, by the pressures inherent in "popularity contests," and by the social weight obligations assigned by all members to other members as a function of small group dynamics.

By the way, this reconciliation phenomenon is not the trial lawyer merely wishfully hoping that the fidelities of a group of voters shift in their client's direction—real action must be taken to gain the advantage. Before the final curtain closes, real action for the trial lawyer at this stage in the production is now quickly scripting, casting, and exhibiting as impressive a mini-dramatic performance as possible, one uniquely tailored to a newly constructed taxonomy: a lineup of "parties-of-one." That is, inducements need to be made in closing to each juror person by person—even looking at each directly and speaking to each directly straight down the line of seats in the box if necessary—encouraging each to acknowledge that who they choose to align with or distance from individually is now no less than a major life decision. Each juror's attention has to be drawn away from the case's parties being the antagonists in the drama and redirected toward *the other jurors* as now being prospective antagonists or collaborators instead. The very nature of their own free will as an individual has to be inferred to now be at stake in this new contest, their vote reflecting their personal integrity as they decide whether to affix to or cleave from others in the box.

Three, a trial lawyer in closing talks to themselves and tells themselves out loud that it is a pretense that jurors are geniuses and that it is also a pretense that jurors are idiots. Infrequently, either pretense can have merit and there have been plenty of trials where treating the jury as "scholars at a table of scholars" or as doltish grade schoolers works out, but the extremes aren't the only choices. It can also be equally effective to tread in the middle ground and let the pool seek comfort in an understanding that all people, juror or otherwise, are mixed bags of dumbness and intellect and are mostly just commonly sensible actors who, if nothing else, hopefully resort to common sense most of the time for most solutions.

Given that all lawyers by definition have a graduate level education which most laypersons do not share, anxieties arise at the very start of *voir dire* over having sufficient knowledge to understand the advocate. That small bit of ever-present relational fear makes it so that jurors *do* like to hear that big brains don't really count for much in jury trials: the middle path eases the anxiety and asserts that no one, juror or otherwise, is always right about assumptions or intuitions and that all people make mistakes. Ironically, the trial lawyer can encourage the jurors to applaud their (the lawyer's) brilliance in noting that brilliance is not needed, in proclaiming that no one, juror or otherwise, should be burdened with an unrealistic expectation of unfaltering wisdom in their decisions—only at most of reasonableness and of best attempts at being reasonable along the way.

In sum, everyone privately and desperately wants to and needs to recognize that screw-ups occur and wants to and needs to feel comfortable excusing themselves from screwing up. Trial lawyers do well to signify that yearning out loud—without of course ever saying any of those actual words yet making sure to subconsciously commend themselves for having thought of and announced the idea.

And the trial lawyer's transmission of all those ideas, those infections, their dogged obedience to all those commands, in order to "get to the jury" and then in order to get the jury to "get to the right verdict" is done in service of someone who is not the trial lawyer in any way: the client. True argument, real Argument with a capital "A" cannot lose focus on the fact that all this manhandling of words, of dress, of voluminous legal authority, is engaged in service of a different citizen, the client, and is done (in the majority of cases) for pay. That a trial lawyer is someone decidedly partisan in another citizen's public contest and is paid to be so is an unremarkable truism simply reflecting what we already know of how the process of representative democracy works in a capitalistic society overall. What *is* remarkable, on the other hand, is the astonishing leeway that such a representative is given to use language to hide that fact by shaping people's minds. It is hardly enough for the trial lawyer to just manipulate language alone in the artificial environment that is the courtroom—they must unquestionably manipulate people as well to reach their goal.

Notes

1 See, e.g., Friedman, Lawrence M. "Law and its language." *The George Washington Law Review* 33 (1964): 563.
2 See generally, Al Pacino in ". . . *And justice for all.*" Columbia Pictures, 1979.
3 See, e.g., Rhode, Deborah L. *The beauty bias: The injustice of appearance in life and law*. Oxford University Press, 2010.
4 Veblen, Thorstein. "The beginnings of ownership." *American Journal of Sociology* 4, no. 3 (1898): 352–65 at pp. 355–6.
5 "Everyone means something different by the word, and a collation of the various definitions and usages of the concept style would illustrate clearly the confusion prevailing in matters of art." Worringer, Wilhelm. *Abstraction and empathy: A contribution to the psychology of style*. Ivan R. Dee, 1997 at p. 33.
6 See, Case, Ermine Cowles. *The dilemma of the paleontologist*. University of Michigan Press, 1951.
7 For a discussion of the phenomenon of "impression management" by lawyers in trials see, Hobbs, Pamela. "'Is that what we're here about?': A lawyer's use of impression management in a closing argument at trial." *Discourse & Society* 14, no. 3 (2003): 273–90.
8 Unger, Peter. *Ignorance: A case for scepticism*. Oxford University Press, 1978 at p. 266. Unger considers that perched inside illocutionary acts are informal rules, what he calls "nests of expectations," which regularly are in force whenever we try to communicate with other people, as in where we represent ourselves as knowing something without actually saying that we know it. This well describes how trial lawyers are indirectly perceived by their audiences, the threads of implied knowledge and authority that appear to wind through their conduct as they make their assurances, corrections, predictions, requests, denials, promises, and the like.
9 The cinematic prototype is Kevin Spacey's character's increasingly insistent exhortations of the simple phrase "Will you go to lunch?" in *Glengarry Glen Ross* (New Line Cinema, 1992).
10 White, James Boyd. *Heracles' bow: Essays on the rhetoric and poetics of the law*. University of Wisconsin Press, 1985 at p. 5.
11 See, e.g., Kooiman, Jan. "Social-political governance: Overview, reflections and design." *Public Management an International Journal of Research and Theory* 1, no. 1 (1999): 67–92.
12 See, Weller, Marc, and Stefan Wolff. *Autonomy, self governance and conflict resolution: Innovative approaches to institutional design in divided societies*. Routledge, 2005.

13 See, Galarsa v. Dolgen California, LLC, 88 Cal App 5th 639, 305 Cal Rptr 3d 15 (2023), as modified on denial of reh'g (Feb. 24, 2023) (explaining the "primary right theory of pleading").

14 See, e.g., Matter of One Hundred Thirty-Seven Thousand Three Hundred Twenty-Five Dollars ($137,325.00) in United States Currency v. State ex rel. Pelahatchie Police Dept., 204 So 3d 317 (Miss Ct App 2016).

15 The possible number of masks to overlay on top of another is one limited only by the actor's skill and the audience's attention span. Outside of Shakespeare's elaborate machinations in that regard, an impressive modern example can be found in Episode 9 of Season 3 of the television series "The Good Place." In a key scene in that episode, the actor D'Arcy Carden (a) pretends to be the character "Janet," (b) who is pretending to be the character "Eleanor," (c) who is pretending to be the character "Jason," (d) while talking to herself in the form of the same character "Janet," (e) who is in this guise is simultaneously pretending to be the character "Chidi." What is in reality a single person talking to themselves presents convincingly as three different people conversing—and wildly, the self-referential topic which "they" are addressing is on who among "them" is playacting and trying to hide from "the others" in doing so. The layering and masking are exquisite in their rendition in a way that all trial lawyers should hope to emulate.

16 See, e.g., Friedman, Lawrence M. "Lexitainment: Legal process as theater." *DePaul Law Review* 50 (2000): 539.

17 See, Solan, Lawrence M. "Lawyers as insincere (but truthful) actors." *Journal of the Legal Profession* 36 (2011): 487.

18 Dawkins, Richard, J.R. and Krebs. "Animal signals: Information or manipulation?" In *Behavioural ecology: An evolutionary approach* (J.R. Krebs and N.B. Davies, eds.). Sinauer, 1987, pp. 380–402.

19 Gotoff, Harold. "Oratory: The art of illusion." *Harvard Studies in Classical Philology* 95 (1993): 289–313.

20 Cicero, Marcus Tullius. *On oratory & orators*. Harper & Bros., 1878.

21 Gustafson, Sandra M. *Eloquence is power: Oratory and performance in early America*. UNC Press Books, 2012.

22 See, e.g., Mitchell, David. *Cloud Atlas: A novel*. Random House, 2008.

23 Ording, Philip. "99 variations on a proof." In *99 variations on a proof*. Princeton University Press, 2019.

24 Siu, Ralph Gun Hoy. *The portable Dragon*. MIT Press, 1971.

25 Queneau, Raymond. *Exercises in style*. Alma Books, 2018.

26 Pétard, Hector. "A contribution to the mathematical theory of big game hunting." *The American Mathematical Monthly* 45 (1938): 446–7.

27 The "thermodynamic method," for example, consists entirely of two analytically breathtaking sentences: "We construct a semi-permeable membrane which lets everything but lions pass through. This we drag across the desert."

28 In fact, Ording mentions both Queneau and "Pétard" in his *Preface*.

29 Joyce, James. "Ulysses. Modern Library." *New York* (1934).

30 See, Ho, Hock Lai. *A philosophy of evidence law: Justice in the search for truth*. Oxford University Press, 2008.

31 Schlagel, Richard H. "Contextualistic realism." *Philosophy and Phenomenological Research* 41, no. 4 (1981): 437–51 at p. 178.

32 See, Walton, Douglas. *Appeal to expert opinion: Arguments from authority*. Penn State Press, 2010.

33 See, Laurence v. Salt River Project Agric. Improvement & Power Dist., 528 P3d 139 (Ariz 2023) ("The doctrine of *stare decisis* is rooted in the public policy that people should be able to rely on judicial precedent to know their rights and order their conduct accordingly").

34 Ording, Philip. "99 variations on a proof." In *99 variations on a proof*. Princeton University Press, 2019 at p. 4.

35 See generally, Lane, Edward William, ed. *The Arabian nights' entertainments*. Lippincott, Grambo, 1855.

36 Melville, Herman. "Moby Dick. New York: Modern Library." (First published 1851).

37 Melville more than most appreciated the necessity of using technical novelty in order to effectively persuade others:

> For be a man's intellectual superiority what it will, it can never assume the practical, available supremacy over other men, without the aid of some sort of external arts and entrenchments, always, in themselves, more or less paltry and base.

From Chapter XXXIII of "Moby Dick."

38 Compare, Walton, Douglas. *Appeal to expert opinion: Arguments from authority*. Penn State Press, 2010.

39 Pease, Barbara, and Allan Pease. *The definitive book of body language: The hidden meaning behind people's gestures and expressions*. Bantam, 2008.

40 Ong, Walter J. *Orality and literacy*. Routledge, 2013 at p. 67.

41 See, Crystal, David, and Randolph Quirk. *Systems of prosodic and paralinguistic features in English*. Vol. 39. Walter de Gruyter GmbH & Co KG, 2021.

42 Cutler, Anne. "The perception of rhythm in spoken and written language." In *Cognition on cognition* (Jacques Mehler and Susana Franck, eds.). MIT Press, 1995 at pp. 283–8.

43 Crystal, David. "Paralinguistics." In *The body as a medium of expression: Essays based on a course of lectures given at the Institute of Contemporary Arts, London* (Jonathan Benthall and Ted Polhemus, eds.). E.P. Dutton and Co., Inc. 1975, at pp. 168–71.

44 See, e.g., McDermott, Josh H. "Auditory preferences and aesthetics: Music, voices, and everyday sounds." In *Neuroscience of preference and choice*, pp. 227–56. Academic Press, 2012.

45 White, James Boyd. *Heracles' bow: Essays on the rhetoric and poetics of the law*. University of Wisconsin Press, 1985 at p. 34.

46 See, Reisigl, Martin. "11. Rhetoric of political speeches." *Handbook of Communication in the Public Sphere* 4 (2008): 243.

47 See, In re Kant's Estate, 265 So 2d 524 (Fla Dist Ct App 1972) (judgment cannot be rendered unless a court's jurisdiction is invoked by commencement of an action or a proceeding before the court); Little v. City of Chattanooga, 650 SW3d 326 (Tenn Ct App 2022), appeal denied (June 14, 2022) ("It is not the role of the courts, trial or appellate, to research or construct a litigant's case or arguments for him or her").

48 See, Isaacs, Nathan. "Limits of judicial discretion." *Yale Law Journal* 32 (1922): 339. "Judicial power, as contradistinguished from the power of the laws, has no existence. Courts… minimize, if not eliminate, the power of the personal judge in the regulation of our affairs."

49 See generally, Pinker, Steven. *The language instinct: How the mind creates language.* Penguin UK, 2003.

50 See, e.g., In re Conduct of Ard, 369 Or 180, 501 P3d 1036 (2021) a case with one of the least helpful and most tautological definitions ever of what is "improper conduct" for a lawyer within the context of rules of professional conduct: "doing something that a lawyer should not do or refraining from doing something that the lawyer should have done."

51 See, e.g., Air Mach. Com SRL v. Superior Court, 186 Cal App 4th 414, 112 Cal Rptr 3d 482 (2010) (characterizing current California law on special and general appearances as "a quagmire filled with traps for the unwary").

52 It does, by the way; see, N.J.R.E 401–3 and 801–8.

53 My apologies to all the offended English teachers out there who just read that sentence, but to me a compelling description of chaos requires some semblance of self-reference in the form of a chaotic sentence structure.

54 See, e.g., Cooper v. Harris, 581 US 285, 137 S Ct 1455, 197 L Ed 2d 837 (2017).

55 See, e.g., Columbia Cas. Co. v. NW. Nat. Ins. Co., 231 Cal App 3d 457, 470, 282 Cal Rptr 389 (Ct App 1991) ("More a vehicle for Jesuitical or Talmudic debate than a definition of the rights and obligations of the parties to the contract, the policy crosses one's eyes and boggles one's mind").

56 See, Searight v. State of N.J., 412 F Supp 413, 414 (DNJ 1976) where the judge was confronted with a plaintiff who claimed that the State of New Jersey had unlawfully injected him in the eye with a radium electric beam with the result that he claimed that someone now talked to him on the inside of his brain. After some careful thought, the judge considered that plaintiff might be presenting "a case of presumably unlicensed radio communication, a matter which comes within the sole jurisdiction of the Federal Communications Commission" but that as a practical matter plaintiff could have simply "blocked the broadcast to the antenna in his brain simply by grounding it [by pinning] to the back of a trouser leg a short chain of paper clips so that the end would touch the ground and prevent anyone from talking to him inside his brain."

57 See e.g., State v. McCarthy, 369 Or 129, 501 P3d 478 (2021) (explaining the doctrine).

58 See, e.g., Bornhoft v. Aubry, 178 Or App 625, 37 P3d 1049 (2002), rev den, 334 Or 260 (2002) (a party owes the trial court the obligation of a sound, clear and articulate motion, objection or exception, so as to permit the trial judge a chance to consider the legal contention).

59 See, Solan, Lawrence M. *The language of judges.* University of Chicago Press, 2010.

60 "Ordinarily, growth of law of private wrongs has been by judicial decision." Hungerford v. Portland Sanitarium & Benev. Ass'n, 235 Or 412, 384 P2d 1009 (1963).

61 The semantics of law is full of what the cognitive scientist and mathematician Douglas Hofstadter would likely characterize as "strange loops": from paragraphs in pleadings incorporating themselves into their own allegations, to courts taking jurisdiction of a case in order to determine if they have jurisdiction of the case, to judicial review providing the avenue for determining the legitimacy of judicial review, self-reference and recursive definitions are innate elements of law, not aberrations. See generally, Hofstadter, Douglas. *Strange Loops.* Basic Books, 2007.

62 Leach, Amy. *Things that are: Essays*. Milkweed Editions, 2012 at p. 10.
63 See, Haack, Susan. *Evidence matters: Science, proof, and truth in the law*. Cambridge University Press, 2014 at p. 51 ("Some assignment of burdens and standards of proof (explicit or implicit) is needed to ensure that a result is reached.")
64 Churchland, Paul. *Scientific realism and the plasticity of mind*. Cambridge University Press, 1979 at pp. 29–30.
65 In re Commitment of Fletcher, 658 SW3d 834 (Tex App 2022).
66 See, Greenberg v. Bekins of S. Florida, 337 So 3d 372 (Fla Dist Ct App 2022).
67 Krauss, Daniel A. *Jury psychology: Social aspects of trial processes: Psychology in the courtroom, Volume I*. Vol. 1. Routledge, 2016.
68 See, Emery, Nathan J., Nicola S. Clayton, and Chris D. Frith. "Introduction. Social intelligence: From brain to culture." *Philosophical Transactions of the Royal Society B: Biological Sciences* 362, no. 1480 (2007): 485–8.
69 Ibid.
70 Hastie, Reid, Steven Penrod, and Nancy Pennington. *Inside the jury*. The Lawbook Exchange, Ltd., 2002.
71 See, e.g., Stone, Vernon A. "A primacy effect in decision-making by jurors." *Journal of Communication* 19, no. 3 (1969): 239–47.
72 Part of what the author David Wexler has nicknamed "argument culture." See, Wexler, D. "The argument culture and the courts." *Court Review* 102, no. 19 (1998): 4–10.
73 See, Morales-Hurtado v. Reinoso, 457 NJ Super 170, 198 A3d 987 (App Div 2018), aff'd, 241 NJ 590, 230 A3d 241 (2020).
74 Ordinarily, the sustaining of an objection to improper argument of an attorney to jury and the instructing of the jury to disregard the argument cures the error. Bratt v. Smith, 180 Or 50, 175 P2d 444 (1946).
75 See, e.g., State v. Murphy, 319 Or App 330, 510 P3d 269 (2022).
76 Cf., Gobert, James J. "In search of the impartial jury." *Journal of Criminal Law and Criminology* 79 (1988): 269. This includes self-vouching, a phenomenon which can only backfire and is signaled by one of the most content-empty phrases a witness might utter: "To tell you the *real* truth . . ." (or its lesser used but equally reprehensible equivalent, "To be perfectly honest…"). Such phrases ironically create in the listener the very opposite of their intended effect; the speaker becomes considered less and less trustworthy with each insistent repetition.
77 Thoreau, Henry David. *Walden*. Yale University Press, 2006 at p. 34.
78 Renteln, Alison Dundes, and Alan Dundes, eds. *Folk law: Essays in the theory and practice of lex non scripta*. Vol. 1. Univ of Wisconsin Press, 1995.
79 See, R.J. Reynolds Tobacco Co. v. Neff, 325 So 3d 872, 882–83 (Fla Dist Ct App 2021), rev den, SC21-1603, 2022 WL 1261381 (Fla Apr 28, 2022) where the appellate court admonished and penalized trial counsel for invoking Dr. Martin Luther King, Jr. in calling for "justice;" quoting at length from Orwell's dystopian novel *1984*; calling appellants "an enterprise of death" and "scoundrels"; suggesting that the jury should punish appellants for harm to others; twice referring to the lack of corporate representation in the courtroom, contrary to an order in limine; and making several other improper comments, and which ended by holding that "This is a case in which the totality of all errors and improprieties is so pervasive as to raise considerable doubts about the overall fairness of the trial court proceedings."

In the same case, a dissent by Justice May made a larger point about rhetoric in general being made purposeless in those closings which reach beyond the pale:

> Creativity in story telling has its place. Use of literary works and quotes can hold the attention of jurors. Were we writing on a clean slate, I would condemn some, and warn against the use of other, references and "creative" name-calling that occurred in this case...[But one] would think that an appellate court would not have to inform counsel or trial court judges of the inappropriateness of comparing the opposing party, directly or circuitously, to historical or fictional villains, such as the Nazis and Big Brother. Likewise, comparisons to the Taliban, Isis, Al Qaeda, Stalin, Pol Pot, Bull Connor, the Unabomber, Cruella de Vil, Hannibal Lecter, the Wicked Witch, Simon Legree, vampires, and zombies are also off limits. *This is not an exhaustive list*. . . . I doubt there is much that plaintiffs' counsel can say that will inflame juries to the point the trial becomes unfair. Admittedly, there are some analogies (Nazis, slavery, the devil, etc.) that cannot be tolerated. It is just so unnecessary in my view.

80 See, e.g., State v. C.J.W., 274 SW3d 547 (Mo Ct App 2008); State v. Gonzalez, 338 Conn 108, 257 A3d 283 (2021).

81 See, e.g., Wilson v. Wilson, 277 Ga 801, 596 SE2d 392 (2004).

82 Hastie, Reid, ed. *Inside the juror: The psychology of juror decision making*. Cambridge University Press, 1993.

83 See, Caplan, David. *Language: Structure, processing, and disorders*. The MIT Press, 1992 at p. 253.

84 See, R.J. Reynolds Tobacco Co. v. Kaplan, 321 So 3d 267 (Fla Dist Ct App 2021), rev granted, decision quashed, SC21-1092, 2022 WL 500293 (Fla Feb 18, 2022).

85 See, e.g., Liang, Zhen, and Jeremy Seligman. "The dynamics of peer pressure." In *Logic, rationality, and interaction: Third international workshop, LORI 2011, Guangzhou, China, October 10-13, 2011. Proceedings 3*. Springer Berlin Heidelberg, 2011, pp. 390–1.

86 Mackay, Charles. *Extraordinary popular delusions and the madness of crowds*. Simon and Schuster, 2012 (originally published in 1841), at p. xix of the Preface to the Edition of 1852.

87 See, Haack, Susan. *Evidence matters: Science, proof, and truth in the law*. Cambridge University Press, 2014 at p. 31.

88 See, e.g., State v. Scruggs, CR020210921S, 2004 WL 1245581 at 7 (Conn Super Ct Mar 8, 2004) upholding the propriety of the prosecutor asking jurors to "vote your conscience on what you truly believe the proper verdicts should be," finding that such a remark, as with invitations to "do the right thing", was nothing more than encouragement for the jury to take their role seriously and act accordingly.

2

The Manipulation of People to Advance Personal Interests

In which the concept of "relative truth" empowers trial lawyers to control social units called "juries" by the costuming, disguise, and selective display of stories via rules of evidence and via uses of trial procedure as supervised by other social units called "judges," and where the trial lawyer's heavily biased expression of opinion, theory, and argument, via style, thus directly leads to the uplift and downfall of the fortunes of other social units called "litigants" so that disputes are actually resolved to a conclusion that directly affects all involved.

Mind Control

All unruly mobs can ultimately be ruled—if not by good old-fashioned physical coercion, then at least perhaps by careful political stratagem, or by targeted financial influence, or maybe simply by object-related misdirection and distraction techniques accompanied by loads of patience and the eventual passage of time.[1] The trial lawyer spurns all those options and rules the "unruly" jury pool (an unruly mob if there ever was one) through mind control alone. No supernatural forces or mysticism, however, is required: the art of oratory, the munificence of trial procedures, and the details of the evidence code all dovetail together to comprise a sufficiently flexible, robust, intricate, and socially approved apparatus for actually controlling the mindsets of small groups—and as we have seen the trial lawyer is armed with, and labors under, oration techniques, confusing evidentiary principles, and procedures and codes, in plenitudes.

Yes, the jury trial is democracy's champion and darling, and yes, all trial lawyers initially stroll into the courtroom ostensibly cloaked with the task and theoretical intention of promoting those democratic goals, including of attaining "justice" and "fair play" for all.[2] Few practitioners sustain that initial noble pursuit, however, and within minutes of entering through the courtroom doors a set of hard realities promptly set in. For one, there turns out to be far too much work to do in the gritty labor of swaying the fact finder to worry much about promoting social ideals, and even a brief amount of rummaging around in their latched trial bags and on their laptops to see what tools are at hand to so sway, quickly informs the trial lawyer that espousing ideals alone throughout the trial process is actually going to be dangerously counter to the end game of effectively serving the client's interests.

The initial tools grasped are semantic ones: mostly those which enable desired images to be generated in the fact finder's minds. There is "cueing," where the speaker actively employs a verbal or pictorial prompt to facilitate the processing of a conceptually related item.[3] As the trial lawyer casually pulls out of their briefcase a large, old-looking, leather-bound volume, artfully places it on the side of the counsel table closest to the jury box, and then inserts the word "authority" into whatever the pending discussion is, the listener is cued to envision those folks who likely wrote that impressive book, the grey hairs and long beards of the past whose sound wisdom must certainly be heeded.

Cueing requires some degree of controlled, voluntary processing on the part of the subject—in a sense it demands a bit of work to join in. With not much else of interest to look at in the mostly staid courtroom, jurors are not remiss in noting the heavy gold-embossed law books, as well as the expensive suits, ties, and dress shoes as cueing devices for the subsurface theme of "serious"; the large binders of paper, stacked banker's boxes, and heavy file folders as cueing devices for the subsurface theme of "complicated"; and the shiny watches, pens, and personal jewelry as cueing devices for the subsurface theme of "valuable," among many others.

There is also the more facile trick of "priming," the seeding of a passive spread of activation through triggering semantic memory.[4] It is a far more unconscious and potentially volatile phenomenon in that the subject does not have to make any explicit judgment concerning the semantic relationship between the prime and the target, nor to actively use the information offered when compiling a reaction. The effect occurs even when little attention is paid to the prime at all. The prime is at the outer periphery of the fact finder's conceptual field of view.

Courts themselves are cognizant of the phenomenon and its effect—the long-standing custom of permitting plaintiff and their counsel to sit at the table closer to the jury box and the defendant and their counsel being relegated to the further away table is a nod to the prime of physical proximity attributing favor. In courtrooms which don't explicitly adhere to such a custom, it is remarkable how many counsel will still seek the priming advantage by arriving early in relation to the time set for trial and subtly or not so subtly maneuvering chairs and tables around the courtroom to achieve the effect independently.

Other semantic tools include generation effects where the listener is urged to construct the topic word for themselves thus making it more memorable[5], and matching effects where the speaker selects aspects of similarity in appearance (or status) to curry an allegiance. As to the first, we have noted above that in most trials jurors are afforded notepads and pens but are unsure about what to actually write down. Urging each to themself generate a particular word which the speaker pretends to struggle with recalling is supremely effective in enabling them to then more vividly recall and employ that word—and its associated theme—during deliberations. As to the second, it is a given that appearances suggesting likeness count for a lot in trial. While *actual* relationships between participants and jurors are prohibited due to the bias implied in consanguinity,[6] nothing really prevents trial lawyers from putting effort into addressing and choosing potential jurors who look or present like their client in key characteristics of dress, age, ethnicity, gender, vocation, or avocation. Minds which occupy similar looking bodies may well think similarly or at least have their owners aligned in more discrete ways, muses the trial lawyer, and even if that belief is not backed up by much empirical support from the psychology literature, still its folk law roots make it a belief compelling and entrenched enough to explain the propensity during *voir dire* to use peremptory challenges to "kick off" potential jurors who simply are members of groups to which the client does not "belong" (albeit at the risk of traipsing on constitutional principles of equal protection).[7]

Mounting Ethical Challenges and Surmounting Ethical Lapses

The next, and more powerful, set of tools for the trial lawyer to retrieve from their bag are rules—and not the easy-to-understand, simply stated, short and sensible rules, but the lengthy, esoteric, baffling, and elaborate variety enumerated above. In their heads, at the counsel table, or somewhere close at hand, every trial lawyer has ready access to stacks and stacks of procedures, guides, and codes, the dogged and clever use of which enables them to delve into the heads of the jury and mess around with any eventual fruition of all those good intentions and lofty principles. We have inspected rules in detail above but need to take special note at this point that the bevy of rules include not just communicative, social, local, and legal ones, but ethical and moral ones as well.

That "messing about" by the trial lawyer in using every linguistic tool available to slant favor toward another is one aspect of a larger schema overshadowing all professional behaviors and interactions, which is the code of ethical conduct for lawyers in general. Lawyer conduct both in and out of the courtroom universally raises concerns about legal ethics, and the fantasy scenario favored by the public (and even by some younger lawyers themselves) is that the profession in general has fallen from some earlier state of grace into an abject and debased condition which needs to be drastically remedied. The reality is that demands for restoration of the legal system back to some historical, traditional level of high functioning professionalism is just that—an illusion, a fantasy. The profession of law has always carried with it irremediable ethical conflicts as an integral component of how law works in an adversarial system and it has done so for at least the last 500 years.

Those conflicts have never been on the threshold of elimination, and likely never will be overcome in any conceivable future. Invoking unreachable ideals, such as expecting that a solid culture of universal "respect" and "honor" will ultimately be installed, is a fool's game—and it ignores the fact that many dilemmas with which lawyers struggle reflect problems that have no connection to deference or esteem, or that simply have no solutions whatsoever regardless of who might deserve admiration. Having to choose between two evils is actually a necessary part of the profession and being practical as opposed to idealistic in the selection is neither disrespectful nor dishonorable in light of the complicated goals of advancing client interests toward which lawyers must always aim. Respect and honor are buzzwords with high emotive content that apparently must be inserted *de rigueur* into every publication about the bench and bar, but they are buzzwords nonetheless, and their assertion as absolutes detracts from the authentic experiences lawyers have in protecting and advancing private interests as opposed to promoting and enshrining civic ones. Mind control, in short, is not an ethics problem disguised as a strategy issue. It is the inverse: a strategy issue that some have cloaked with the costume of ethical concerns.

Part of why legal ethics is so confounding in its implementation is that the lay public mistakes it for what it is not. Asked to locate ethical obligations from the lengthy list of rules noted above, the layperson points to the Model Rules of Professional Conduct—the MRPC—a detailed list of practice-related commands with which all lawyers are hopefully familiar and which all states' respective bars impose for that jurisdiction's practitioners to follow or be sanctioned under.[8] But those lists are not ethical codes even though they certainly have some ethical components and have historical foundations in legislative concerns about general ethical behavior. The public likely considers that if a lawyer has violated a certain MRPC section, that they must have then necessarily committed an ethical breach, but that is not nearly so.

One, in between an ethical act and an MRPC phrase lies the client. The framework on which lawyers impose constraints and restrictions on themselves as to how to act and on what to do as representatives of others is a framework which those whom they represent have had a hand in constructing and who deserve priority treatment. Providing a client with an informed understanding of their rights and obligations and explaining practical implications of the same to them cannot be subsumed to a non-client's interest such as a communal ethical interest in "being prompt and diligent." Zealously asserting a client's position in an adversarial proceeding cannot be subsumed to a non-client's interest such as a communal ethical interest in "displaying candor." Seeking results advantageous to a client or examining a client's legal affairs cannot be subsumed to a non-client's interest, such as a communal ethical interest in "dealing honestly with others."

To truly act on behalf of another means that elements of the other's personal history, personal proclivities, and personal needs must be taken into account. Honoring community aspirations isn't what's at stake in the representation game—honoring individual aspirations is. Certainly, some individual's interests may make it easy to comport with general legislated commands to engage in ethical behavior—but some may be directly contrary to doing anything "ethical" for the community at all. Since client-based priorities cannot be cavalierly abandoned, then insoluble tensions between the client's need and the community's need necessarily surface with each new representation.

Two, it is wildly inaccurate to say that a lawyer does or does not behave ethically for social purposes simply because they do or do not comport with a state-mandated responsibility list devoted to itemized confidences, privileges, and conflicts of interest. Individualized rationalizations as to why a lawyer has selected to say a particular word, or to take a certain step forward or backward in pursuit of a case, may be entirely disconnected from a mundane check off of whether a set of privileges have been respected or a set of conflicts attended to. Lawyer behavior, for example, is deeply influenced by secular or religious group precepts which a licensee may have adopted, family customs which they may have grown up with, or complex philosophical theories which they may have fashioned about how people operate alone and in concert. From intimate personal anxieties which inhabit their inner natures to intensely private feelings of guilt or burden they are likely saddled with via their upbringing, private phenomena become key components to evolving one's moral decision-making and personality that easily can bypass the weaker force of "social ethics." For lawyers, "doing law" and "acting morally" are not just intimately connected activities, they are intimately *conflicting* activities as well; the very boundaries of the latter are defined in many ways by the lawyer engaging in the former:

> If I were to write a long treatise devoted to developing and maintaining a sharp distinction between the concepts "pie" and "cake," disposing definitively of all the hard borderline cases, like Boston cream pie and upside-down cake, I could scarcely look forward to being congratulated on my contribution to the clarification of a difficult subject. Nor will it do to say that the efforts made to distinguish law and morality are justified by the importance of the subject matter involved, any more than I could support my exercise in culinary taxonomy by pointing out that it dealt with the important subject of human nutriment. The question is not whether law and morality are important. The question is whether drawing a sharp line between the two is important.[9]

Many people, including judges and jurors, mistakenly conflate responsibility rules with ethical conduct. Law school courses and bar associations are not immune from making such an error, and indeed the "ethics and professional responsibility" component of bar exams is invariably merely a test of re-reciting the content of such rules. It is a further confusion that neither is legal ethics the equivalent of the private or personal moralities of individual lawyers, however. It is not automatically so that an ethical standard is triggered whenever a particular lawyer has selected to make what seems like an "ethical" (read, laudable or socially approved) decision on responding to a challenge or question in their capacity as a lawyer. Lawyers may well push or be pushed to perform or refrain from actions where doing so appears noble, or appears to transcend a personal desire, but the internal rationale for doing so (or for not doing so) may not be the output of purposely attending to an ethical obligation.

Alternatively, lawyerly conduct professedly *catering* to legislated ethical norms may fall far short of its mark morally. For instance, the lawyer who loudly proclaims on their Facebook page that they refuse to assist any client who eats meat because killing animals for food is "morally wrong" and who refuse to support clients engaging in such practices, is not following ethical codes of conduct at all even as they might well believe that such is the only ethically rational position to take. Serious ethical lapses occur in trumpeting such moronic announcements, including the derogation of basic jurisprudential principles of equal access to justice and the disrespect of rights to exercise core freedoms of association and belief.

Ethics are controlled by large-scale and large-scope mandates handed down historically though the evolving influences of social groups on their members, not by the spontaneity, fickleness, or happenstance of individual determinants which happen to be coincident with those influences.[10] No differently than with other professions, lawyers do not get to pick and choose, unimpeded, those rules they agree with and those they find repellent, and other than being part of the legislative body that enacts the rules, lawyers have no lasting influence over what is codified as command and penalty. For all those reasons, no personal morality principles can truly hold sway to construct or transcend historically based ethical codes which press their weight down over all lawyers, in all practices, and across all jurisdictions.

At the same time, nevertheless, ethical conduct is still a component of a certain type of social *identity*, and the layered identities of lawyers as the public shadows of others are, by definition, identities that are both constantly shifting and multi-factorial; the varying roles lawyers have to inhabit during their workday make their public personas overflow with nuances which interlock only loosely with legislated ethical behavior. Compliance with ethical norms is directly affected by where they might stand, who they might stand in front of, and why they might be standing there at that particular moment. MRPC sections struggle with this problem of identity and clumsily make categorical distinctions in the form of lawyers as being "advocates," or separately as being "officers of the court," or separately again as being "counselors" or "advisors." Those raw divisions, to some degree, make sense to keep functions compartmentalized in terms of outlining generic responsibilities to distinct laypeople in distinct (and often quite artificial) legal situations. The undeniable overlap in all those positions which every lawyer actually embraces in practice, however, makes things far messier than those divisions can possibly account for or acknowledge off the books.

For instance, a lawyer in a courtroom proceeding may at one moment be speaking to a judge "on the record" and be making a highly biased argument on a legal proposition in the most public of settings, and then, within seconds of a break being held in the proceeding, may well be talking privately with their client in the most protected and unbiased of secret discussions saying things flatly counter to what was just said on the record moments before. The close proximity in time, location, and setting suggests that only one set of rules are operative when clearly several sets are in overlap and quite likely in antagonism to each other.

The disparity spans the spectrum of how people interact as to their words chosen, their posture and stance, as to their tone and demeanor: the lawyer must stand, must use honorifics, must act courteous, patient, and formal with the judge—and then in the space of a single breath may need to switch to be extremely secretive, to have to talk in colloquialisms, to need pretense and laxity as rhetorical aids, and to be discourteous as all get out with the client standing right at their side.

As to communicative content, that is often mediated by whom the recipient is: the lawyer has an ethical obligation to provide supporting authority and to disclose adverse authority to the judge, while they do not have to, and frequently won't, support even one single statement to the opponent or adjacent client with anything better than purely subjective opinion, bombast, or uncertain conjecture. Straight to the judge's face or out of the side of their mouth to their client or colleague they may offer recounts of past experiences mixed with expressions of self-effacement or egotistical boast, any or all as advancement of a position in the case may warrant. Posturing as an activity is ethically complex, yet constantly posturing with a host of strangers in real time is the bread and butter of every lawyer's in-courtroom and out-of-courtroom experience. By talking at all, they are attending to duties as counselor and advocate nearly simultaneously yet can have wildly different aims with each sentence asserted—on the one hand to advance the client's goal of prevailing in a contested dispute and on the other hand to possibly save the client from themselves or at least from their next terrible decision they may make in a more private part of the process that may not even be contested at all by anyone. Assigning the lawyer then to an artificially constructed legislative category in some ways hurts, not helps, the system as a whole gauge the true range of their ever-shifting "ethical" responsibilities.

Additionally, ethical obligations tangle with truth as a relative concept in a way that the codified rules find abhorrent in their pretense that there is a universal and objective "truth" out there which society demands that all lawyers protect at all costs. Even juries know better: asked to believe that a trial lawyer is telling them something unquestionably reliable in statements at the start or end of a trial, jurors—being people and thus by definition organisms adapted by evolutionary forces to be self protective and cynical of the foreign—recognize right away that the speaker has a champion, a favorite, and that the words spoken are in service of a "side" not necessarily in service of the "concrete truth." In that aspect, juries swiftly accept a reality that the MRPC turns a blind eye toward. In daily instances both trivial and overwhelming, there is immense pressure on lawyers to *not* "tell the truth and nothing but the truth," not just to a jury but to many others around them as well. While an MRPC rule might demand otherwise, it is not an ethical lapse to be *less* than truthful with people who are not the client, and it is not an ethical lapse to be *selectively* truthful with the client.

Consider an "objectively" true proposition to be "my client's core position in this dispute is factually and legally weak." Were the lawyer to say those words to the court in a public proceeding as a candid concession, they would then seriously disserve their role as zealous advocate and likely be subject to some state bar-related or consequential financial sanction from the client. While that proposition might be highly advisable to convey to the client themselves (but not be pushed to explore all legal bases for saying it), in contrast it would be highly *unadvisable* to truthfully inform the opponent or decision-maker of such a belief. Candor is not a virtue in either arena, it is a vice through and through and lawyers know that and have to deal with that whether as advocate, or advisor, or as officer of the court.

Lawyers lie, but they need to.[11] The practically ethical lawyer (as opposed to the ideally ethical lawyer) is frequently untruthful about weaknesses, is frequently overly exaggerative about strengths, and is selectively ambiguous about nearly everything in between. Candor to the client may be paramount, but candor that derails the client's reliance on the representative role or that drains confidence in the judicial system or in the specific proceeding or adjudicator, or which dismantles the lawyer's core abilities to assist and promote the interest at issue, is candor that is *eroding* a potentially protective result, not enhancing it.

Consider this conceptual parallel. The Fifth Amendment to the US Constitution represents our civilized protest against using torture to extract confessions.[12] What it essentially prohibits is one citizen benefiting from another's involuntary speech. It does not, however, prohibit *all* confessions; self-incriminating testimony is easily permitted by the Fifth Amendment so long as it is voluntary and not compelled. *External* influence is the core concern. The Halakhah of the Talmud, in distinction, prohibits *all* confessions, whether involuntarily induced or not.[13] Its protest is against humanity's own destructive inclinations, protecting people not just from other people but from themselves as well. *Internal* influence is the core concern. Both forms of law worry about undue influence, but the Halakhah gets it that undue influence has hidden as well as overt sources and that an acceptance of human nature means that a broader form of protection is necessary.[14]

In this country we play many roles as we govern ourselves. One is to represent ourselves, one is to judge ourselves, and one is to talk publicly to ourselves as that representation and judging process unfolds. An appreciation of the need for lawyers to lie tracks a Halakhah-like appreciation that in an adversarial system of justice influence has hidden as well as overt sources and if a scheme of partisanship allows for influence, it must embrace allowances for external *and* internal influence. If it is unjust to demand that a criminal defendant be obliged to speak truthfully about their own complicity in a crime—and it is—it then must be unjust to expect those who represent others to have to disclose all truths to those who listen and judge, to make the representative confess all, even in spite of whether that confession better comports with an ethical directive, or better informs another section of the citizenry.

Law is not the pursuit of "better" or "more" information for all, as science is. Law is not the pursuit of better ethical behavior for all, as philosophy is. Law is the pursuit of better protections for individuals, and that protection is for both client *and* lawyer as individuals, protecting the latter from having to compromise an internal strength or expose an internal weakness which might harm the former externally. The necessarily broader form of protecting the need for lawyers to be deceitful, the Halakhah-like form, is one which walks in tandem with (a) the interpretation of information sufficient to require comparatively weighing relative strengths of proofs and (b) the retooling of information sufficient to require withholding and concealment of relative truths from one citizen to another.

Navigating Informational Exchanges

In that complex sense, a lawyer's "ethical" conduct is closely entangled with strategy and with the art of decision-making guided toward reaching a desired goal that is directly antagonistic to another, competing, lawyer's desired goal. There are backstops of course: no one would contest that it would be highly unethical for anyone, lawyers included, to outright physically hurt or kill someone in order to accomplish a professional objective on behalf of a client. In addition to being criminalized, those backstops develop by relying on drawing lines between words and deeds and the lawyer's professional life is tangled in the use of words far more than in the execution of deeds. The nuances arise then independent of the backstops: while most would agree that it would be unethical for a businessperson to blatantly lie to obtain a profit, there is considerable and legitimate disagreement over whether it is unethical for a lawyer to lie to a jury to obtain a verdict from them from which a businessperson could then use to obtain a profit.

As a guidepost for ethical conduct, the standard obligation that a lawyer must display "candor toward the tribunal" only leads so far toward the river but stops well short of the bank. If it were genuinely a command to be complied with without exception or reserve, every lawyer would need to constantly be calling or e-mailing each judge's chambers to keep them updated as to the latest truth that they need the judge to be aware of—a literally impossible, institutionally destructive, and socially unworkable scenario. Clearly, the abstract candor placed on display to judges is highly selective, not just to time, place, and case, but to important and conflicting concerns of confidentiality and advocacy.

As another guidepost for ethical conduct, the gold standard of maintaining civility to one's opponent has similar problems attached. Unyielding civility across the board would flatly dismantle a lawyer's strategic options about acceding to or declining requests for continuances, extensions, stipulations, and exceptions. The client would be disserved were their representative to compromise their advantage in exchange for their opponent or the system being assisted; the imbalance created by unchecked civility fast makes the lawyer potentially *unethical* with each new conversation. There is not just a nuance to choosing what to say to another person based on who that person is to the lawyer speaking, there is a nuance to changing up the decision with each case and each new conversation and not following any blanket rule at all, but fluidly rolling with each circumstantial twist in the dispute to decide what next to say in spite of what one may have just said a second previous or in a case just before.

Part of the nuance is created by the fact that a lawyer's practice necessarily involves repeated interactions with other lawyers, judges, officials, clerks, the public, clients, assistants, experts, and witnesses, and as a result the lawyer easily acquires substantial amounts of unique information on a daily basis which others can't access. That personally held information, in turn, translates into personally held power. Beyond the fact that this data bank is simply significantly larger than that which the average citizen accumulates in their daily lives, there is also the fact that it is data significantly more specific to a client's active case than anyone else around might be in possession or control of. Such acquisition, within an environment devoted to protecting secrets and privacy, creates a tremendous information disparity between lawyers and everyone else, one which can be and must be leveraged to gain advantage.

There is a very practical reason why clients (and judges and other lawyers) are regularly asking lawyers as client representatives for new information, for updates, for status checks, for additional briefing, for scheduling cooperation, and for consents or objections, and there are some ethical reasons why lawyers regularly are expected to provide the same, but there is a *strategic* reason why compliance might well be in different amounts and in different forms depending on who is asking and why—and withheld entirely if need be. "Buying time" or "pressing for time" by selectively deciding who to call or e-mail back that day, exactly when to do so, and with what words, are crucial strategic tasks for the lawyer which only an *imbalance* of information can make valuable and which only some managed craftiness can make practically effective. The lawyer not answering the phone call from the court which they see ringing right in front of them is a lawyer engaging in a form of deceit—and deceit which is mandated by what the client needs in priority and in antagonism to what the caller might need.

Knowing things that the client or others do not know is thus a massive advantage to the lawyer in practice, can be a massive danger to the client if used poorly, is a massive inequity and vulnerability locked into the juridical system, and produces a massive gap of power inequality which professional responsibility rules and legal proceedings brusquely pay lip service to and even more often just outright ignore. Ethical obligations to be an information conduit (yet in a rather restrictive and discretionary sense) at the same time as they are an informational checkpoint, filter, and stopgap, are forces which transform lawyers into alternatively nervous and confident bundles of competing influences. No professional responsibility rule can close the informational disparity gaps, nor completely temper the background disquiet constantly accompanying decisions needed to be made as to what information should flow in what direction and in what configuration. If representational protections were to bend a knee to every jurist's command for complete disclosure, our adversarial system would be in utter crisis, not in uneasy balance.

As noted, behavior consistent with one's own moral compass is also not the real address of legal ethics. For one thing, attending to such behavior just isn't the exclusive province of lawyers in the first place—hopefully that attendance occurs regardless of one's vocation or profession and social forces direct it to transcend the immateriality of what one's particular job might that day require. For another thing, it seems highly likely that there are as many moral compasses as there are people; not only are universals thus hard to come by in that very large area, but formulating rules for "all moral compasses everywhere" to adhere to would be as incapable of definition as it would be impossible to enforce. While it was admirable for Moses to propose that he could do it in ten, or for Martin Luther to propose that he could do it in ninety-nine, outside of the context of religious fantasies we easily recognize that publicly proclaimed versions are mostly notable in their impracticality and their violation; far more often than not in everyday life each individual is constantly constructing their own personalized list of which moral commands to embrace and which to reject.[15]

The theme of manipulating to persuade relies on appreciating intricate details of the encounters which lawyers have with clients and others in practice, aspects of how the substantial power wielded plays out across the myriad opportunities to use that power. The practitioner can use the calling card of "lawyer" to initially solicit others to provide them private facts to work with (and to be paid to do so). They can use the clout accompanying the role of "advisor" to attribute and arrange value to some of the facts relative to others, to draw in new facts and toss away old ones. They can block all others from learning about not just the facts they have come into possession of, but even the fact that they have a certain client or a case at all. They can unilaterally select which rules to tell the client about, apply personal judgments to decisions to suppress or reveal certain facts, and massage the import of both rules and facts to non-clients. They can invoke the attorney-client privilege to protect themselves from being forced to disclose private communications, and can invoke the confidentiality privilege to protect themselves from being forced to disclose private information. They can employ and manipulate the marital and self-incrimination privileges (along with parts of the evidence code such as the hearsay rule and its bewildering exceptions) to derail numerous lines of inquiry into exposing those privately machined facts and laws.

Don't think, by the way, that just because a client exists in the equation that this is all done at the behest of the client with their full awareness and support—it is not. The truism that many of the rules recited above have been designed to protect the client and not the lawyer doesn't mean that the client appreciates the rules or even knows anything about them. Certainly, many clients, in their naivete, may idiotically desire others to learn in full what the lawyer realizes cannot be divulged at all costs, and even clients who are intelligent people *yet who are not trial lawyers* can cheerfully rush toward perils which must be skirted by sophisticated maneuvers utilizing this privilege and that refusal. The earnest shout from a client demanding that "I just want to tell my story," is often a noble call-out in drama and literature, but can be an absolute disaster in litigation or during the unfolding of hearing or trial. Protecting a client's interest means keeping an eye out for threats on all sides, including internal ones.

All those manipulations of words that lawyers wish to use or hide behind can be actions in compliance with ethical obligations to protect and represent clients as those who need to be protected—from rules and from themselves as much as from other people. The decision to raise an objection to a witness reciting inadmissible hearsay or, alternatively and just as importantly, to select to not speak and *decline* to raise an obviously applicable hearsay objection, is a wielding of that power in service of a larger goal and is one unattached to expressing one's conscience or following an MRPC rule, regulations which mandate protections in ignorance of what those protections are ultimately in service of. Lawyers consider and insert their own litigation and life experiences, their own special legal and educational knowledge, and their own creative and gut instincts in a courtroom setting into a complicated philosophical equation. The variables and functions in that equation tend to generate decisions that reflect strategical insight into the lawyer complying primarily with their representational role; concessions to regulatory mandates imposed on the lawyer in their communal role may be factored lower or perhaps subtracted altogether as protection of that particular client may require.

In an adversarial system of law, all advocacy is intensely partisan—it could be no other way. The hallmark of such a system is not honesty, but scrutiny. Even the derogatory remark that a lawyer is "speaking out of both sides of their mouth" is an observation of that partisanship disguised in the form of an insult. It is no less true for being demeaning—the task of emphatically embracing two polarizing or diametrically opposed viewpoints depending on the client or the case or the moment is nothing to be scorned. Both "sides" of the mouth must be employed if there are audiences in both directions to address. And in addressing them to scrutinize the evidence while doing so is to scrutinize *all* of it, including and especially that evidence which the opponent uses or hopes to eventually use; adversarial conduct means that there must be some serious effort put in to prevent adversaries from using it as well.

A mouth having two sides, a presentation having two audiences—these are each bite-sized samples of an impressive buffet of polarities invading all aspects of law. Polarities infect every level of "ethical" legal practice. Polarities run counter to fairness. Advancing a client's interests almost by necessity means that an opponent's interests are harmed in the process (or at least made subservient to the client's interests). Not always, but frequently, the "prevailing party" rule in court cases demands that a jurist or jury locate and present one and only one true winner and one true loser in the battle.[16] Casting back at the essential precept that competing influences are what propel legal inquiries, then fundamental ethics grasp that it was not a breach for the winner's counsel to have crafted strategies and worked around procedural and evidentiary rules in the most partisan of partisan conduct to get them ultimately put into that triumphant position.

Up to No Good

Here then is the consequential truism that the law schools and the MRPC would never fess up to but ultimately cannot deny: Lawyers are not obligated to pursue the community's common good—they are devoted to promotion of *individual* interests not communal interests. Protecting lives, liberties, social order, property, those are all poetically noble aims, but they are the aims of the citizenry in general, of political bodies, of novel writers and legal philosophers, and of religious and social service organizations. If lawyers are able to advance the cause of liberty *at the same time* as they advance the client's interest, so much the better, but that outcome is purely icing on the cake not at all the cake itself, and an approach to the goal of protecting a client may quickly diverge and almost certainly eventually conflict with some loftier communal goal.

Lawyers do not have an obligation to promote liberty. They do not seek justice. They do not serve society. They do not work to better communities. They do not uphold equality. They do not act in the service of truth. Again, any or all of those events might coincidentally occur but if they ever do it is fully tangential to and only indirectly connected with what the lawyer is peculiarly manufactured and aligned to accomplish in their professional role. That role is acutely centered on the protection of one solitary member of a community alone, on the protection of the tiniest segment of all society, on a social unit whose protection may require *opposing* liberty, outright *hostility* to social equilibrium, destructive *intrusions* on communities, and a blunt *antagonism* toward the exposure of various truths.

An individual's justice is not justice for all and ethically protecting an individual via the law might in fact detour far off a path of justice for any, especially given that what "justice requires" is not an abstract activity but is always culturally and historically conditioned.[17] Again, institutional and ideological pressure is frequently exerted on lawyers to protect the weak and needy, and to the extent that the particular client that day happens to be themselves weak or needy then by fortuity the lawyer's project might nicely line up with that institutional and ideological aspiration.

As the next day's client is rich and powerful, however, the ethical commands on the lawyer are not to then abandon that client in favor of finding and helping a weaker or needier one, or to ruin or compromise the rich client's interests merely because their interests now conflict with the institutional aspirations. The realistically ethical lawyer then shifts—and employs strategy, intuition, experience, knowledge, and power in pursuit of protection of simply a different member of society now, perhaps one with no vulnerabilities and more than enough resources, but one who still deserves and is owed competent and effective representation nevertheless:

> I know I do not represent only the noble and the good. Most of my clients are good enough in an ordinary way, but basically unthinking and rather selfish; some are in my view pretty despicable people engaged in pretty despicable enterprises. I help them not only when I think they are in the right, but when I think they are in the wrong. So long as they are not legally wrong or morally wrong as to be intolerable. In many of the cases I have litigated I am inclined to believe that justice was on the other side, though I have not really asked myself that question in a disciplined way.[18]

Protection of the client's interests is a professional goal and is (hopefully) disconnected from the representative's own personal beliefs. The lawyer's *sincerity* in trial is as artificial as is their *insincerity*—no one in a courtroom truly has the conviction that the trial lawyer is exactly the client nor that the trial lawyer has nothing at all to do with the client, and all grasp that the lawyer/client entity in front of them is an amalgam of measured and connected interests, much of which is simply financial. "Well, that's what they're paid to do" is an observer's sentiment clumsily recognizing that the speech that emanates from the one emanates from both and that economic motivations exist for the words spoken to be meaningful for, and also about, both entities.

Folded into the "being paid" part of the sentiment is the begrudging recognition that there is an acquired skill being employed that has real material and economic value to others, crediting the tacit admission that most laypeople simply cannot speak in an effective fashion in a formal setting. As articulate and analytical as many people are, presenting a skewed storyline and a set of honed and pertinent observations to another in a streamlined and persuasive way without violating a bevy of technical regulations is usually well outside their ken.

Abbreviating an incident straight down into its core components and leaving out all the detritus is something that invariably needs to be done while litigating a case, yet takes a trial lawyer alone to actually accomplish. The client again wants to "tell my story," informs the trial lawyer of that desire, and may even instruct the trial lawyer to enable them to do so. As an advocate with a pointed agenda of protection, however, the trial lawyer may not want any story mentioned at all or may want some distorted version of the story to be conveyed but only in a manner far differently than the client is capable of—even while as a counselor the trial lawyer may feel bound at some vague professional level to follow certain client instructions. That new tension created between the dual roles is not easily resolved and signals that, unquestionably, certain sacrifices are going to have to be made by someone. Overall, the client's autonomy as an individual can likely be preserved but there may well be a hard hit to their pride along the way, and it may take not so gently guiding them to a version of a trial in which desired facts are entirely absent or necessary facts are far more carefully controlled in their telling than any layperson may realize or appreciate.

In this respect, the realistically ethical lawyer does not suppress their own judgment; they give voice to the voiceless by maintaining the fidelity of the task—convincing the fact finder but not jeopardizing the myriad protections at play while doing so and while effectively getting the prominently biased parts of the story out into the light. A commitment to the end goal without capitulation to flattering another's ego, without allowing personal sympathies or naivete to override the wise use of technique, and without enabling the inexperienced client to submarine the experienced practitioner, is key.

Intimately tied to that attempted preservation of autonomy is a sensitivity to conflicts of interest which might adversely affect the lawyer-client relationship itself. It is important to recognize that society does not want ordinary self-interest to guide the decisions on those whom we might crucially depend; we want the representative of others to be, in a basic sense, as independent, impartial, and unbiased as we want the decision-maker to be in the dispute between the representatives. If we think of a profession as a number of individuals in the same occupation voluntarily organized to earn a living by openly serving a certain ideal in a morally permissible and socially sanctioned way, then that organization provides us an alternative to self-interest that has a larger social benefit than self-interest does alone. We achieve something socially valuable by having representatives delimit conflicts which might adversely affect the quality and efficacy of the representational act.[19]

Lawyers communicate in large part by confidently asserting things to be so and those things aren't always empirical facts about the world. They include not just quasi-facts, but nonessential facts, and trivial facts, and facts disguised as opinions as well as those opinions which were once facts and then re-disguised back one second later as an array of different and new facts. Assertiveness in all those respects can take the lousy empirical facts about what "really happened to Smith" in a real-world incident involving both Smith and Jones, and still achieve a reasonable and valuable result or award based on the art of manipulating and then presenting something else entirely to the fact finder to ponder about alternative facsimiles of both Smith and Jones—Bizzarro-Smith and Bizzaro-Jones as it were.

No ethical rules are broken by manipulated presentations, by hiding or distracting from the entire picture or from the most important parts. While no trial lawyer can completely escape *all* bad facts (or, says the highly egotistical trial lawyer, *can* they?), good lawyering can at least orchestrate it so that most of the worst facts are eliminated from being major components in the fact finders' calculations leading to the outcome. No ethical rules are broken by using rules regarding exclusion and elimination to remove statements and documents as records of facts from analysis and equation. More crucially, no ethical rules are broken by a trial lawyer using communication skills and deceitful strategies to redefine and then dictate what is entailed in a good outcome for that client's interests in those circumstances.

Constructing an Analytical Shelter in an Informational Storm

As a parallel, neither are ethical concerns compromised by trial lawyers doing so by engaging in cost-benefit evaluations. The legal scholar Richard Posner illustrated the aptness of such evaluations in decision-making through the analogy of leaving the house in inclement weather.[20] He mused that if the weather forecast was for rain, he would then have to decide whether to take an umbrella with him when he left the house. To do so, he would likely consider a short idiosyncratic list of possible annoyances and pleasures and execute a quick "off the cuff" gauge of probabilities, including one, that the forecast is even correct and that it will affect him personally, and two, whether the need or interest in staying dry for some unknown period of time is worth avoiding the discomforts of getting wet and of carrying or perhaps losing the umbrella.

Posner's larger point was that it was commonplace to do these calculations quickly, nearly unconsciously, and privately—without the need for a calculator or for verification from an outside source, or to even have to explain any of them to himself later. That deliberation—an easily recognizable cost-benefit analysis—he concluded, is a key element to engaging in rational thought, and is classically how lawyers reason to conclusions. It also is an analytic tool that has a long-standing evolutionary precedent as being an adaptive feature for all humans,[21] is an important tool for non-lawyers as well to implement in just about every cognitive activity, and is one therefore included in the processes of legal reasoning and decision-making.

The trial lawyer's choice between adhering to or ignoring alternative legal rules often depends on them making acutely pragmatic decisions about which rule might have a closer fit with a certain goal. As the goals shift and as the smorgasbord of rules evolve and present themselves for selection, the decisions made are not significantly distinct from the quick "off the cuff" ones that idiosyncratic people make every day about minutiae such as the use of umbrellas. Costs and benefits are always being weighed at every moment of waking life whether one consciously identifies that they are actually doing so or not, and it is part of the realistically ethical trial lawyer's job to do so with the client as a joint exercise and also without the client as a private exercise. Folding in all identified costs, all appreciable benefits, and all conclusions from their harmonizing together to direct the client and the fact finder to reach a certain decision is unabashedly "manipulation" and is "game-playing," but at the same time it is neither "unethical" nor "antagonistic" to the client's interests—it is how the complicated version of legal conduct and reasoning operates via logical constructs toward achieving privately beneficial results employing attention to both costs and benefits.

For the most part we have been considering the interplay of the key actors in our odd theatrical set piece, the trial lawyers and their litigious clients. Inserting the play's intended audience, the fact finder (for our purposes here, the jury), into the equation means that we have to start by acknowledging another classic truism: that juries are for the most part kept in the complete dark about nearly everything, especially about the juiciest stuff of which the judge, litigants, and trial lawyers are all, behind and on the stage, keenly aware.[22] Yet the reason for such shielding is not because there is a danger in providing them the information, it is a reason related to that information disparity and to those regulatory protections we noted above. In a sense it is because the trial lawyer is empowered with ways to construct the shelter and does so to protect or advance the client's personal interests—again a directed endpoint which may be light years distant from the fulfillment of any idealistic democratic concern.

The "play" which every participant circles around in our model is of course a public trial. Trials are conceptually more freeform than one might initially grasp; they don't have to be, though usually are, held inside courtrooms, they don't have to involve, though usually do, testifying witnesses, and they don't have to be, though usually are, public events that are recorded for posterity. To the extent that they are plays, they are plays on stages which are floating about quite a bit in conceptual space: a five-minute semi-cooperative exchange between lawyers and a judge "on the record" in chambers may constitute a "trial" not legally distinct from a three week-long slog under a rotunda with thirty active participants, 300 exhibits, and a packed gallery of journalists.

Nevertheless, there is a conceptual infrastructure to all trials. State constitutions and statutes form the basic foundations and issue the legislative commands that a trial may be held at all, and detailed rules of civil and criminal procedure then construct the parameters around which those events are ultimately scheduled, how their workable details are made concrete, and how their formal outcomes are made consequential.[23] Judges run trials and are supposedly in control of their progress but their power is not without limit and they certainly are not "umpire-equivalents."[24] Most importantly, lawyer participation at all ports is equally integral. As trials float along on their stages, the shipping weight of all that process is first launched by the legislator's words, true, and is then helmed by the judge's words, also true, but it is ultimately buoyed, transported, and finally ported, anchored, or sunk by trial lawyers' words critically and separately.

Except for the extremely unusual circumstance where both sides are acting *in pro per*, every trial is essentially a vessel powered by the words of trial lawyers arguing selected laws and selected facts. Throughout the process, rhetoric paraded about on the floating stage can masquerade as fact and appeals to authority can masquerade as fiction. Judge and jury are on board, but neither plays any part as contributors to those words, with the former simply sifting through what words the latter can receive and consider. A jury is a passive receptacle of discretely filtered information with no say in what information has managed to reach them, and only some say in what to do with it.

The movement of all that data and process back and forth between the other players is substantial but what is heard by the jury is a highly restricted rendering. By the time one gets to a civil or criminal action's culmination, a lot has been learned, shared, and utilized by the other participants but only a smattering by the jury. As trial unfolds, juries don't know much to start with, are told stories by laypeople as the evidence gets displayed, are instructed by judges as to only distilled parts of laws said applicable to the stories, are told more complex stories (including entire alternative realities) by trial lawyers as the evidence/stories get interpreted, and as the thing concludes, remain excluded from being privy to considerable packs of factual and legal knowledge as to other stories never told at all and as to important chapters of the stories that were told.

None of this would be so were it not for trial lawyers and their two-sided mouthfuls of manipulative sounds and words. Take, for instance, all those objections that trial lawyers seem to be making all the time. The superficial point of objection is to propose the application of a rule of evidence to a question asked in examination or an exhibit offered into evidence in order to give the court a chance to consider the legal contention being made.[25] The deeper point of an objection is to *restrict the flow of information to the jury*. Objections are tools of constraint and they assist the trial lawyer in having their manufacture of a client-skewed storyline be a successful venture. Constructing a selectively beneficial narrative requires manipulating a balance of true and false statements in favor of false ones being taken as true, an adaptive trick to obtain some advantage from those on the receiving end which every one of us has learned from childhood on.[26] That can't occur until and unless there are only limited choices of true and false statements available on the menu. If the menu of choices is too expansive, then the consumer is afforded the dangerous liberty of weighing each candidate against a large field; thoroughly informed receivers tend to more thoroughly assess credibility. If the menu is narrow, on the other hand, then the consumer is left to choose from a small subset of propositions, and credibility assessments are made far more difficult. The trial lawyer's tasks include making a skewed subset of facts (ones favorable to the client) the *only* subset. Schooled in the intricacies of the evidence codes, good trial lawyers realize that if objectively true statements of what really happened interfere with the goal of selecting the lawyer's storyline, then objectively true facts have to be brutally eradicated from the equation.

In that schema, an objection is an important mechanism for reducing information flow. It stops answers, stops questions, narrows the data stream, and puts limits on the prevailing narrative. Objections such as *hearsay*, *relevance*, and *lack of foundation* are those interruptions that posit that other people's versions of truth are untrustworthy or incomplete. The trial lawyer uses those objections to remove the expression and receipt of unfriendly facts. Objections such as *best evidence* and *unauthenticated documents* are those that imply that what one reads can't be trusted. The trial lawyer uses those objections to remove the sources of actual and prospectively unfriendly facts. At the heart of all objections is the allusion that the lawyer's data control is protective of the jury: that the listener should be suspicious of what the opponent is presenting and should depend on the trial lawyer's professional interference in spotlighting the truly useful bits. At the end of all objections, however, is the muted, suppressed, lawyer-only-interpreted versions of the original information where usefulness and protection are hardly the real objectives.

Cross-examination is different, in a somewhat delicate manner, from objection. Since, by definition, the very act of a lawyer engaging in cross *increases* the volume of both questions and answers, it is not an information barrier-type mechanism but is additive. Nonetheless, it is still comparatively restrictive, manipulative, in its own right. It surprises no one, practitioner or layperson, to get it that in cross trial lawyers regularly ask questions to which they already know the answers. The juror believes that the point of this mini-game apparently is for one to cleverly reveal what another hoped to cleverly hide. Yet for the most part, truths aren't actually "uncovered" in cross, more just repositioned to line up with the mile markers already posted along an advocate's narrative path.

A large chunk of that is that the crossing lawyer likely desires to construct another image for themselves to layer on top of the rest—the muckraker. They puff their chest out and jut their jaw forward, now positioned as the intrepid investigative journalist, doggedly uncovering secrets about which it is absolutely imperative the jury must be made aware. Are these truly secrets? Must one necessarily learn them? Perhaps, but then again perhaps not at all. Far more crucial is that the witness' answer should *appear* to be a secret forced into the light, regardless of whether the answer actually enlightened any issue. In the end, crossing is, of course, just another mask to don, helpful since it imbues admirable qualities of grit and determination, and potentially infectious since it suggests a David-Goliath plot which some jurors might find appealing as consonant with their moral sensibilities. The best grilling in cross isn't truly the functional equivalent of a crucial reveal—it is instead the hero's quip to the villain's rant, pure (and powerful) theater carefully displayed to assure the audience that their champion has listened attentively to a key detail sufficient to have called it out and thereby earned both admiration and trust.

Resistance Is (Kind Of) Futile

Procedural rules prohibit jurors from being part of the filtering process; they certainly have no hand in the selection of what can and can't be heard or read, so reliances become necessary. Left with no choice but to repose trust in someone else to do so, they find that the choices are quite limited in the courtroom environment: trial lawyer or judge is it. Judges are more trustworthy of course but are not the active players in gathering and presenting evidence. They are passive acceptors of evidence that has already been gathered and presented by the litigants' representatives and it is not uncommon that neither has selected to do so with some piece of evidence that would have been supremely helpful to have seen or heard. An adversarial system such as ours puts the combatants in control and relegates the judge to be largely another information filter.

Included in the restriction of information to the jury is the necessity of making sure they are deprived of any usable knowledge about legal rules in general. They certainly don't get any access to research tools at all, much less actual law books, databases, or legal educational resources; they are not told anything about the broad range of statutes, ordinances, or case law which might apply to the facts of the case they are sitting in decision on; they don't get legal questions answered by anyone nor hear explanations from the judge about legal concerns or issues; and they are actively shut down in their attempts to inquire or obtain any of that. Not only are jurors not expected to know law, no one in the courtroom truly wants them to be familiar with law overall, jury instructions notwithstanding. A form of myopia is desired instead in which it is deemed best to strictly narrow their vision down to only a tiny few selected excerpts of a tiny few selected statutes garnished with a tiny few selected propositions from a tiny few selected cases.

Thus from the start of, as well as throughout, the trial, the trial lawyers are prohibited from telling them about law. It is partly for that reason that objections cannot be explained to the jury nor can the significance or basis for rulings on objections be mentioned to the jury in the same respect that going beyond stating the legal ground for an objection ("speaking objections") are prohibited.[27] It seems odd on its face that in front of the jury the trial lawyer may not justify the raising of objection with authority and is only allowed to identify the evidentiary name for the objection and then stop talking to avoid reprimand. That seems petty and artificial but has a purpose—again to make sure that the jury is sheltered from legal knowledge, from the wrong information, and from a surfeit of information, right or wrong. By the end of the trial, the abbreviated raft of issued jury instructions, and the trial lawyers' creative interpretations of those instructions (and supposedly nothing beyond those instructions), are the be-all and end-all of the jury's legal education.

This seems strange. On the face of it, trials seem like they should be infected throughout with Law adorned with a capital L. Isn't the entire point of a "courtroom" for society to create a physical forum by which to publicly present legal disputes for resolution? Isn't the entire point of a "litigant" for a citizen to have a fair route to access laws to resolve their disputes? Isn't the entire point of a "trial lawyer" for society to create surrogates for the disputing litigants in order to best advocate their competing legal positions? Who is being served by such a paucity of the one subject that should be at the forefront of the engagement? It is not just ironic, it is downright anxiety-provoking that the decision-makers of those disputes which get presented are aggressively being *shielded* from learning actual law.

A consequence of the shielding is that the trial lawyer speaking in the courtroom during court proceedings is guided to speak in code. The code utilized has to be closely managed or it loses its effect. Any other process would be a completely different system of justice, would enable the jury to learn the rules of procedure and evidence and start to apply them. The divisions between litigant, representative, and decision-maker would be trespassed, the compartmentalization of those in dispute from those in judgment of their dispute would be seriously collapsed in turn, and the goals of socially mandated contest would be potentially deconstructed as a consequence. Trials would turn into nightmarishly exploratory free-for-alls. The resulting calamity would be that the province of the court to adhere to its judicial role, the province of the trial lawyer to adhere to their advocacy and representational role, and the province of the jury to adhere to their decisional rule, would each be so eroded as to have the system's goals of resolution traversed in which the laws would not then be administered effectively or completely and would be devalued as Law.

Being pressed to talk in code makes the trial lawyer's journey as advocate a lengthy and arduous affair. As they set off on the path, the trial lawyer first needs to educate themselves as to what type of code will be needed and how the code is going to operate. Doing that requires identifying the client's objective. Meetings occur and a private arrangement is established in light of a collaborative task—the trial lawyer and the client are the only participants and both have the joint goal of figuring out what is really wanted by the latter. At this juncture, additional education occurs, this time the lawyer privately educating the client about all pertinent law, good and bad, a lesson the reconstruction of which is going to be crucial to future success.

Once that step has been accomplished, the trial lawyer next needs to list and identify the best legal maneuvers available toward achieving the arranged objective. Doing that is also private, but now is not collaborative at all—the trial lawyer is the only member involved and the client's participation is neither enlisted nor desired. No external education efforts are engaged in between trial lawyer and client, what is learned is all internal to the trial lawyer alone. Sources of information to make wise selections include chats with colleagues, review of past experiences, legal research, and some hot and heavy introspection into style and options thereof.

Finally, the trial lawyer needs to implement the maneuvers which they have ultimately identified. Working on that final task moves along an entirely different intellectual track than the first two. It is now a quite public arrangement and a quite anti-collaborative task—the trial lawyer and everyone else in the world are the participants and active fighting, not getting along, is the strict order of the day. It is a step highly antagonistic to education being any sort of goal.

For one thing it is a task which involves people who are not the client and whom the trial lawyer doesn't particularly want to be educated about anything, including and especially about laws. Trial lawyers want their opponents and their decision-makers to know *less* law than they do, or at least to know only certain laws and not others. For another, this task is anti-collaborative in that people are expressly disinvited to work together. The trial lawyer wants the clerk to not help the other litigant, wants the witness to not help the other witness, wants the judge to not help the jury, wants the jury to not help each other, and wants the outsider to just go away altogether and not interfere with anyone. Excluding witnesses from courtrooms, screening judges from *ex parte* contacts, not contacting the other side's client, redacting testimony, limiting e-mail chains, shielding the identity of experts, and sequestering juries are all part and parcel of this keep-people-in-the-dark structure:

> Symbolic language, whether in a newspaper or in a court of law, is all too often no more than 'empty speech', which does not implicate the subject's desire. Such speech, in contrast to 'full speech', is in the service not of truth, but of deception, and not of understanding but of successful miscommunication. In particular, the parties in a legal process try to control the interpretation and ultimate meaning of their words *before* their utterance . . . Law, in other words, aims at the level of the subject's utterance, rather than at the truth of the subject.[28]

True Lies

To prevail in the last step the trial lawyer must keep their eye on the prize discerned in the first step—they not only can't lose sight of the marked objective, they also can't be distracted by obstacles or diversions once the specific legal maneuvers and styles are chosen or employed. That means that they have to ditch the relatively dead weight of appeasing others and catering to others and worrying about others whom they encounter along the path—unless of course the goal requires it. They also have to recalibrate others' purported "truths" to meet their agenda's specifications. To do that means painstakingly close attention to administering what "truths" are getting lovingly told and what "truths" are getting rudely pushed aside. "I'm telling you that is what happened—it's an absolute fact" cries the litigant, or opponent, or jurist, or witness, and the heated exclamation pinpoints the need for the trial lawyer, not to fold and simply accede to the assertion, but to exploit and manage it.[29] Should its acceptance assist the client, the trial lawyer must find ways to confirm or emphasize the proclamation. Alternatively, should it be averse to the client's interest, the now clearly shameless boast must be ridiculed, or perhaps minimized and drained of import, including by hiding it or by maneuvering procedures and rules around to keep it from being heard in the first place.

A "style" then is not merely an argumentative aid but is a very personalized and specialized apparatus by which to have the right people stay focused on necessary (relative) "truths" and by which to draw focus *away* from those that are unnecessary or harmful, all in order to accomplish a very specific result. Adopting styles is how the coded language delivers its best effect internally and externally. As the legal researcher Susan Daicoff espoused, certain decision-making preferences or styles do predominate for trial lawyers, primarily styles that emphasize logical analysis, cool and impersonal reasoning, and cost-benefit analyses, people engaging in a peculiar mode that "tends to deemphasize harmony, personal relationships, pleasing others, and avoiding conflict and criticism."[30] Every courtroom wall reverberates with the transmission of such styles. But those are not the only items on the available menu, and the fortuities of that day's case might make it so that the more effective choice foregoes logic, reasoning, or analysis altogether.

A large part of the code in which trial lawyers develop and eventually speak arises from their chosen style enabling them to evade those distractions, those obstacles raised by having to consider the emotional well-being of others, including even of the client themselves. As the client hears their own lawyer comment that "I'm thinking about that option" or "That's not what I feel will work best," they are often hearing the coded versions of decisional processing which they are simply the beneficiary of, not the focus of or partner to. Everything gets managed, words, the truths which the words claim to back, the people who claim to be in charge of those words, and the rules which govern who can make such claims, when, and how. As a trial elapses, management balloons.

And here comes another real pinch: the management steps, the chosen styles, the resultant code, the to-be-achieved goal, again, *they all require subterfuge*. Even with Daicoff's "logical analysis, cool and impersonal reasoning, and cost-benefit analysis" style, even with the most common and classic approach, a trial lawyer must still lie—even the "telling it like it is" lawyer whom we encountered above will grudgingly agree to such a ground level necessity, there is just no way around it. Every tailored question to a witness demands it. Every idiom use demands it. Every argument presentment demands it. Every representation to a judge demands it. Every piece of advice to every client demands it. Every lawyerly act *in toto* demands it. In the manner that collaboration needs to be encouraged or stymied along parts of the path, truths need to be suppressed, subdued, and concealed in order to have lawyering as a social concept of individual protection in a representative system work. Simple recalcitrance or a stubborn unresponsiveness is not enough to get the job done; active untruthfulness has to be inserted—and then leveraged and exploited.

A sidebar is vital at this juncture. I do not feel that I will have earned any privilege to go around making claims about lawyers necessarily lying unless I at least make some attempt to tackle head on what I believe the phenomenon of "lying" itself actually encompasses. Most definitions posit that for a lie to occur two things alone must happen: the author (a) must manifest a clearly identified mental state (being "deliberate" or "purposeful"), while (b) engaging in a not-very-clearly identified act ("issuing some sort of false utterance").[31] To put it more colloquially, one has to say something incorrect that they know is incorrect while they are saying it. Few definitions address the multifaceted variety of recipients or the multifaceted variety of social circumstances which many lies involve, and most definitions tend to consider writing or talking as the only conduits and tend to repeatedly circle around a single and mundane definitional requisite: that in lying one is "asserting a false statement." As falsity is contingent on truth, however, then a tautology thereby arises since one may then validly say that lying is simply "not being truthful" while being truthful is simply "not lying." Tautologies, of course, are supremely unhelpful to gaining any valuable understanding of basic semantic or philosophical concepts, so a less slippery explanation seems necessary.

One would think that a more helpful and less tautological definition would be one simply narrower and pickier, that is, some hyper-technical definition which specifies that true "lying" demands compliance with all the following criteria:

a) a discrete, carefully worded, declaration to another which the other actually receives;
b) which the author purposely or deliberately makes and themselves comprehends;
c) designed to deceive another to the author's advantage or to the other's detriment;
d) where the goal of harm to the other, or benefit to the author, is clearly in the author's mind when made;
e) where the declaration is one that the author themselves does not believe at all to be true; and,
f) where the act of making it violates some moral standard of the community.[32]

Yet such an artificially restrictive definition is agonistic to the remarkable plasticity which deceit exhibits as a millennia-old evolutionary adaptation. "Lying" is integral to how our human nature developed and its waters fill an impressively deep well: not just the boringly deliberate falsehood of a low budget TV police procedural show, but also the poorly thought through and purely thoughtless remark; the rude off-the-cuff vehement denial; the plain old "honest mistake"; the self-deception and self-delusion of the recited fever dream; the romantic relationship fake-outs to a love object; the little white lies meant to soothe and placate; the untimely whispered asides within the bellowing crowd; a religious speaker's proclamation about a deity; and the muted absurdities lurking within nearly all joking and sarcastic comments. To immerse myself in that well, to subvert the reader's expectations, and to prove my larger point, therefore, I wish to therefore define lying in the *broadest* of possible terms, as in anything which happens to present as antithetical in any manner to another's perception of some event. That makes "lying" include things like:

1. Failing to acknowledge that someone in fact perceived an event at all;
2. Omitting the mention of a perceived event;
3. Exaggerating the details of or subtly distorting a perceived event;
4. Pretending that one event perceived was actually a different one instead;
5. Offering impressions of perceived events filtered through one's own perceptions;
6. Making efforts to prevent one's perception of an event; and,
7. Making efforts to alter the effects of an event to change how it is perceived,

among numerous others, including all the wild predictions, deliciously stated ironies, fudging of technical terms, off-hand pointless comments, and idiotic misstatements mentioned above. With that, putting on makeup or a wig is "lying," even where the makeup or wig is so poorly done or clearly signaled that no one in their right mind would actually be deceived by the sorry attempt. Using an alias or pretending to be another is lying. Proposing alternative futures but not describing them specifically as pure hypotheticals is lying. Choosing to say only three words alone when a critical fourth or fifth would have been essential to a more complete explanation of a perception is lying. Dreamily posing wishful scenarios, meanly ridiculing another's proposed future, and actively restricting another's ability to explain an event's perception to a third—all these are "lying" as well.

Are any of these starting to sound familiar? The trial lawyer, judge, and juror now chime in to say they certainly do and to also grudgingly admit that none are entirely unexpected nor are entirely prohibited, and a number are even favored. They are all language acts one finds being used in trials, ones which happen to be separated from truth and antithetical to perceptions, ones which span the art of rhetoric and which handily fit within the mold of a representative's art of persuasion.

Tellingly, lying is not unique to law; all walks of life involve contorting the veracity of what one is being told and is telling others. The philosopher Salman Akhtar has proffered a brutal bullet point set of realities nearly impossible for any candid, functioning adult to honestly refute:

- Everyone lies.
- Anyone who claims to be forever truthful is telling a lie.
- It is undesirable to be truthful under all circumstances.
- Lying is essential for smooth social dialogue and interpersonal politeness.
- Different forms and varying extents of lying are integral to many socially useful lines of work.
- Lying can at times save lives
- Since all sorts of gray areas exist between what constitutes a lie and what constitutes a truth, it is not always easy to separate the two out.[33]

What is not mentioned in that list, yet forms a vital component of it, is the idea that a substantial *cost* is always imposed on the activity of being deceptive. Because trustworthiness is not an observable trait but must be displayed, then false displays carry with them a suite of social expenses. One, behind-the-scenes construction of the trust display takes real time and effort; costuming, set design, rehearsal, background research, all incur their price. Two, the fidelity of the display is usually proportional to that effort: duck hunters, celebrity impersonators, and film technicians will all agree that more expensively constructed decoys tend to lead to more believable displays and thus tend to generate higher rates of acceptance and thus higher yields in return on imparted production value. The philosopher Kim Sterelny captured a glimpse of the expense that the lie exacts and the reward that it seeks by comparing it to the low cost involved in making honest displays on the same topic:

> It is easy and cheap for me to present credibly as an Australian birder, because I am an Australian birder. The resources needed to make my birding credentials credible have been assembled automatically, as a side effect of my birding, and independently of any need to signal that characteristic. Becoming an Australian birder was not effortless. But once I became a moderately competent birder, signaling that trait became effortless. Indeed, often I do not need to signal; this information leaks from my ordinary life activities. Suppose someone with no birding skills wanted to credibly impersonate being an Australian birder. That would impose high signal costs. They would have to outlay funds on peripherals: optics, field guides. They would have to spend time and energy acquiring at least a passing knowledge of the birds, especially if they could not rely on an utterly ignorant audience. It is possible to fake birding interest and expertise, but it would be expensive. It is cheap for me and expensive for a fraud. If the profit of deception is low, this asymmetry in itself might suffice to keep signals honest.[34]

But of course the "profit" of the lawyer's deception is not low, but high. Still, pure cynicism about acquiring benefits aside, there should be nothing revelatory to the sophisticated reader about acknowledging that trial lawyers, in that sense described above, lie and lie all the time, as well as that they both benefit from, and simultaneously pay a price for, such conduct. There *should* be, however, something revelatory about realizing that the price paid is not a "penalty," it is just simply a price, and that the lying they are doing is an integral component of their job as is the paying for it. An adversarial representational system posits an appreciation of the need for the shielding of the jury from bad law and bad facts (bad for the client, that is), the need for a coded language to be used on and on behalf of the client, and the need for an eye-on-the-prize-always type obligation to manipulate others in order to be effective, and are all insights which lead to such a revelation.

It is also important to acknowledge that the deceit in which lawyers must engage has numerous empirical and phenomenological limitations. All of it must at least stay within the confines of realities which no listener, no matter how gullible, could be swayed to reject. Basic frameworks about how the world operates undeniably pen in the trial layer no differently than they do anyone else on a mission to persuade. That lying mandatorily occurs is not an observation that all truths are then consequently strangled or that all beliefs are thereby suspended:

> I have been told by a number of extremely objective, rational, "tough-minded" people (in England and Scotland), whose judgment I would unhesitatingly accept in other matters, of certain peculiar experiences (some of which they could report firsthand) which, *if authentic*, would necessitate a radical revision in our conception of man and "life after death." Nevertheless, I continue to think of ghosts as "unreal" and to question the "authenticity" of the evidence offered by these persons. Why is this so? Surely it is not a question of my not having seen a ghost, since I believe in all sorts of things I have not seen, such as electric currents, light and sound waves, mesons, and the like. No, it is simply that the properties of ghosts (as characterized by people who have "encountered" them) do not conform to my categorical scheme . . . they do not behave as do the physical objects around us (they cannot be publicly observed, they cannot be photographed, they have an anomalous space-time existence, and so forth) and their presence cannot be experimentally confirmed, unlike unobservable scientific entities.[35]

Articulating a rationale for such a proclamation—that trial lawyers must lie to the public to do their jobs properly, to protect the client and advance interests—also requires tackling the question of why it is that client interests should have such supremacy, that is, take such an acute precedence, over public interests to begin with. In other words, it seems more reasonable to accept this decree (or at least deem it less problematic) if we are able to justify putting clients in such a priority position over everyone else that lies are considered not just appropriate but outright necessary to assist them.

Doing that starts with appreciating that any lawyer's duties to their client result directly from the existence of the client's individual legal rights. To the extent that the law grants a client some sort of recognized legal interest, the lawyer then has a legal duty to protect that interest. We can also note that it is the law of agency which provides the foundational structure for nearly all the consequences that follow from satisfying those duties within the lawyer-client relationship.[36] An agent's loyalty to the interests of the principal dominates their interactions at every turn; it obliterates the point of the entire relationship if the agent doesn't follow commands, that is, is disloyal. In a fundamental sense, principals and agents together form single conceptual units with the agent being the physical embodiment, the extension of the principal's own will and directive. Now certainly agents can sometimes act outside their authority and thus loosen the bonds of the relationship enough that the unit is dissolved back into two separate entities exposing the individuals to individual liability, but unless and until that happens the one remains the pure mask of the other.[37] Where the relationship stays intact, an agent acting to protect the self-interest of the principal does not themselves express any self-interest in doing so—interest protection is merely an assignment handed down, another obligation which the job entails.

Where the legal system is concerned, we have seen that some complication occurs if the quotients in the equation are client = principal and lawyer = agent; the MRPC and the various privileges legislatively inserted into lawyer-client relationships messes a bit with the law of agency being the *only* defining set of rules. Nonetheless, in no small part the lawyer's lie is, must be, the client's lie even where the client is oblivious to the details of which actual lie is being uttered, to whom, and when. The safeguards of (a) an opposing client and opposing trial lawyer, (b) an attentive judge, and (c) a discriminating jury panel may out the lie or distill it of its intended effect, of course, but its assertion is part and parcel of how agency works. The derogatory term "mouthpiece" is a crass encapsulation of the sophisticated notion that the person talking is doing so with someone else's voice. Massive historical and political forces have compelled this special protection: a client has a position and wants to convince others to accept that position, does not themselves have the requisite skills, tools, education, or experience to do so effectively, but is entitled to and benefited by a system that authorizes them to employ a surrogate through which effective convincing occurs.

And not just any surrogate, any pulpit preacher or sharp-tongued telemarketer who happens to be around, but one trained in and armed with all that peculiar "legal" knowledge and the wherewithal as to how to leverage it against an opponent who likely has the exact same. This is surrogacy where wielding power is contingent on exercising a special skill set in ritualistic combat where all combatants are tasked with doing all they can to influence while staying within the pages of a voluminous playbook which has been handed out to all titled "What Is And Is Not Allowed In Influencing Others." Manipulation is mandatory on that battlefield. Deceit is mandatory on that battlefield. And since effective deceit on another's behalf demands proficiency and sophistication in being deceitful, then each combatant has to carefully think about the elaborate cognitive ability which lying will involve and which legal knowledge may sharpen.[38]

First, the liar needs to make the false statement. This is not innate but is learned; constructing genuinely workable falsehoods takes adult knowledge and adult experience in cleaving true from false propositions made by others. Lawyers hear all sorts of false statements (and *possibly* false statements and flatly non-provable statements) every day, from the morning's new consult to the evening's case list wrap-up. They are surrounded at every turn by others hoping to convince them of "what really happened" and they eventually develop a pretty good ear for the inadvertent and deliberate omissions hiding within the interstices. In turn, gaining knowledge and experience in constructing alternate versions of others' stories and in deconstructing the alternate versions of others' stories eventually becomes most lawyers' stock-in-trade.

Second, the liar needs to cautiously control their visual and aural appearance during the lie; facial and micro-facial expressions[39], vocalizations, and posture need to be well managed and to do that the liar needs to have a good handle on what an "innocent" appearance regularly looks like and sounds like in others and to others. This requires being cognizant of cultural norms of truth-telling and then adapting one's words and affect to fit the right circumstances. The appearance of confidence in one's own words being true has a tangible component, as do non-spoken representations of veracity—and again manifesting confidence is classic lawyer behavior with a long history and pedigree. As a component of representing private interests, lawyers work intimately with secrets of all sorts and gain a strong familiarity with the public versions of represented truths in the form of sealed records, sworn oaths, spoken affirmations, written and attested declarations, and notarized affidavits as part of their job.

Third and most importantly, the liar needs to know quite a bit about what the listener does and does not know for the lie to actually work. Being physically near the listener to observe them helps. Questioning the listener closely helps. Comparing the listener to other listeners helps. Attention to the most trivial detail is awarded. And if a barrier is erected by others to protect the listener's privacy and to limit interactions with the listener, then projecting into the mind of the listener to apprehend and postulate their specific level of knowledge and awareness of the message contents, as well as anticipating their likely reaction to the message's delivery, is definitely mandated.

To that end, legal knowledge and legal technique is enormously beneficial to mind influencing and mind projection projects. The lawyer reads, writes, and recites day in and day out all with an aim toward gauging what others might know about or not know about or think about as they hear and read the product of those efforts. Assessing the informational content of others is a mental game which draws on noting suites of socially significant behaviors working successfully in tandem with a cooperative social environment to reveal the content. Expertise in reading, writing, and talking is expertise conducive to the liar having the necessary apparatus to get themselves and their readers or listeners in conjunction with the presented lie as it occurs in the conversation. As we have seen, informational transactions—and the ability to attain advantage through imbalances in those transactions—sit at the very core of law practices, especially in litigation environments and trial circumstances, and informational wealth along with expert communication skills foment the opportunity for deception to work well.

In short, the really desirable type of manipulation is a developmental skill.[40] Honing it demands transcending the naivete of only honest expressions. Honing it demands fine-tuning some workable level of fakery. Sure, faking involves a cost that honesty does not. The cost that is tagged on to the fakery inherently mandated in the practice of law, nevertheless, is one built into the very fabric of becoming a lawyer in the first place. Law schools unknowingly teach the fakery. Legal research unknowingly empowers the fakery. Bar associations and law firms unknowingly resource the fakery. Courtroom experience both knowingly and unknowingly hones the fakery. As one in the throes of discerning, identifying, suppressing, subduing, and concealing facts and law harmful to the client, the trial lawyer should adapt and evolve throughout their upbringing and education to become well suited to playing all those cognitive games and playing them well.

Ever present and swirling around the trial lawyer's coded language and the procedurally tricky steps taken on the path to the goal is a bevy of concerns about the client's interests being protected and advanced. Argumentative devices are used to push those interests firmly along such a path. As agents uniquely suited to protect their principals using specialized legal knowledge, experientially developed linguistic skills, and seat-of-the-pants fashioned presentational tricks, trial lawyers are pressed to merge their personas and their specialized talk into a thing called Argument which is necessarily some truth, some lies, some facts, some law, some falsehoods, some sincerity, much that is a mixture of all that and much that is none of that. Argument is both the perquisite to and the outcome of making trials work as representative-driven, socially valuable, dispute resolution phenomena.

Clouding the Issues

A lawyer-centric view of all that simultaneously beauteous and wretched lying requires that we keep in mind that Argument capitalized is not necessarily "arguing" in its lowercase form. Lowercase arguing in real time is mostly a series of punctuated interruptions where each participant inserts inflection and tone to try to gain the upper hand, where each strains to control the response and reaction of the other, where each leans in to the goal of "scoring a point" yet may be sidetracked from that goal by shifts in volume and tension of the exchange. Most lowercase "social" arguments have a brute cadence, an uneven back and forth of loud insistence and slight concession, with some verbal overlap depending on the vehemence of the participants.

Capitalized upper case Arguing in the trial lawyer's extraordinary biome is different. With turns being regimented, interruption and overlap is absent. With the sequence of participation being supervised by an outsider, the exchange cadence is far more stilted. With the use of a courtroom stage, and the artificiality of each actor getting to be the only one on the courtroom stage who may talk with no formal time limitations, there is far more theatricality to the transaction. Notably, the art of dramaturgy also provides the trial lawyer with an extra prop bag of semantically emphatic devices that most social arguers would never deign to utilize: the conspiratorial wink, the breathy sigh, the hearty "genuine appreciation" laugh, the upraised finger, the crocodile tears, the flattering aside, the beseeching alto, the menacing bass, the jaw drop, the eyelid flutter, the stuttering interruption, the conciliatory shoulder shrug, and the narrowed squint—a list limited only by whatever the prevailing culture combined with one's personality suggests may be appealing to others.

Additionally, the art of rhetoric has gifted trial lawyers with the use of what can be extraordinarily understated and muted messages veiled behind whatever is overtly being transmitted. Trite as it may sound, even minute and particular hand and finger placements provide signals, micro-gestures operating as a subtle communicative force between orators and their audiences.[41] Not looking at the receiving person being spoken to accompanied by delicate pronoun shifts from "we" to "them" while locking eyes with the judge is a powerful ploy to employ in any argumentative exchange; alternatively, "distracted disinterest" by the trial lawyer in the courtroom carries a different rhetorical weight, evoking images of the scholar's thoughtful reflection, the religious official's decorum-related emotional distancing, and the college professor's insertion of intellectual or academic superiority.

Never forget that the undercurrent of fabrication on a stage maintains its presence throughout. For one, absolutely none of those invocations recited above may be justly earned, and the bulk of them are easily stagecraft alone, perhaps even mere mannerisms alone. Stagecraft in general is all about patent deceptions most of which are nonverbal; looking away at the precise moment that a point needs emphasis, the visual equivalent of the pause, a subliminal message that the speaker is not one of the gang but is in control of or above the gang.[42] Stagecraft is the laugh and sideways glance but executed at the precise moment that another's point needs to be *deemphasized*, the visual equivalent of the new arrival's claim of joinder, "I am one of you." Arguing mandates stagecraft. And because audiences clearly know initially that this is a stage and that *some* sort of acting is going on in front of them, the best deceits are those which escape detection as deceits. The most monumental successes arise where the listeners lose sight of the stage altogether, accept the actor's monologue as society's received truth, and adopt the offered script as a digest of real-world beliefs.

Disguising an entire stage is hard to do. Making the inauthentic seem authentic equally so. Conveyance of sincerity is an essential element of effective lying—but it must be anything but blunt. Barren exhortations of "You've got to believe me" and "I am really telling you the truth" won't cut it at all. Those crude emphatics *raise* alarm bells in most listeners and drive them away from a lie's acceptance. Productive sincerity formations instead require tailoring the message to the recipient in such a way as to make *them* do the work of convincing, have *them* desire the speaker to be genuine because doing so seems like the best choice among a limited field of poorer choices. Evangelists swoon to this idea—it is the speaker who claims to be the bitter skeptic and who rhetorically insists that the audience consider *disbelieving* a message. If rejection of the message is subtly designed to be unpalatable, the audience works its way toward convincing themselves of the alternative as the attractive one. In that way, many of the best liars don't assert their sincerity at all, stepping back and working indirectly to get it granted to them through managing internal expectations.

"Know your audience," the lawyer says: Arguing capitalized weaves effects back and forth in relation to *who* is being argued to. We all get it that while highly susceptible listeners such as toddlers will accept nearly any proposition at face value, anyone older than four pretty much needs to at least be spoken to in their working language to be swayed.[43] So what is the language which six or twelve adult strangers seated uncomfortably in a courtroom box "speak" in? That massive unknown demands massive social projections and sparks massive legal ingenuity. Colloquialisms and idiomatic phrases work in some few instances, a humbling self-effacement approach of short, blunt noun-verb pairings works in others. One thing is for sure: the vernacular used must sound like how a "normal person" talks and thinks, not how a lawyer or judge or expert talks and thinks.[44]

The language which the *court* "speaks in" is something of a different matter (although not entirely): with the judge, the trial lawyer is hemmed in at all sides by the demands of an exquisitely precise technical vocabulary, a lexicon that demands professional minds to be linguistically aligned. Effective talk to a judge is to have the judge "think just like" the trial lawyer, and the speech patterns, shorthand, and references are all akin to how trial lawyers talk in and among their own conspecifics. In contrast, with the jury, the trial lawyer jettisons any special language, aims to have hearts aligned, not minds, that is, projects speech patterns along an arc designed to have the jury "feel like" the trial lawyer's client or the bystander witness, really someone, anyone, who is anything *but* a lawyer. To the jury, talk must sound universes distant from how a "trial lawyer" presumably sounds to colleagues or authorities.

In speaking to a judge, intellectual control and transferred direction are a trial lawyer's sharpest tools. Use authority shorthand such as "the case," not full-on citations to Smith v. Jones, since abbreviated references imply that lawyer and judge have both already smartly done the same background research, are already close study partners who can rely on the other's brain being pre-prepared. Use muted, low volume, casual nods to applicable rules and principles so that each part of the full argument feels like a set of side projects engaged in jointly; better to listen to the lawyer's annotated version than waste time and resources reading other versions in full to get to the same message. Soft peddle global concerns, hard peddle local ones. Judges—who are also lawyers—need to be coaxed into being scholarly compatriots who can comfortably trust their close legal colleagues. Argument to them doesn't just provide a testing ground for their judicial contemplation, it subtly sets the boundaries of what that testing ground even encompasses and what it leaves outside.

In speaking to a jury, emotional misdirection and transferred attention are the sharpest tools. Use folk law shorthand such as "the king can do no wrong" rather than stilted, established, annoying legal phrases. Use terminology which their own spouse or buddy might use cavalierly at a barbeque and then position the opposing lawyer as the uninvited neighbor spouting inane vitriol over the backyard fence and interrupting a fun event; imply that there are clear allegiances to embrace and clear invites to disdain. Use earnest call outs to small group togetherness so that each part of the full argument feels like a set of handshakes being made on obviously smart decisions. Soft peddle strangers' concerns, hard peddle family ones. Jurors need to be coaxed into being familial compatriots. Argument to them doesn't just provide an emotive context to join or disband particular groups, it provides the boundaries of classification and category to mandate that the jury accept who is in and who is out of any group at all, to locate others to even have emotional reactions directed toward in the first place. Alignment is key in both instances, but the players and the words being aligned are orders of magnitude apart.

And the trappings of a "stage" are ever present in both conversations. The demands of a stage make arguing require some object somewhere to be the visual and conceptual central reference point for that audience to note and relate to, thereby to align with or separate from. Listening and looking go hand in hand for audiences. Words and objects must connect in the conceptual space provided to them, and must connect in location, significance, and in timing of consideration. A few cases lend themselves well to naturally identifying a unique object of interest: the weapon used in the commission of a crime sitting on the counsel table with an exhibit tag attached to it is easy to draw attention to. Even then, the object has to be given a legal significance. The speaker must think of the core propositions available to them to impart that significance. Most involve a "timeline" of the object as it sits on a conceptually elevated platform.

Three questions come to mind in that regard: One, does the proposition review the object's past? Two, does the proposition survey the object's current present state? Three, does the proposition predict the object's future or propose a new future for it?

Perhaps it does none or all those things. Choices in and fluctuations around those timelines are directed by the trial lawyer's words and motions on the stage because those timelines and motions can have intellectual and emotive interest to (a) listeners who are professionally invested, as with judges, or (b) listeners who are situationally invested, as with juries, in deciding something about the object's "meaning" to a final decision about a litigant. The significance of the object is a function of the basic information provided about the object and why it is placed *there* and the trial lawyer is in strong control of that information—and distributes the information sparingly using screens, curtains, props, and spotlights.

Most cases, however, have no physical item at hand for reference, or at most involve places, interactions, mechanisms, discussions, or arrangements which can at best be indirectly illustrated but never handled or touched. And every case, regardless of demonstrative exhibits, include abstractions for which there is simply no pictorial or physical assistance available for demonstrating. To that end, the most important challenge for the trial lawyer is to somehow make abstractions into tangible props during the course of the play. Doing so requires visualization of where an abstraction, like a physical object, might also "sit" as one thinks about it in normal time and space. At heart, the words used about abstractions need to produce a powerful mental imagery that goes beyond inanimate objects altogether and draw interest about that one thing which is most interesting to all people—other people. Abstract concepts and physical objects must be linked to *people* to have any impact on the minds of decision-makers. They need to be transformed into the personalized: things fought over, worked on, disdained by, sympathized over, by people deeply invested in doing so.

Control, therefore, is key. Contention, collaboration, acrimony, consolation—all need control to work. Information flow must be forcefully regulated. It is hard to grasp the complexity of the epistemological question of why the law constructs the phenomenon of some key participants in a case (the litigants) being provided a lot of information while other participants in the case (the deciders) are regularly precluded from obtaining the same. One part of the explanation is that lawsuits, cases, are simply not democratic phenomena even though they are generally governed by and historically originate from the application of democratic principles. There is little that is equally or evenly distributed among the participants in a case—much like imbalances in evidentiary burdens and financial resources, imbalances of power are the norm in a lawsuit, not the exception. Rules and court procedures vest power in some players which is purposely antagonistic to that wielded by others, and that power includes access to information and the ability to limit access. Sharing is discouraged in favor of much more important jurisprudential considerations such as finality and reliability. True democratic distributions would enable litigants "second and third and fourth chances" to fix legally insufficient missteps, perhaps, or retry factually insufficient assertions, but the public policy bases for doctrines such as collateral estoppel and *res judicata* brook no such opportunities.

A second part of the explanation is that law is a process which embraces the odd value of an independent decision-maker being a non-knowing entity, particularly via the purposeful "not knowing" aspect of exclusionary rules which have been specifically designed by jurists and legislators to stop people such as jurors from learning irrelevant or prejudicial information throughout a trial. In two classic short words, the trial lawyer's interjection of "Objection, relevance" presents in shorthand the necessity that trials and hearings at their heart are narrow disputes about singular historical events which occurred between private parties and which need to be kept narrow and singular in order to enable an overburdened and antiquated justice system to manage them to a feasible, workable resolution. Of course, in pursuit of that fantasy "justice," there are always some legal theoreticians who dreamily believe it should be otherwise:

> How supportive evidence is of a claim depends on how well it anchors the claim in experience, and how well it integrates it into an explanatory account; i.e., on how good the circumstances of any relevant observations were, and how well the claim in question fits into an explanatory story with the other relevant facts presumed known. But supportiveness is not enough; the warrant of a claim also depends on how warranted the reasons that support it are, independent of the claim itself. . . . But even supportiveness and independent security together are not enough; the warrant of a claim also depends on how much of the relevant evidence the evidence includes—for however supportive and however secure the evidence is, it won't give strong warrant to the claim in question if it omits some essential facts.[45]

But "omitting essential facts" is a mandatory practice in trial, not the least reason for which is that trials would fail at a fundamental level if omissions were prohibited and completely full inquiry and disclosure made the gold standard instead. We have an adversarial system, not an inquisitorial one; we traffic in hard realities of choosing facts from two combatants' pre-culled lists, and we definitely do not bask in the luxuries of calmly locating every essential fact there is to present for healthy and thorough consideration. Disputes, being antagonistic by their very nature, must be antagonistically teed up, antagonistically confronted, and antagonistically disposed of, or law will turn into a fruitless and wasted academic endeavor pivoting to communal goals in rejection of personal ones. Utility and self-interest, however, actually run the game and utilitarian principles say that in order to manage knowledge of discrete events, a deliberate ignorance of other different events, other different persons, and other different disputes, has to be managed as well. To shed light, one has to create focus and one has to create darkness, or otherwise the light being shed will not be distinguished from the general ambience, and the subject and background will sadly and meaninglessly merge into non-information.

This concept in court cases translates into focused and darkened (i.e., offered and eliminated) areas of competing knowledge, that is, agnostic effects. Investigators in agnotology and the sociology of ignorance[46] analyze the production and maintenance of ignorance in all sorts of human pursuits, law among them. Demands imposed by relevance can help us understand how it has come to be that in an age of high-level concern over curtailing ever-growing and desired ignorance, we nevertheless work systematically to promote and secure less knowledgeable fact finders—and characterize our doing so as "just."

At least the manipulation of juries by trial lawyers to stay within the confines of the relevant doesn't tread the classic agnotologist path, the sad walkway of deliberate or inadvertent neglect, poor reasoning, definitional blindness, unquestioned tradition, and nonscientific selectivity which some people and many political groups employ to keep both themselves and others completely ignorant of important social or political truths. Lawsuits are different than social service projects or politically directed campaigns in that respect for many reasons.

One, the calculus of jury manipulation does not deny real world influences but to the contrary *accounts* for them. We are cognizant of jurors' desires to insert their personal preferences into the trial outcome and we deliberately adjust for that desire by using judicial power to prohibit their personal contributions, silencing their own potential prejudices and interferences by a communally accepted agreement, as it were.

Two, the ignorance which the law and the trial lawyer jointly craft is not disadvantageous to the juror as it is to the ignoramus; the barriers are erected in recognition of the jurors as individuals with individual lives, and thus help limit personal exposure (as well as reduce potentials for retribution and retaliation). Rights of privacy, as well as of safety and security, are respected by delimiting certain informational exchanges.

Three, trial lawyers for all their faults are at least somewhat sensitive to the fact that it is not always the case that knowledge *is* power; some forms of knowledge can create unproductive distractions in the recipient at best and a complete paralysis in the system at worst. Where time is at a premium, as it is in the sheer number and progress of trials through an overburdened system, then knowledge limitations which promote efficiency are valuable. Wastes of time and energy are avoided by curtailing knowledge.

Four, the practice of law in public settings with judicial oversight must stay keenly aware of the fact that many important social relations depend on systemic ignorance arrangements such as trust and politeness. Not just decorum in trial proceedings, but reliance on the authority distributions between bench and bar, are functions of the jury's knowledge being restricted in important aspects; the effective administration and operation of a trial frequently hinge on confidence in the knowledge of others and a need for propriety as to that confidence being as highly valued as the accumulation of one's own knowledge.

Deliberately placing gaps between what jurors already know and what they don't need to know is an important activity since constitutional parameters constructed to create fairness and due process in the entire judicial system—from *voir dire* to jury instructions—are boundaries devoted to getting them to only what they *need* to know so that other players, the litigants, are not disserved by unfair knowledge disparities. Correspondingly, evidence rules and trial procedures are only partially devoted to creating agnostic effects. Additionally, at least the overt intentions of the exclusionary rules and procedures we are discussing are not aimed to cloud or confuse any particular person, but are aimed to protect a particular ideal in light of a particular reality.

Moreover, the blinders placed on jurors are provisional, are used to keep jury panels in the dark only for a *temporary* time period, that is, until a judgment finally issues. Once that occurs, the former jurors are now certainly welcome to learn anything and everything about what they were not told earlier. Many courts take advantage of the lifting of the exclusionary rules after the close of the case to get judge and jury together after everyone else has gone home to talk about what was kept from the panel in the heat of all that battle. Absolutely nothing later prevents former jurors from revisiting the case via accessing other informational sources, from dockets to statutes to news reports, including even fashioning a "speculative history" retooling of the dispute as to what missing witnesses and eliminated evidence *would* have shown the case was truly about.

That timing factor allays the creation of further uncertainty and confusion, something which willful transmissions of ignorance in other strata of society don't support and don't account for. To that end, juries are not informationally discontent for long, only for a truncated period; their obliviousness is not due to their own desire or disregard to be so or to remain so, it is a desire and disregard manufactured by others for them and only provisionally with a respite from the ignorance eventually afforded in full.

It is also significant that jury ignorance does not materially affect jury rationality. Jurors, like all people, are pretty familiar with the universal presence of the con artist, the sideshow charlatan, the great pretender; most cynical adults get it that there are always unreasonable people who may masquerade as founts of reason.[47] Every adult in every courtroom also "gets it" that the exclusion of knowledge of particular facts is not also the exclusion of the use of reason or of common sense. It is unremarkable to recognize that institutions and individuals often work quite hard to confuse and cloud any evidence that might show people what is actually happening in particular places, but that confusion and clouding have their upper limits in the face of rational thinking.

As we saw with Schlagel's refusal to believe in ghosts noted above, as with the difference between a person saying "He is asleep" and saying "I am asleep," the proposed truth of many statements can simply be rejected on purely logical grounds.[48] Even if one is not a committed skeptic, in the "who is really asleep" example, the first assertion (about *another's* status) can simply be evaluated with behavioral criteria as observed or recited by a credible observer and thus it has a chance of acceptance (in light of course of its particular delivery by the speaker). The second statement, on the other hand (being about one's *own* status that, if true, would not logically allow the statement to be made in the first place), presents as a pure self-contradiction; it is what is often called "playful nonsense" and no one who is rational accepts it, regardless of its delivery or its speaker.

Finally, the exclusions are not products of cooperative ventures; it is the unilateral use of the rules and procedures by the trial lawyer that tamps down the flow of information, not the request or voluntary embracement of them by the jury themselves. That one-sidedness does not mean that the jury is disserved, merely that it is reliant on another's help. Sociologists recognize that such a dynamic is a universal part of the human condition:

> At times, all individuals find themselves participants in interpersonal interactions characterized by an asymmetrical structure: they help or are helped; they advise or are advised; they abandon or are abandoned.[49]

And not just help and advice and instructions, but substantial information itself is in fact eventually provided them; juries receive personal deliveries of witnesses, documents, records, and citations to lawful authority that are each truly meaningful packets of data, and which in isolation and in tandem reflect an accurate use of authority—just not *all* of it. The asymmetry, the imbalance, is not a reflection of any underlying coercion or collusion to keep the public in the dark. It is a motif constructed in the service of keeping the public informed and functional simultaneously; establishing a socially acceptable form of relevance personified and of finality implemented.

Our legal system recognizes the great social benefit of curbing private combats. There is enormous social value in unevenly matched players on an uneven playing field agreeing to be bound by artificial limitations and accepting conclusive decisional acts in order to satisfy their own personal gripes. It is a joint project not executed in the service of Justice with a big J or high social ideals about Truth and Fair Play with their own capitalizations—it is executed with an eye toward addressing the necessarily pickier and smaller components attendant to accomplishing manageable and effective dispute resolution among the citizenry. The larger projects aimed at accomplishing social good are puzzles to piece together by other players in different professions and via the protocols of different institutions, not law.

Truth, Law, and Evidence

One evening I was talking with my daughter about her master's thesis on artificial intelligence's influence on medical ethics and we touched on the topic of how doctors (in comparison and contrast to AI programs) reach their diagnoses. She talked a bit about the processes involved in physicians carefully "reasoning to a conclusion" and comprehensively describing to their patients the logical diagnostic path along which they traveled to determine what the patient's condition was, as well as what could or should be done about it. As we both mulled over the details of reasoning as a mental process, I thought about my own profession and how lawyers express to others how they "reason to their conclusions" (to the extent that they do so at all). One fundamental distinction between doctor-patient and lawyer-client explanations seems to me to arise straight from the conceptually distinct nature of doctor-patient and lawyer-client relationships themselves.

Doctors are separate conceptual entities from their patients. Protection of the patient mandates that the patient obtain an explanation about the protection because the patient's interests are independent of the doctor's interests. Being fundamentally disconnected units, the doctor can't *share* the patient's interests, but can only try to *protect* those interests from the outside. In example, if Smith is diagnosed with a diseased liver, then protecting his body means treating his liver, which in turn perhaps means selecting the appropriate pharmaceutical. While the doctor can and should learn the various rationales, Smith is the only one around who can be provided any rationale about the pharmaceutical options, and, to get his body fixed, Smith has to know something about the anatomy and physiology going on inside of him which the pharmaceutical will hopefully affect so that his exertion of decisional power has a valid empirical foundation.

Lawyers, on the other hand, are *not* separate conceptual entities from their clients; they are conceptually connected instead under the strange umbrella of being their "representatives." Protection of the client's rights may or may not need to involve *explaining* the protection to the client as long as the client is simply aware that the protection is occurring since the one is, for all intents and purposes, the other. In other words, unlike the doctor, the lawyer can explain to themselves, in the shared role as client, the rationale for any protection to be instituted.

In example, if Smith is unlawfully arrested, then protecting his rights means dismissing a criminal charge filed against him, which in turn means perhaps selecting the appropriate motion by which to do so. Here, Smith does not *have* to get a rationale about the motion options (although nothing prohibits it) since his lawyer developing the rationale is enough. To fix his legal problems, Smith doesn't have to know anything about motions or rights—as long as his lawyer does, the exertion of decisional power is protected. Smith really just needs the lawyer to stand in his shoes and figure all that out *as if the lawyer were him*. Indeed, since figuring all that out includes persuading a judge to grant the motion, and since persuading is an art not a science, then asserting objective truths and employing empirical reasons to do so—even to Smith himself—might hamper, not foster, the effort.

The telling of truths is thereby a drastically different pursuit between the professions. Doctors are slaves to empirical truths—there is zero benefit to anyone, only enormous detriment to everyone, in "shining on" the patient about what organic problems their blood chemistry panel discloses. Lawyers, as representatives looking out for guarding shared social interests, really shouldn't be telling very many truths at all—in an adversarial system of justice the goal of "truth-telling" is actually "truth-obscuration." The use of reason, the proffering of empirical facts, and the employment of style in law traverse conflicting pathways since lawyers often don't *want* to use reason as an analytic device to uncover "what really happened" when (a) relative truths about what happened are often independent of reason, and (b) emotion can be a far more effective tool available for getting to the endgame of having another accept a favorable, if factually skewed, version of "what really happened." Moreover, law, vastly unlike medicine, is a competitive sport not a collaborative one,[50] and a good (read, effective) style can be analytical, surely, yet at the same time can evade, deride, or even transcend cooperation and cooperative reasoning altogether.

From the Star Chamber to Modern Legal "Truths"

The deformation and manipulation of reason is no bug in our legal system—it is a crucial feature. It is critical to appreciate that in an adversarial system of justice the goal of law is not the search for one truth but to the contrary is actually the shuffling and obscuration of multiple alternative truths. To grasp this insight, one must first step back to the late fifteenth century when the Court of Star Chamber arose in England, a special legal body made up of jurists and counselors tasked with fixing a long broken justice system and initially conceived as a modest supplement to the more standard common law courts of the time.[51] While the Court of Star Chamber started off with good intentions under Henry VII as a vehicle to enforce certain laws which other courts would not enforce, and to grant remedies which were politically unavailable as a practical matter within the common law system, Charles I quickly exploited it to enforce harsh political goals instead, and in doing so converted it into what we recognize today as a classic symbol of political oppression.[52]

Deriving support from the king's sovereign powers, the Court of Star Chamber enjoyed significant muscle and flexibility in procedures and format distinct from all other courts. Initiating and concluding decisional power was vested in individuals not in groups; juries and grand juries were not needed to obtain either an indictment at the beginning of a case or a verdict at the end of one, and a petition of an individual complainant alone was sufficient to trigger jurisdiction and to obtain a conviction. The art of factual inquiry was heavily malformed in favor of accuser and against accused, the latter who was in each case personally put on oath whether they liked it or not and was compelled to directly answer not just the originating complaint but all subsequent questions.[53]

Most importantly, the Court's procedural requirement that the accused have an advocate alongside them throughout operated to convert two individuals into one unit, but in the harshest possible way—by making the client personally responsible for what their representative advocated, including to the extent that if the representative failed to vouch for the client's words under oath, the client was not only precluded from presenting their version but was deemed to have simply confessed completely.[54] Having both representatives and oaths imposed substantial burdens on the accused by exposing them to contempt and punishment for answering as well as for not answering questions, regardless of whether the question was favorable or hostile or to whom the question happened to be directed. The combined effect of forced advocate and forced oath in order to present "the truth" in the Court of Star Chamber was to have individuals tread a painfully narrow and dangerous path, one beset on all sides with grave consequences for both travelers, the accused *and* their counsel.

Now, it is less than astonishing to recognize that truth and the justice system have always historically been at odds, and the inquisitional mode of the Court of Star Chamber was merely one mode of getting at what the party in power that day wished the truth to be. "Lawyers," as a social construct, arose from the Court of Star Chamber in the form of personified tools which both sides—accuser and accused—exerted to pry their version of truth out of public inquiries while navigating through obstacles such as inescapable oaths that the system itself had strewn about to penalize participants during the course of the inquiry.[55]

The eventual end of the Court of Star Chamber certainly did not end the serious commands which political systems imposed upon the citizenry to expose, deliver, and promote personally skewed truisms in order to achieve legal goals. The processes inherited from the Star Chamber, and the tricks and techniques developed by the functional stand-ins now known as lawyers, inflamed everything. Our current legal system, a descendant of the ancestral Star Chamber, has embraced the notion that where truth actually reposes in the practice of law is necessarily a function of two interconnected phenomenon: just who specifically claims to speak the truth, and just whom the speaker must specifically persuade.

In law as in other social institutions, truths are frequently exposed, delivered, and promoted by relying on the speaker's and the recipient's level of awareness and personal judgment; as those levels vary wildly from person to person, the truth that is revealed in transmission from speaker to audience necessarily varies wildly in turn—*and becomes relative*. Reconciling one's personal cognition with the object of that cognition "subjectifies" each person's views about that object, and no absolute "truth" is available.[56] The idea of using an advocate to discern relative truths on behalf of everyone being questioned—whether it is someone for the accused or against them—developed first to support and then later to counteract the one-sided inquisitional mode of the Star Chamber.

Certainly, the justice system which evolved in the United States from the late 1700s on sought to pointedly avoid the injustices fomented on the participants within the Court of Star Chamber.[57] It rejected the inquisitorial model and instead adopted an adversarial model which entrusted power to a third group purportedly distinct from accuser and accused: "fact finders," those assigned to select the best "truth" among the competing choices offered by the other two. In such a system, the result for all is that truth ends up being whatever a fact finder (in the form of either judge or jury) ultimately decides it is.

Such a system demands, as a necessary corollary, that the advocate's role is then not to reconcile anyone's beliefs at all with anything universal and objective (truth with a capital "T") but rather to mold or deform such beliefs toward the goal of convincing the fact finder that their version (of truth with a lowercase "t") is superior to another's and should be selected from between the two.[58] Adversarial controversies create adversarial offerings of truth, and such offerings in turn create offerors who are heavily invested in making the best offer of a version favorable to them. The recipient of the offerings distills truth not just from versions of the same set of facts but from what set of facts is even available to consider in the first place—and is led to actively disregard what should have been available but which was, for whatever reason, absent.

In escaping the political injustices of the Court of Star Chamber, our system has created different, though less philosophical, injustices where fact finders not only do not purport to know the truth, neither do they even work to seek it out for themselves and are discouraged from doing so. Instead, they take a far more passive role and are directed to simply wait to receive what others claim the truth may be. Jurors are much more "those who must choose," that is, dependents, than they are "those who get to decide," that is, independents. Since lawyers evolved as tools to uncover relative truths, and since fact finders are charged with determining relative truths, then lawyers are specifically designed to prey on dependencies inherent in that dynamic and influence fact finders in a highly relative manner. Hence, the insertion (and systemic support) of "being a good influencer of dependents" into the law equation is made an inherent power and an inherent trait of its practitioners.

Contrary to public perception then, the discovery of one singular truth in our process is often *incidental* to the process and is frequently rejected outright. In the law as it works at present, we have constructed a lavish buffet of codes, rules, and procedures which all work to hamper, not encourage, exposure. These include detailed evidentiary exclusion rules leading to motions to suppress; lofty and picayune rules of professional responsibility designed to protect privileges and confidentiality; and ever-shifting conduct and practice rules (broad societal concerns really) about courts doing everything possible to avoid that terrible boogeyman called "prejudice."[59] The union of those rules and principles operates to constrain and constrict the presentation of evidence of what might have actually happened in any particular incident. All the rules recognize and impart high value to the concept that the protection of competing social goals often requires a suppression, a shutting-down, of truths far more than an advancement or revelation of them.[60] And the result? Essential facts get omitted. Essential truths get censored. Essential points get dropped. Essential information gets dumped. "Tough," says the post-Star Chamber practitioner, "at least the client is served."

In our justice system courts do recognize an ideal which is aspirationally called "truth,"[61] but absolute truths simply do not exist and the consequential (and competing) relative truths are all fair game. It is not for lack of trying that participants in trial attempt to convince each other of themselves being the Real Keeper of All Truth: the phrase "fact checking" implies it, as does "in the court of public opinion," and "the honest truth," and "undeniable evidence," and "to a moral certainty," along with a hundred other more or less poetic exhortations that what one is saying is unassailable in its pure honesty. But all those phrases consist simply of words offering subjective versions of measuring credibility of other words, most of them via the employment of symbolically emotional modifiers and culturally sensitive terminology ("As God is my witness, I am telling you that . . . ," etc.) Throughout each case one side is (a) employing the most effective of those phrases with a trembling hand and tremulous voice all while, (b) trying to deeply bury the other side's version of events, and at the same time (c) unearthing and displaying their own favored version. The players in charge of doing the interment and the resurrections are paid advocates tasked with using implements of suppression and restraint effectively to advance a client's individual interest in having their "*more* truthful" version championed.

Weirdly, a just result does lay at the end of the endeavor, but it is not necessarily *everyone's* just result, simply one combatant's just result—and the trial lawyer's heavily directed efforts to persuade are what point the way on one path and foreclose all other paths to attain the desired goal. Society, curiously, is okay with that and has been for some time even though trial judges, legal commentators, and gallery observers would be loathe to concede the point.

You Say *Bravado*, I Say *Bravura*

Relative truths are the subtle shades and hues of grey drawn out from the absolute blacks and whites of overt truths and overt falsehoods. Handed only the greys to examine and assess, fact finders have no choice but to select what they ultimately *like* aesthetically in terms of the restricted options lining the palette. The offering is done through plaintiff's counsel's and defense counsel's competing "styles." The selection made has consequences for both. Given that the trial lawyer's role is not to decide but to persuade, and to persuade as well as possible, then not only is it that successful operation of the system mandates that the advocate's functions and the fact finder's functions are kept separate and apart, but it is also that the fact finder be made aware of the consequence. A well utilized fact finder has to come to recognize that some sort of penalty accompanies poor persuasion and some sort of reward accompanies good persuasion. An advocate works to guide the fact finder in differentiating the same, but avoids at all costs reminding them that the guiding efforts are motivated by the consequences.

At one level, it is obvious; no juror is ever fooled into thinking that the advocates are not partisan, especially because jurors are told straight out by the judge at the start that they are there to decide a private dispute and clearly those in dispute wish to influence that decision. Jurors accept partiality as a given but are uncomfortable with it being unadulterated. Bluster and obvious sophistry do not go over well. Trickery and cleverness alone and on the surface, the overt or poorly hidden type which shows itself as what it is, is swiftly rejected by jurors as being unpersuasive. The trial lawyer therefore needs to create other more deeply hidden and nested levels of discourse. Doing so requires burying the paraphernalia of partiality, using persuasion techniques so subtle or layered as to not appear to even *be* persuasion at all. Requiring such nuance in order to get to those consequential detriments and incentives dictates that it is the *manner* in which relative truths are presented that becomes paramount for the advocate in order to be successful.

This is not easy. For one, as we have noted above, every juror is, naturally, a born skeptic. Within a second of sitting down in the box, every juror almost automatically adopts the mantra "be wary of strangers." Within a second of seeing a trial lawyer stand up and walk toward them, every juror, if only out of emotional self-preservation, looks at the trial lawyer and unconsciously flinches, thinking something along the lines of "here comes trouble," not "here comes assistance."[62] The flags are red in part because the environment the juror has been placed in is a foreign one filled with strangers, and evolution has adapted them (all of us really) to be guarded and distrustful in unknown (and thus potentially hostile) conditions. Moreover, the legal "environment" in which the juror is involuntarily immersed is more complex than just the physical spaces alone—it isn't really old courtroom walls and floors, archaic pieces of furniture, and musty suits and judicial robes that create the real baseline anxieties, it is all those rules in all those books on all those walls surrounding the dais and the chairs that winnow sharp into their psyches, that dig in the most to make things so nerve-wracking to the neophyte.[63]

The standard juror knows little about what law is composed of, but what they do know is that they don't particularly like its complexity whatever it is. As jurors register some displeasure with legal rules and procedures in general, the subtext about the rules is usually that (a) they are unnecessarily obtuse, (b) they are too voluminous, and (c) they seem written more to bewilder and confuse than to actually aid and enlighten.[64] What the layperson thinks should be a fairly short and straight path between raising a basic social concern to eventually obtaining relief for it, hardly seems short or straight in any manner at all. If jurors learn anything at the outset of a trial, they learn quickly that rule-related obstacles rise up at every turn, small burdens and large curves thrown in the way by laws, by judges, and especially by those strangers pretending to be friends who supposedly are meant to be helping clear the way but are instead clouding it, that is by all those damn lawyers loudly reciting every last one of their damn thoughts about all those damn rules.

In that respect, the litigants get something of a break: as jurors turn attention away from the trial lawyers, they see the parties themselves sitting next to their eager stand ins and are not without sympathy to those poor souls who, hunched uncomfortably at the fringe of the counsel table, look like they may have become trapped in an unending, confusing, and expensive lawsuit. The clients, plaintiff or defendant, may visually present as ordinary people wearing the miserable costumes of sad sacks besieged on all sides by troubles, likely financial as well as obviously legal. Most people feel some personal concern for litigants simply as a general principle.

Keep in mind that jurors aren't socially naïve, only jurisprudentially naïve: they are familiar with informal dispute dynamics, and most will have some camaraderie with the general gripe any plaintiff has that they were hurt and the general recoil any defendant experiences in being wrongfully accused.[65] In their own domestic and work lives, jurors also know all too well what litigants are faced with in the form of bureaucratic annoyances accompanying lawsuits, such as time-sensitive deadlines, required confirmations, mandated office forms, official interviews, and the expenses generated by all those things. Reading a verdict form and a jury instruction reminds them in their own lives of necessarily wrangling with confusingly worded legalese-sounding documents in order to get differences finally resolved and bills finally paid.

In all that, it isn't that difficult for jurors to envision legal formality as *counter* to success, to feel that legal procedures (and those responsible for and advocating use of legal procedures) to be hostile forces blocking, not easing, access to a normal solution to a normal problem. Lawyers who sound like lawyers therefore seem to be the very opposite of help. Yet lawyers also seem to be inescapable. Juror wariness about the nicely suited person earnestly marching toward them is only matched by juror resignation that they better deal with it, since the most available face to put on both the solution and the frustration to the solution is the face of the person standing directly in front of their box and who, like it or not, has been inserted into the process with approval by society (whom everyone is a member of) and the judge (whom everyone respects). Everywhere the juror turns to look they see another lawyer who somehow sprang up from some side room somewhere to raise an objection, insert a comment, delay a decision—in a sense, argue.

And they don't discount the alienating effect of the surroundings in which the trial lawyers act and interact; all this annoyance occurs in a room visually unlike anything compared to their homes, schools, and offices. Asked in *voir dire* about their initial impressions of potentially participating in a trial, many jurors focus on locale right off the bat with some form of "Well, I've never been in a courtroom before." Even though it really should not be, far *unlike* a stage in a theater, a courtroom can be one of the most discomforting places on earth—an unsettling and sporadically frantic place inhabited by people who are cold strangers to the newcomer but warmly familiar with each other, an in-group conversing in cheerful or solemn voices while tossing off important sounding phrases to other strangers and to the room at large about some of the most private matters in another person's life, and blithely ignoring the out-groups of observers seated right behind them.[66]

Jurors, very much like litigants themselves, may often feel in a courtroom that there is a secret script which everyone has access to read from except them, and that if they were to blink for even a moment something critical may have passed where an opportunity is lost, a dollar has floated away, a ruling has been made, or what should not have been done has been done and can never be undone, regardless of officially signed form, bold date stamp, clear precedent, clear justice, or clear need.

If trial lawyers were *just* hindrances and nothing more, it would be easy for the juror to merely lower their gazes and patiently outwait them. The complexity is that the lawyer presents promise as well. Some potential usefulness, some help, some capacity to be likable, to make things better rather than worse, seems to accompany these strangers which cannot be entirely ignored. The juror grasps that lawyers are things the populace has specially machined to supposedly provide guidance and assistance as litigant substitutes, and who are clearly being paid considerable sums to attend to all those obstacles while navigating (or offering to navigate) a path to a solution. The fact that lawyers are "paid talkers" is pretty impressive to jurors, more than one might realize.

From their own domestic and work lives, jurors appreciate the power of the profit motive to get jobs done, and it does not escape their attention (or esteem) that they mentally note lawyers have been hired as *de facto* workers to do a good job for *de facto* customers called clients and that the entirety of the job seems to be complicated ways of talking.[67] They get it that lawyers make a living erecting things similar to consumer goods but out of words alone, weird things called suits and claims and arguments and verdicts; they get it that lawyers (a) are partially self-directed and partially customer-instructed to manufacture the good efficiently, (b) need to act sharply and not be unnerved by panic while doing so, (c) must know and use all those thousands of rules to assist in a decisive manner with addressing "issues" and obtaining "orders" and "judgments," and (d) emphatically exude, or at least put on a show of, confidence in the process.[68] Work for profit can impress, work done well can impress, and trial lawyers can and do impress jurors both by what they actually say as well as what they represent socially as they talk, talk, talk, and talk.

But blending relative truths with nuanced deliveries to realize rewards makes it so that the actual way trial lawyers meet those expectations in providing all that assistance is not by "playing fair." It is not by "getting the truth out." It is not by "seeking justice." The actual way diverges from all those ideals and digs deep into the harsh realities of what private representation of others truly entails: gamesmanship, partisanship, exploitation of rules, leveraging of advantages, application of the technical and the obscure, strategic maneuvering around human nature—and, by definition, the manipulation of people while doing all those things. Their manipulation is intimately connected to, and a function of, those earlier imbalances of information and power which we acknowledged above are integral to the working of the judicial system. Never forget that while jurors and witnesses are placed under oath in a trial, lawyers are not. Ironically, though they talk the most in trials, they have not been sworn to "tell the whole truth under penalty of perjury" in doing so; the Star Chamber compulsion to join in blood oaths with their clients turned to dust long ago. They are free and not free at the same time and the forces compelling them to act are not promises to be truthful to all but promises to be protective only of some.

So, the juror's instinct about caution is a good one: they *should* be wary of the trial lawyer—what the trial lawyer is up to is not in either the juror's own interests, or in the interest of pursuing the juror's ideals or really *any* ideals. While the trial lawyer's work is not purposely antagonistic to those things the juror may hold dear, in advocating for the client the trial lawyer has to step very carefully around the instincts and the caution and do what they can to assuage anxiety all while zealously attacking the opponent. Advantage-taking, in essence, is key.

And the art of litigation is particularly favorable to people utilizing that especial tactic of capitalizing on an opening created by another's misstep. In that way it's like chess but only if chess had twenty people instead of two moving the pieces, had thousands more of applicable rules, and had a lot more pushing and shoving than turn-taking and strategizing. Realistically, everyone involved in litigation is, at a basic "chess-playing" type level, taking advantage of everyone else as the game, that is, "cases," progress: *pro se* plaintiffs and represented defendants take advantage of each other's knowledge or ignorance of certain facts and events; deposition takers take advantage of deponents' inattentiveness or innocence; movants take advantage of opponents' lack of relevant authority; all litigants take advantage of missed deadlines and missed statutory requirements; experts take advantage of novices' misunderstandings and ignorances; judicial assistants (mostly) take advantage of the noncompliant; and judges (mostly) take advantage of the unprepared.

Manipulation of weaknesses or hesitations, squeezing value out of misinformation as life hacks, as strategies to move forward successfully in the world against others trying to do the same, is not a trick used only by trial lawyers. Getting one over on the other guy is certainly not unfamiliar to a lot of people but is instead, if not customary, at least to be expected in nearly all goal-directed activities. Put another way, lawsuits are microcosms of contests between people in all sorts of forms. Ording and Siu and Queneau and Boas and Smithie, along with every evolutionary biologist ever, would be mostly unsurprised by any of these realizations:

> Apart from its practicality, manipulation is possible only if manipulators have and can be known to have relevant information and ways of making it available. If they are expected to share it, they may manipulate by withholding it while providing other information. Otherwise they may signal unreliably. Among the more obvious circumstances in which to expect attempts to manipulate is when the individuals who interact have only ephemeral or rapidly changing relationships.[69]

Try in good faith to name a relationship in which the participants *don't*, at some level, manipulate each other to some sort of advantage. Even the fiction author, with only the most ephemeral of relationships possible with their unknown and unknowable readers, can be expected to manipulate. Trial lawyers, also with only an ephemeral relationship with their jurors, can be expected to manipulate as well. Given the legal system and the roles assigned within the system before and at trial, it can be no other way. Ubiquity is not its own justification, true. But ubiquity not uncommonly reflects attention being paid to impart value to some communal need. Manipulating another is a basic need with strong evolutionary underpinnings.

Not only is the relationship between trial lawyer and juror simultaneously antagonistic and mutualistic in that sense, but it is also transitory and rapidly changing within a matter of hours or days, and is certainly not one founded on any mutual agreement to even *be* in a relationship. Nor are the specific persons involved self-selected—instead, like in a deviant rom-com, the crazy coincidences of a registered voter record, a bailiff's chance lottery selection, and the fortuity of the last peremptory challenge in *voir dire* having been exhausted, all combine to throw a pairing of utter strangers together in spite of each not knowing who the other is or either wanting to autonomously create a genuine relationship with the other.

Of course the juror, somewhat like the fiction reader, *expects* the trial lawyer to manipulate and of course the trial lawyer is faced with an awareness that their listener/reader's expectations that someone is out to fool them (and the accompanying suspicion and distrust) are likely the order of the day from the start. Nevertheless, this is a compelled reading: juror and trial lawyer find themselves face to face and tasked with the former having to listen to the latter use one type of talk to circumvent another type of talk, including referents to "trust" and "confidence" which neither particularly has (at least at first) in the other. Both opposing trial lawyers possess a ton of information, the juror warms up to the notion that society must want them to snag at least some of that information, the judge hopefully watches eagle-eyed as each of the two trial lawyers parsimoniously doles part of the information out, and each trial lawyer in their role as a litigation opponent will be sure to raise hue and cry if the transmission is too much or is of the wrong content or is done at the wrong time or in the wrong manner.

Any initial expectations only get more confounded from there. For one, the real-world trial lawyer's dialectal selections can be and often are quite contrary to laypersons' naïve expectations of what that oratory *should* be; remember what is expected is mostly derived from entertainment media depictions of actors playing lawyers, itself a deception twice removed. The best trial lawyers, disguising the fact that persuasion is occurring, work to subvert expectations.

For instance, a very effective method of argument from a premise to a conclusion in argument involves the employment of contradictions, as in proposing or inferring that a thing must be true as long as its mirror image is unquestionably false.[70] Ording refers to the principle of explosion in logic which tracks that selfsame idea. Trial lawyers (to whom logic may display only a passing fancy when they are in their formal argumentative mode) are no strangers to the "explosion" of an idea by broadcasting its contradiction as an unacceptable premise, while not necessarily rationalizing the idea with any direct logical or evidentiary foundation.

Yet contradicting by simply saying "No" to another's "Yes" is not the effective type of contradicting, albeit that the schoolchild likely calls that puerile game "arguing." Contradicting by pointing out that the "Yes" has such a gaping hole at its positional center that the "No" is the only way in which the hole can be filled, on the other hand, is a far more workable operational route—and doing so also while running out a timed clock, while making the point to the fact finder when they are most psychologically vulnerable to receiving its impact, and while enlisting appealing word choices, inserting subliminal components of body language, and triggering thematic devices to hammer the point home, all lockstep together as argumentative mechanisms combined in service of a manipulator's goal of prevailing on the pending point, perhaps without ever saying the word "No" even once.

The quaint (and flat wrong) notion that legal argument is synonymous with "debate" is a notion that tragically misconceives of a trial lawyer as a formal presenter at a podium with a timer, taking measured turns with a colleague overseeing as presenter, politely pointing and counterpointing each other to a neat and tidy conclusion. Nothing could be further from the truth—debaters for the most part make terrible trial lawyers. The crucially valuable legal argument eschews every podium offered, flaunts any timer's warning beep, throws wrenches into prim proposals of democratic turn-taking, and denies the significance of counterpoints made being actually "counter" to anything. Hands are waved, not clasped. Points are recalibrated, not scored. Turns are co-opted, not taken. Verbal and conceptual *messiness*, not tidiness, is often the result of good legal argument, and the impact on the receiver is hopefully a function of being impressed with the aesthetic surmounting of, not the measured concession to, normal rules of formal debate.

This distinction cannot be overstated or underrated: a valuable argument at trial and a useful style really must be anything it can to escape the anathema of debate. For instance, debaters rail heavily against use of what they call the "*ads*"—the argument "*ad populem*" as a speaker's illicit appeal to popular sentiment; the argument "*ad misericordiam*" as an illicit appeal to pity; the argument "*ad baculum*" as an illicit appeal to threat; the argument "*ad hominem*" as a personal attack against the arguer; and the argument "*ad ignorantiam*" as an illicit appeal to ignorance.[71] Categorized derogatively as logical "fallacies," the *ads* earn ire from the debate hall judges but can earn verdicts in the courtroom. Trial lawyers don't need accolades, they need favorable decisions. In different amounts and with some discretion as to target, every one of those *ad* stratagems is a found coin for the trial lawyer to relish spending, not to toss aside. Indeed, the entire doctrine of "impeachment' of a witness is a slightly reworked form of *ad hominem* argument; claiming to disclose via cross-examination that a witness has made inconsistent statements, that they are personally biased in favor or against a litigant, or that their character for truth and veracity is bad, are at one and the same time both intimate condemnations of a person themselves and legitimate argumentative devices authorized for deployment by the evidence code to sway a fact finder about "truth."[72] Impeachment is gold for trial lawyers, dross for debaters.

The disparate nature of what debaters do as opposed to what trial lawyers do is also uncovered by their disparate goals. The one seeks to accumulate non-monetized points in an artificial contest where certain points are given for the employment of logic and other points are taken away for quarreling or being contentious. The other is inapposite and seeks to attain an economically beneficial "judgment" in a very real contest where no points whatsoever are tallied or weighed by anyone, and where logic can be detrimental, where quarrel and contention is expected and admired, and where the hasty generalization and the specious accusation can greatly aid, not hamper, the arguer in ultimately prevailing. The debater abhors pity because pity is irrational. The trial lawyer courts pity because pity can justify the acceptance of a conclusion which, rational or not, might otherwise be rejected. The fact that pity is cathartic is a boon to the trial lawyer and of no interest to the debater, and their paths to their goals thus sharply diverge at that and several other branching points, including more sordid motivating forces like profit motive, guilt, and social prejudice.

It has been said that oratory in legal proceedings is less interesting than in political or important social issue contexts since the former ultimately has no great questions to answer or address whereas the latter is often stuffed to the very gills with them.[73] Yet interest is a function of more than simply the orator's topic alone, it is also a function of their audience and of their delivery. With private disputes made public, interest might be cultivated by the universality of some legal principle applied to communities, true, but might be elicited equally by the trivial, perhaps via an intense dissection of some small personal concern of importance only to one man or woman. And politicians as well as actors would agree that interest is often a correlate of presentation format; as Cato's ceaseless poking of the Roman Senate with his "*Carthago delenda est*" demonstrates, a compelling approach in focusing on the commonplace has just as sharp a potential to burrow its way into the listener's psyche as does any haughty universal plea for righteousness to all the gods in heaven.[74]

A Garden of Versus

Such is not of course to discount theme as its own strong reason to garner interest in the realm of jury trials: like a good war movie, the civil or criminal lawsuit also gets the benefit of emotionally triggering its audience with that perennial favorite topic of human nature, hand to hand combat. The trial lawyer gets to take advantage of offering up a lurid fight between matched antagonists and is aided in that effort by how the practice of law in general embodies and relies upon the quality of polarity. Dichotomies in the form of oppositional concepts such as us/them, win/lose, for/against, support/oppose, grant/deny, sustain/overrule, plaintiff/defendant, complainant/respondent, positive/negative, and right/wrong infuse all legal proceedings, even the most collaborative.

The polar nature of law doesn't just apply to the participants, it applies to the ideas that are enshrined in legal processes and it applies to every step in the jury trial sequence as well. In law, many, many things are sharply positioned *against* other things—not just people poised against other people, but ideas and interests slated against other ideas and interests, and words announced and thrown against other words in antagonism.

Oppositional concepts in law run far deeper than the layperson casually assumes and can carve out ways to appeal to human instinctual desires to compete, or, at the very least, to participate from the sidelines as others spar. The attendant psychological weight of watching antagonistic forces battle to an outcome is ripe for the trial lawyer to exploit in order to engage a viewer's emotional participation.

Initially, the very caption of a pleading brandishes the word "versus" even if no adversarial positions can be immediately pinpointed in the allegations that directly follow. Pleadings merely frame the issues and issues stack up against other issues in a manner not necessarily commensurate with either the number of parties involved nor with the types of relief sought. One plaintiff can construct seventeen unrelated issues via a single pleading and two defendants can then multiply that number threefold, including by constructing six new issues cross-wise between themselves which don't even involve the plaintiff at all. In lawsuits, threats beget threats: complaints lead readily to counter-complaints and cross-complaints and third-party complaints and amended complaints and supplemental complaints and pleas in indemnity and interpleader as well as in abatement, additur, and remittitur. The status list is neither short nor intuitive.

From there, conflict scenarios multiply like rabbits. Procedurally, the real and imaginary feuds which the allegations originally announce may swiftly inflate or deflate through a bevy of competing "pleadings motions" by both sides seeking to test the legal validity of what has been pleaded. Contemporaneously with the pleadings, during the stage called discovery (where each side learns what objective evidentiary support supposedly lies behind the allegations and defenses) methodological fighting tends to polarize the combatants even further; this stage is characterized by the motion to compel and the resultant sanction. As it does in all litigation stages, money talks loudly in discovery and the expense generated in parlaying knowledge back and forth can be quite palpable: sides threatening to "bury" the other in a mountain of produced documents signals how easily financial pressures can be weaponized. Similarly, insertion of an overweening threat of an opponent paying a sum (in fines or attorney fees) to the other for a discovery rule transgression is a driving force in making the compulsion even more bitterly divisive. Because relative truths are at stake, there is as much information-avoiding behavior going on in discovery as there is information-attracting behavior. Mutual avoidance in disclosure means that discovery as a battle tactic ends up being far more an exercise in frustration than it is an exercise in catharsis.

More motion practice then follows to again narrow (rarely to expand) what a fact finder will eventually be able to consider, and the collateral indignancy associated with warding off motions hither and yon impacts not just the boundaries of the dispute but the personal resolve of the combatants to remain in the combat to the end. Finally, the concluding campaign of a jury trial culminates in a victor (perhaps) with the jury verdict proclaiming a situationally absolute winner and loser (again perhaps), the last and most sought-after division in the battlefield of all (if it even occurs). The modifier "situationally" is used since it is absolute only in the relative sense given that there exist the legal spoilsports of the "motion for reconsideration," the "motion for JNOV (judgment notwithstanding the verdict)," and the "motion for a new trial," along with motions for remittitur and additur, any one of which may puncture what seemed to be a certain victory or invert what seemed to be a resounding defeat. In turn, the appellate systems may then trigger a reviewing court to affirm, reverse, or remand that initial depiction and outcome and send all scrambling back to the trenches with different armor and different arms. The status categories get renewed and revamped and now appellants and respondents, and cross-appellants and cross-respondents, appear to couch old factual allegations in the new uniforms of new legal conclusions and push on to fight once more.

Integral to all these skirmishes is the linguistic viewfinder through which such conflict and its combatants are being observed by the field officers. Polarities such as plaintiff/defendant or winner/loser are created by assigning designations, and the designations subsequently demand the production of other polarities in the form of labels then affixed to the actors' statuses and activities, specifically, labels connected to shifting burdens of proof and levels of culpability. From distinguishing a "misdemeanor" from a "felony" while calling both accusations "crimes," to distinguishing a "preponderance" from "clear and convincing" or "proof beyond a reasonable doubt" while calling all those standards "burdens," lawyers (akin to taxonomists and in their limited role as social scientists), unceasingly engage in the art and artifice of classifying.

Considerably *unlike* those in the hard sciences, trial lawyers attach prices to their classification schemes; there are very real "expenses" incurred with each designation. The protest that litigation is always "costly" is not simply a reference to the bare dollars spent and gained which are clearly attendant to fee agreements, retainers, trust accounts, and jury awards—it is a reference as well to the more subtle but equally impressive prices exacted for having a burden of proof imposed or rebutted, and the situational costs expended or saved in being transformed from a plaintiff to a counterdefendant or to a judgment creditor or judgment debtor.

Long Story Short

All this polarity is a manifestation of the post-Star Chamber effort to replace real fighting with ritualized fighting and unfair fighting with fair fighting. Society has an interest in its members' concerns getting addressed without real violence being engaged and at least being addressed somewhat equitably. We aren't foolish enough to believe that fighting won't occur, so we don't direct energy into *completely* quelling it, we simply work to redirect manageable parts of it into judicial forums and via judicial formats that tamp down as much of the potential bloodshed as possible.

Not just arranging legal topics into systems[75], but also placing people and events into outlined categories and then placing those categories into ordered (or seemingly ordered) hierarchies, is a very human activity that serves a number of these goals which the trial process promotes and which trial lawyers are thus interested in toying with.[76] For the trial lawyer's professional aspirations, among those goals is that of creating frameworks for arguments in trial in which they can better (or completely) control a narrative. Another is to use polarizing language meaningful to a specific segment of society to leverage an advantage as to them, and even to use constructed legal terminology to simply *sound* smart while doing so regardless of whether the speaker actually is smart or has a smart position to advance.[77] The employment of complex classification schemes can accomplish all those aims and more.

The trial lawyer does not have to create such schemes whole cloth; analyses from other disciplines can offer up a variety of models to exploit and work with. Evolutionary biologists, for instance, have developed an entire field of classification called taxonomy and its offspring, cladistics.[78] Taxonomists in the biological sciences for their part have been themselves meta-classified into "lumpers and splitters," the former as those who want to create less classification divisions and the latter as those who want to create more. Charles Darwin, writing in a letter to the botanist Joseph Dalton Hooker about the classification of genera and species in plants, is normally credited with that self-referential division; in his concern over the problem of how to separate one biological species from another Darwin posited the concept that those who "make" (define or name) many species are the splitters, and those who make few are the lumpers.[79]

The terms have since been taken up in other disciplines, in contexts between those who prefer the "more" of precise and minute distinctions and those seeking the "less" of larger and more encompassing organizing categories. The world of inquiry needs both, Darwin suggested, and perhaps further intimated that each of us needs to entertain both modes of thought in our own research: without his fine-line divisions of the peculiar varieties of Galapagos finch beaks into separate categories, larger theories about all life in general may never have arisen.[80] All lumpers seek general unifying characteristics and broad categories of analysis. All splitters seek tight definitions and locate finer and finer dividing lines.

In a classic monograph on the topic, the biologist George Gaylord Simpson humorously exaggerated the pattern: "Splitters make very small units—their opponents say that if they can tell two animals apart, they place them in different genera, and if they cannot tell them apart, they place them in different species. Lumpers make large units—their opponents say that if a carnivore is neither a dog nor a bear they call it a cat."[81] Substitute "issues" for animals in the quote, and it becomes a rather on point observation about how trial lawyers may and often do adopt those taxonomic strategies in their litigation-oriented endeavors.

Available polarities in the ritualized fighting that is trial work enables trial lawyers as lumpers to employ general unifying characteristics and broad categories of analysis to entice the decision-maker to insert themselves into a cohesive, unified story line—the popular magazine type of enticement of joining the party, of "how well did you do on our test?" From start to finish, the lumping lawyer proposes consolidating a pleading alleging six alternative theories for relief into one universal and generic dispute, proposes treating everyone on one side of the courtroom as "those people," proposes that "all of the evidence together only points one way," and proposes coalitions of factual events and legal issues whose integration has the decision-maker at the center of a larger whole. Lumpers desire unity.

Lawyers as splitters seek not just precise definitions and hope to hone in on differences wherever they may be suggested, but also want their audience to be discriminating as well. The splitting lawyer proposes that a pleading has not been crafted carefully enough and has missed an important separation of distinct legal principles, proposes that parties and topics be severed from one another given their unique elements, proposes that only one word from one witness makes all the difference, and proposes that the decision to be made is unique and does not possibly affect and is clearly unaffected by other decisions and other fights going on elsewhere. To the jury, the enticement of careful splitting advises the recognition of, and perhaps prejudice against, an "out-group" as opposed to the "in-group"—the latter to which the trial lawyer wants them to belong along with the client in solitude and solidarity. Splitters desire distinction.

Both lumping and splitting work in general in the sense that dualism and classification work in general, placing ideas in contexts that have an appeal to a sense of balance through organization, of equity arising via inclusion and exclusion used reasonably. More importantly to this topic, both tactics work in a more detailed fashion at trial by lining the jury up with the dichotomies which the trial lawyer wants them to join and dividing the jury away from those categories the trial lawyer wants them to abjure. People being somewhat natural lumpers and splitters in their daily lives depending on the circumstance, jurors are often keen to be enticed into or out of a suggested select grouping depending on the factual offering creating the circumstance. The trial being both temporary and artificial, and the assignations being conceptual not real, then the only way in which the selections can be made are just that—by the power of verbal suggestion alone. In each strategy, *words* control and there is no denying that the trial lawyer's words are the ones in charge of the overall taxonomic operation.

Successfully banding the jury and the client together is accomplished through carefully proffering classifying words at every opportunity. The arranged classifications are part of a calculus, moreover, in which the magnitude of emotive force depends on the recipients' peculiar preferences as to certain hierarchies—and since there is no way to know what those preferences truly are, then which classifying schemes are chosen is necessarily freeform and relies partly on knowing a lot about human nature and partly on gleaning any insights possible in *voir dire*. A trial lawyer's taxonomic choices flourish as equal parts advance planning and extemporaneity. This, by the way, is a project with extensive historical roots: 2300 years ago, Aristotle (in his guise as splitter) demarked modes of persuasion into those he felt were in the character of the speaker ("ethos"), those he considered disposed the listener in some manner ("pathos"), and those meant to show something in the argument itself ("logos").[82] Those tripartite divisions reflected a belief—which later legal scholars have shared—that arousing the emotions of one's audience couldn't be simply a function of skill alone, but had to be governed by particularly directed inclinations of the listener as well.[83]

An Exercise in Style Exemplified

In example, let's imagine a female client's claim of civil assault, specifically that during a row with her ex-boyfriend she had a "reasonable apprehension of imminent offensive physical contact" by him sufficient to cause her emotional distress.[84] The mutually agreed upon objective becomes to get financial compensation for her distress and to get it paid directly from the pocket of the ex. As the plaintiff's trial lawyer initially sizes up their client to present most favorably as "a socially-inept, short-statured female especially vulnerable to emotional influence" and the defendant to likely present as a "socially-accomplished, wealthy, aggressive large male," one possible plan to employ a style requiring taxonomic divisions unfolds.

The style, we will call it *Seclusion*, has its genesis in a pleading alleging the defendant's conduct to be "menacing" and "purely deliberate," the former allegation to trigger him emotionally and the latter allegation to foreclose the potential for any insurance coverage. It then builds through getting the defendant in deposition to protest about use of the word "menacing" and to agree that he was more social than she was in the relationship. At pre-trial it continues with a motion *in limine* excluding all references to "domestic partners" and, as the jury pool is brought into the courtroom, having the client seated at the far end of counsel table by herself with only a small purse in front of her. *Voir dire* focuses on friendly questions to the unattached about dating mishaps and challenging questions to the married about faithfulness and errant spouses, and peremptory strikes are taken against two married males and one large size unmarried male in the prospective panel.

Counsel's opening is more casual than formal, describes the litigants as "mismatched," and implies that economic disparity—both in society in general and with the parties in particular—is gender-dependent. Retooled a bit based on juror reactions to both counsel's questions in voir dire and both counsel's openings, it is a style then refined through eliciting very specific testimony, specifically the plaintiff's about her size and loneliness and the defendant's regarding his numerous male friends and physical activities being isolated from hers. Cross of the ex-boyfriend harps on his athleticism and his resources, and positions the answers as benefiting from the client's vulnerabilities.

At the close of the trial things are narrowed down further with a jury instruction about "physical facts" reminding the jury about how personal certain types of "touching" between males and females can be, and it culminates via a closing where the trial lawyer (a) stands uncomfortably close to the panel, (b) remarks in near whispers on the voracity of defendant's protestations about menacing, (c) comments almost cavalierly on size discrepancies in opposite sex couples, and (d) cites a compelling statistic on common perceptions that smaller size people have about larger size people as well as making the psychologist's observation on certain peculiar anxieties many females have about males overall. The word "unfairness" in a few derivatives is used throughout.

The project is finally measured for results by a checked line on a verdict form testing the trial lawyer's pending taxonomic theory that the jurors needed to split all people into couples, then all couples into the aggressive and the susceptible, then all of the susceptible into "this one poor woman," and finally that at least four of the six jurors needed to emotionally affiliate with her isolation alone. It may well have been that no "concrete facts," that is, direct witness testimony, actually established either his overt threat or her overt apprehension, but no matter—words start to end, the bulk of which were her splitting lawyer's, many of which were either untrue or neither false nor true but simply opinion, and the only ones of which mattered, were those which lead four strangers to make a checkmark on a piece of paper about another stranger.

The empirical plausibility of a certain fact or of a set of facts regarding an actual assault was never really at the heart of the venture, only configurations and relationships as perceived through a continually distorted lens affixed to a distorted scope cautiously viewing how people might potentially align in a social environment. Remarkable above all is the clandestine nature of that *Seclusion* style (or of any utilized style) in that it seems facially (including at the close of trial), as if it had been entirely adlibbed when in fact it had been engineered down to the very rivets. Ethos, pathos, and logos are all employed to arouse the panel's emotions to a targeted end.

The adversarial system creates plentiful opportunities at numerous loci to make taxonomic offerings by the lumping or splitting trial lawyer—from when the courtroom lights are first turned on until deliberations begin—to propose to the jury (a) that certain groups exist at all, (b) why one group is preferable to support, and (c) the benefits to joining it instead of being left out in the cold. It is all a metaphysical fantasy of course, since no person in the courtroom, litigant or juror, is physically or situationally impacted by accepting or rejecting the trial lawyer's hierarchy. Human nature and adaptive influences, however, make most people inclined to embrace group acceptance and disinclined to be subject to group extirpation. These are evolutionary derived needs and drives (closely akin to the evolutionary need for manipulation of others which we noted above) and can be and are exploited by the trial lawyer on behalf of a client who stands to best the other side by their representative's unique option of grouping being the finally chosen set.

Aristotle's rhetorical formatting reminds us that argument as a concept has its own dualities, including that of promise/threat, and speakers throughout history have been known to reach passionately to both ends of that spectrum in order to accomplish some oratorical objective. Both promise and threat can be highly effective as tools of persuasion (just ask any law enforcement officer, school principal, or parent) and both techniques stem from principles of negotiation. In the analysis of negotiation as a rule-governed interaction among social groups, both promises and threats are core devices in bargaining theory and suggesting a penalty or a reward for performing or not performing a certain action is normative, not deviant.[85]

It is naïve to think that lawyers only negotiate with each other in settlement discussions alone—lawyers negotiate with *everyone* in *every* discussion. A colloquy with a judge is a negotiation, an aside to a client at counsel table is a negotiation, a friendly chat with a potential witness in a hallway is a negotiation, as are opening and closings and e-mail "reply all"s, and a thousand other conversations. Promises being liberally shouted or cautiously sprinkled throughout those exchanges can seem innocuous enough, but threats can present as considerably more distasteful. That disparity is likely only because (a) one may be equating threat with fear alone, and (b) one may not be considering the immeasurable subtlety with which threat may be truly levied.

The prospect of a lawyer actually threatening a jury with words predicting that some physical harm will befall them is ludicrous and can make one visibly wince. Of course, overt threat in such circumstances would not just be tactically problematic, but also highly unethical, judicially sanctionable, and morally repellent to boot. But the finesse of a threat that some more *conceptual* harm will befall such listeners is a distinction with a serious difference. "If you do not convict, a murderer will run free" is a negotiation threat to the jury in their largest, lumpiest, role as representing all of society together, and is a vastly useful one to stir just the right individual emotions (fear among them, but others as well) and command just the right group reaction.[86] In short, argument does not invariably tilt exclusively toward promise alone as the chosen tack; by its nature, promise is simply the one usually easier to observe bobbing about on the surface of the pending "discussion."

Obviously, juries and trial lawyers do not truly mutually negotiate anything, nor do they enter into enforceable contracts nor execute formal agreements, so regardless of whether a promise or threat is subtle or overt, jurors rest assured that no consequences attach which would ever affect them personally. The trial lawyer is thus tasked with making the impending verdict be something they will feel *extra*-personally, locating for them a justification to be legitimately concerned for the fate of another individual or of a larger group of people. The trial lawyer fails if the jury concludes that whether the promise or threat will be fulfilled or abandoned is merely the stuff of useless speculation, is ultimately inconsequential to anyone real. What comes at the end of deliberations must have a moral bite. To effect that, it becomes necessary to get jurors to muse seriously over distributions of power: what power the judge has, what power the trial lawyers have, and what power they themselves have—and not merely power over controlling the immediate effects of a case, but over controlling the later effects of people's lives and of the trajectory, control, or health of entire communities. Groupthink and group-directed action is thus mandated. Again, taxonomies are key.

Certainly, it is necessary that the trial lawyer has the jury experience the lawyer's own influence, perhaps through apprehension group members sometimes have about group leaders "living up to their word," but it is absolutely essential that they also experience the moral anxiety which comes with themselves executing influence over another. The trial lawyer exercises influence but also hands out influence to be exercised. How does one "hand out influence" exactly? It is an illusion: accomplished by the right words as they are annealed by the right choice of style. It is an illusion: accomplished by creating anxiety and guilt in the recipient that they actually already have it but may have been misusing it. It is an illusion: accomplished by creating pride and desire in the recipient that they must want more of it but aren't aware of the best sources by which to access it. It is an illusion: accomplished by creating concern and responsibility in the recipient that it is so critical and important that they are going to need assistance and guidance from the lawyer in responsibly employing it. It is an illusion: accomplished overall by stories and control and theatricality and taxonomy and careful word choice—all are paramount.

Doggedness and Dogmatism in Dog Bite Cases

It seems helpful to my thesis to keep returning to the practical, so let's do so. Alongside the everyday disputes we recognize repeatedly occurring between automobile drivers and others while on the road, between customers and shopkeepers while in the store, and between landlords and tenants while at the rental unit, we might consider the everyday dispute arising between two people on either end of a dog leash while walking on a street—specifically as to the event of a dog biting a person. A dog bite is an act with a modicum of legal and social significance and one that can be and has historically been exploited by all sorts of lawyers for economic gain.[87]

In exploring the relativity of that type of event through the lens of legal style, including via the guided aims of Ording, Siu, Queneau, and Boas and Smithee to entertain, educate, and puncture the misunderstandings and myths which many laypersons hold about many professionals, it is also an event which as a model may help to deflate many of the inflated, myopic, and misguided concepts that the public frequently has about what trial lawyers really are, what trial lawyers really do, and what jury trials really involve.

For one, a model "dog bite case" offers up a manuscript attendant to many different styles of jurisprudential proof. Argument options present alternative ways of rooting out the salient portions of the same fact pattern within the boundaries of the related rules of law—and enable the players to insert or withhold drama as needed.[88] Dog bite incidents are ubiquitous enough to present a wealth of "on all four" possibilities. Consider a made-up but exemplary case we will call Smith v. Jones being presented in summary fashion as follows:

> On January 1st, plaintiff Smith was bitten on the ankle by defendant Jones' dog while walking in front of Jones' house. Smith claims Jones was careless in controlling the dog. Jones denies being careless. Smith seeks compensation for medical expenses to repair the wound and for the pain experienced in the incident. Jones denies that Smith is entitled to any compensation at all.

Out of those 63 relatively neutral words, a trial lawyer could easily envision constructing argument on the hypothetical Smith v. Jones case enveloping 630, or 6,300, or more, nonneutral words, building discourse to span a wide range of six different styles, including ones inspired by reference to topical events, by claims of precedential experiences common to all dog owners, by social conventions related to animals in general, by a participant's own quirky personality traits, by an insertion of popular culture references, or by a pretense that there are larger regional socio-political influences at work, among other even more inspired sources.

A little creative effort could quickly encompass the attempted inclusion of present time governmental animal control rules and the attempted exclusion of similar past incidents and of privately resolved transgressions. It could summon polarities by the truckload and engender the creation of lawyer-manufactured classification schemes of dog/cat, owner/non-owner, pet/stray, obedience/disobedience, and safety/danger among other even bolder candidates. The rhetoric of fear and influence of moral righteousness could be massaged to tangle and untangle certain facts with or from each other as dramatically significant, each corresponding sentence being levied against its fellow to advantage a client's status. In format, an argument erected out of those sixty-three words would initiate in the mendacity of a multi-page pleading document, would be used to both bury and exhume hundreds of pages of records through the discovery and motion process, and would transform and culminate in hours, days, and weeks of trial lawyers' speech acts transmitted across the theatrical stage of a courtroom. The promise of a good fight being staged and judged is palpable throughout.

Let's therefore imagine that our fake Smith v. Jones case has now been fully litigated and has culminated in a somewhat abbreviated, yet fairly robust jury trial. Six witnesses, say, have now testified in detail: Smith themselves, Jones themselves, a nearby neighbor of both, an animal control officer, a local veterinarian, and Smith's medical doctor, each person carefully examined, cross-examined, and redirect examined for about an hour total apiece. Six documents, say, have been admitted into evidence and published to the jury: a photo of Jones' dog, a veterinary evaluation of Jones' dog, an animal control report, a doctor's report of Smith's injuries, and a photo of Smith's wound.

From those resources a closing argument must be made by Smith's trial lawyer to convince the jury that Jones is clearly liable, and a competing closing argument made by Jones' trial lawyer that Jones is certainly not. We recognize that it is highly *undesirable* for either lawyer to recount, word-for-word, the exact information elicited by the witnesses and documents, and that a healthy amount of reimagining (at most) and consolidation (at least) is unquestionably necessary. At the same time, we recognize that brevity is hazardous since a final decision may hinge on the recall of a particularly telling sentence from that lot and that a failure to highlight the good stuff and to disdain the bad stuff would be a sadly lost opportunity for each advocate. We also recognize that the jury should be made to personally care about attending to the selected data as paramount elements to use in coming to a disposition and should be convinced to personally disdain all the rest of the data as unhelpful detritus.

Relentless selections both judicious and preferential therefore have to be continually made by each trial lawyer, and each has to deliver their parsed and summed selections in as attractive and convincing a manner as is possible without tipping to the jury that they are doing so as the one person in the courtroom who "does not have any dog in the fight," to put it bluntly. The speaker's personal appearance, physical attributes, and environmental limitations, those vocal and visual, must be accounted for. Projections must be made about how jurors might feel about (a) dogs in general, (b) Jones' dog specifically, (c) bite wounds in general, (d) Smith's bite wound specifically, (e) dog owner responsibility in general, and (f) Jones' responsibility specifically, all which is just the raw stuff to start with.

Almost equally importantly, projections must also be made about how jurors feel about law, lawyers, judges, and trials in general and about those two trial lawyers primping about at the heart of this one case specifically. Those projections can only be based on what each trial lawyer knows about the jurors, information which for its part is extraordinarily slim being merely those snippets learned in *voir dire* (not much) along with those slim visual cues hopefully noted in their reactions to the participants' actions and words during the trial (even less). And each lawyer has to keep in mind overall that lumping dogs and splitting people is a bonus for Smith; vice versa for Jones.

This is a one-off experiment. To use Stephen Jay Gould's metaphor, the tape cannot be run a second time.[89] The working hypothesis for each trial lawyer is that the jurors will eventually vote in favor of their side, but there is no way to really know for sure which factor is the control and which factor is the variable. The variables in particular are frustratingly slippery and there is no way to completely account for interference from a host of unknown, outside factors—yes, the laboratory (courtroom) doors close, but realistically they only close so tightly and only for so long. Infection is unavoidable. Infection, by the way, is also encouraged by the experimenters themselves. Most odd is that the outcome of this weird single use experiment personally affects the experimenter and the subjects alike, and spreads disproportionate financial impacts among many (but not all) involved in the process.

Being confounded as a *scientist*, the trial lawyer then most likely does what an *actor* would do instead: manipulate *all* the factors, be those language, people, and/or objects. Triumphantly hold high the photo of the dog and contemptuously toss aside the photo of the wound (if Jones' lawyer) or do the exact opposite (if Smith's lawyer). To themselves privately, the trial lawyer issues instructions: since the audience is an alienated and disenfranchised one that will not really react explicitly no matter what you do, then just react for them by asking yourself rhetorical questions and answering your own questions about concerns you might have if *you* were them—about the animal control officer's poorly stated and stuttering answer in cross-examination, for instance, or about the medical doctor's odd hesitation to a key question in direct. Pretend you are one of the parties and point the finger at the other party for what they claimed happened but clearly didn't explain as the dog approached. Pretend you are the judge and the jury by remonstrating about the other counsel's failure to place into evidence those facts about biting that should have been shown and clearly weren't. Pretend that you are one of the witnesses and repeat (slantedly) the juiciest quotes and reenact the most telling pauses. Pretend that you are society in general and either laud or lambast the rules about how dog owners and bite victims are treated in light of the principles of justice that society should venerate and respect.

Critically, the trial lawyer must be anything and everything *that is not actually the lawyer themselves*. Pretense and disguise, acting and emoting, classifying and categorizing, lumping and splitting, accusing and justifying, teaching and scolding, and hiding and exposing, all that and more is the objective of discourse and is the representative's crucial task in representing at a trial. If there is a "spotlight" in a courtroom as a stage would have during a play, the trial lawyer maneuvers to stay right *outside* its margins but can never stray too far from where it is pointing.

The trial lawyer moves about energetically on the stage at the spotlight's fringes beseeching the audience to constantly look at what is in the spotlight itself but not at them as they beseech. Sometimes what is in the spotlight is an idea and the suggestion might even be to those listening and looking to close their eyes and ears to better concentrate on its thematic importance. Other times what is in the spotlight is an object such as a document or item and the suggestion might be to intimately examine it or touch it to better appreciate its temporal and physical value as a decisional aid.[90]

When what is in the spotlight is a *person*, unique problems arise. We note that as one of the actors in the play, the client is certainly on the stage and should technically be directly in the spotlight but litigants in practical effect are mostly just unhelpful visual distractions. Other than when plunked down on the witness stand to testify (even that only sometimes and definitely not always), the client's actual activity level at trial is quite low and for the most part they do nothing but sit and occasionally fidget and nod.[91] Their appearance is truly unhelpful to the case; the trial lawyer does it all as the *doppelganger*: they ask questions for the client as if they were them, they respond for the client as if they were them, they intently walk back and forth to the box and the bench in their stead, they write furiously and remark passionately as they stand in their shoes, and they react to each unfolding moment in the courtroom *as if* their own lives and fortunes were the true focus of the entire play, yet never daring to say out loud that their own lives and fortunes are actually not involved at all.

As noted, jurors get this at the same time that they don't get this. Schooled on media-distorted versions of trials, they grasp that the trial lawyers are there doing a job, yet the *pathos* consternation remains: the disjoint which arises from holding the folk belief that public disputes are appeased best by those affected being the ones who should take direct action.[92] When lined up against what one would expect in an informal social interaction, it is perfectly understandable that jurors might be bothered by the fact that the people most intimately involved in the suit sit silent while the people who are not the ones actually fighting are the ones so emphatically vocal. The contrived, artificial aspect of trials being voiced by representatives seems intuitively wrong, backwards, to most laypeople who are confident that the process would benefit most from just a real person straightforwardly telling their real story themselves.

While the private yearning to replace "all the lawyer talk" goes unfulfilled (at least in most trials), for the lawyer its specter cannot be ignored. Ironically, a concern over the absence of directly delivered stories in a play where they were rightfully expected is a concern resolved only by *more* playacting. The trial lawyer must now pretend to not be the one whose machinations created the absence, must pretend to disapprove of those wretched other lawyers who have done so, to step up and take sides with the jury against this outrage, to bitterly complain about the unfairness in not hearing direct recitations, and to demand explanations from the system or from the opponent, either or both of whom must be the target of all that wrath. The trial lawyer must pretend that a situation they knowingly helped make is not of their own making. Of all the problematic undertakings a trial lawyer is tasked with, probably the most delicate of the lot is to garner support from their listeners that lawyer talk is bad—while being a lawyer who is standing right in front of them talking to them about how bad it is.

First Impressions, Second Chances, Third Strikes

As we consider the participation and framework of the trial lawyer involved in such a matter eventually "arguing" all their interpretations to a jury, be it about a dog bite or any other dispute, we need to pause for a moment, however, and step back to recognize that "arguing" in the law is not only not debate, it is also not what juror or reader likely thinks it is. A substantial reality check against misunderstanding the process is to grasp that this is where "argument" in the colloquial sense diverges from "Argument" in the jurisprudential sense, and that in the latter event the stages of the litigation matter greatly. Important transformations take place at different steps which directly impact just what the trial lawyer is allowed to use to exploit. Among other related phenomena, we return to highlighting a significant difference in legal practice between an opening statement and a closing argument as well as appreciating a sharp circumscription as to what the trial lawyer is really doing when they engage in either task.[93]

In the former case, the trial has not yet begun and thus no evidence at all has yet been taken nor any law yet identified—there are only contentions alone floating wild and free, that is, proclaimed beliefs by the plaintiff that a viable and valuable claim somehow exists and that a remedy is desperately needed, and the combatant's proclaimed beliefs (i.e., by the defendant's answer) that no viable and valuable claim is presented and that no remedy is required at all (or at least only a minor one). Opening statements are exactly as named: "opening" in the sense that they are made in order to begin an exposure of all that lay ahead—the projections about what the complicated trial process is about to entail—and "statements" in the sense that they are mere narrative descriptions of what the representative for each side predicts will be eventually established during that process. They are certainly not themselves evidence, nor particularly crucial, nor ultimately usable in any real jurisprudential sense—they are merely stage-setting devices of relatively limited case value but of interesting rhetorical help and persuasive value as educated peeks into one of several possible futures. Moreover, they offer early opportunities to classify and to promote suggestions as to who the lumped and the split are likely going to be as well as what issues or objects exactly are going to be affected. Dichotomies and alignments all sprout from seeds subtly planted at this critical step.

As to the latter step, closing argument, the trial has now (well, nearly) concluded in that all the evidence has at least finally been presented and there is no further evidence that can be added, heard, removed, or alternatively considered. The questions which remain are not predictive anymore, but to the contrary are retrospective and deliberative, those matters of personal opinion swirling around as to what to now think about, how to now weigh, how to now arrange and organize, and just where to anoint significances. Closing is a critical glance back into the past in the form of summing evidence which has been, carefully or carelessly, marshalled by the players under the supervision of the court.

Closing arguments are also well named: they end or "close" the case at its finale where procedural doors have been shut and they finally allow a trial lawyer to "argue" in the small sense for how the trial lawyer themselves may believe the fact finder should best think about and rule upon the issues left at hand. Taxonomies set in place long before now may come to bear fruit, and there are tangible remnants of offered and admitted evidence to work with, objects now viewed as models on which to hang positional markers, the Exhibit #102 or Witness #3, being guideposts arranged for the jury to follow on its path to concluding that they are finally with or against one of the parties.

The stages connect as a rhetorical sequence. Openings offer first impressions of what lay on the surface, the presentation of evidence is replete with second chances to correct those impressions, and closings can summon forth the idea of "third strike and you're out" type symbolism suggestive of the impressions hitting or missing, the last dichotomy of a winner and loser finally identified. Both the former and latter steps share some similarities; as combatants are well aware, marks imprinted at the very outset of a fight and marks left uncovered by the very end of a fight may retain more than just symbolic significance to those deciding the fight.

As a substitute for physical combat, all three trial steps share the common trait of manifesting exclusively through the use of linguistic, as opposed to physical, acts; the speakers at each stage are (supposedly) professionally trained storytellers who are specially authorized and empowered by a judge to make some sort of public speech at a specified time in a proceeding.[94] In all three steps, the speaker takes pains to identify details about the players, the setting, and the events which the audience is being asked to consider. In all three steps, themes are expressed, themes which the speaker personally feels are the most crucial to highlight or disregard in their respective tales. As promised, a fight really does unfold but it does so entirely verbally. That makes the prospect of anti-climatic disappointment quite real. It's the modern equivalent of a Roman citizen entering the Colosseum to enjoy a gory fight between a lion and a tiger only to find a poet standing in an empty arena reciting a ballad describing their dramatization of the animals' encounter having already happened somewhere else.[95]

In a sense, that's okay. It's not that horribly disappointing to the jury to have had fists replaced with phrases; at least a dramatic arc of some sort has still been provided. Even if no one actually punched anyone in the nose at least a narrative *about* people punching other people in the nose was incidentally enjoyed. We have immersed ourselves in stories about fights almost as long as we have immersed ourselves in fighting. Storytelling in general is as ancient a human practice as is battle and from the mythology and fables of pre-Hellenic times to the modern bedtime story, the practice of pressing parable, folklore, legend, Just-So-Story, and cautionary tale into an entertainment and educational mold to convince and persuade a listener to feel or act in a certain way is clearly at the forefront.[96] Some trial lawyers are quite adept at the narrating game, others not so much, some trial lawyers are adept at the fighting game, others not so much, and all are constrained in their role by the circumstances of the courtroom environment and the evidence code as applied by the particular judge presiding over the event. As actors in a theater, they are also unloosed or constrained by the ofttimes awkward and ofttimes beauteous activity of trying, while "storytelling," to simultaneously talk, think, remember, emote, and convince all at the same time:

> [T]o solve effectively the problem of retaining and retrieving carefully articulated thought, you have to do your thinking in mnemonic patterns, shaped for ready oral recurrence. Your thoughts must come into being in heavily rhythmic, balanced patterns, in repetitions or antitheses, in alliterations and assonances, in epithetic and other formulary expressions, in standard thematic settings (the assembly, the meal, the duel, the hero's "helper", and so on), in proverbs which are constantly heard by everyone so that they come to mind readily and which themselves are patterned for retention and ready recall, or in other mnemonic form. Serious thought is intertwined with memory systems.[97]

Whether it is opening (again, where the speaker's aim is to project speculatively into one likely future among many), examination (where the speaker's aim is to reveal discretely selected present events through the interplay of question and answer), or it is closing (again, where the speaker's aim is to direct attention to those events of the past which the speaker feels are the truly meaningful ones as buttressed by the question-answer results), it at least seems on the face of it that "telling a good story" and "telling a good story about a good fight" must always be the focus at every phase.

It's not. The layperson may be surprised to learn that "storytelling" is not what effective trial lawyers should do at all, *especially* in either opening or closing. That practice is mostly disastrous as many new practitioners all too soon discover. "Story*manipulating*" is what is really mandated in order to achieve a good result for the client and in that respect, subjectivity rules the day. The teller's work is to pretend that they are telling an objectively true story but to hide the truth that the nature of its telling is unavoidably subjective, is really a monstrously biased and quite personal *deformation* of one possible story among a field of equivalents.[98] The teller also has to draw attention away from the fact that it is only storytelling which is happening. A key trick for the trial lawyer engaged in either opening or closing is to take what are indisputably severely skewed opinions and beliefs of a single person and make them seem like empirical, public, group-approved proclamations filled with independent authority and profoundly generalized social import. Stories alone can't possibly accomplish that result.

To that end, openings and closings are frequently garnished with references to the majesty and seriousness of the courtroom, of the legal system as an institution, and of society in general, with inspiring callouts to ideals such as "justice" and "responsibility" and "duty," and with heartfelt appeals to a host of familiar abstractions and common concepts as to what people "must" and "must not" do when operating in their group form. A "big" message evades a "small" story. Closings—again because now there is at least concrete evidence in the form of exhibits, witness statements, and documents to particularly point to and identify for detailed discussion—are composites of even "bigger" messages which intermix those abstractions with harder inescapable realities, the "it cannot be denied" of what extremely notable word one witness may have actually said under oath on the stand, or what extremely notable term one piece of paper may have actually broadcast in a signed writing.

To repeat: Argument should *not* be storytelling. Trial lawyers should *not* be storytellers. Trials should *not* be stories being told. For one thing, trial lawyers don't need to tell stories in part because they are constantly handed stories that already exist and which, if they need to be simply *told*, can be told by examination alone of percipient witnesses who are real (though not necessarily better) storytellers by definition and design. Trial lawyers are there to manage the storytelling of others by cutting, pasting, trimming, and folding elements of others' stories into their subtly crafted messages, to regulate the "real" storytellers so that only very certain selections in a far longer potential narration are heard and assimilated.

We are all familiar with the speech which goes on too long and the presenter who just doesn't know when to shut up. Without culling, without editing, the undirected and unlimited tale of tales can be an irritant of the highest order. With a tight conceptual schedule to stick to, and with direct and cross-examination as the backdrop, the trial lawyer is both scriptwriter and stage director and in those dual capacities must often enlist usage of the giant hook reaching out from the wings of the stage reeling in the vaudeville act which has overstayed its welcome and which has left its audience impatient for the hopefully more visually interesting, more meaningful, finale.

Of course, in vaudeville the hook can come out as many times as there are faltering acts to reel in. In trials, on the other hand, the opportunities are far fewer and institutional limitations abound. Trial lawyers—being not just socially constructed devices akin to play directors armed with vaudeville hooks, but also being individuals with personalities and personal histories—don't fit as neatly as they should within the confines of adhering to the first impressions adduced in *voir dire* and opening, the second chances attendant to getting to examine all those witnesses, and the "three strikes and you're out" finality offered in some closings. Those trial stages, those local rules and MRPC warnings, impose real restraints.

Accordingly, not a few trial lawyers try to escape the boundaries encircling them as they speak in normal courtroom practice. The escape may be done *temporally*, by speaking when there isn't a specific event on the trial schedule really allowing it, and it may be done *thematically*, by speaking over and off topic on issues beyond those which the moment is supposed to be engaged with.

As to the first type, the more assertive trial lawyer may take advantage of pauses and hesitations by other speakers as occasions arise; as to the second type, the more loquacious trial lawyers will try the patience of opposing counsel and the bench by pontificating too long and overbroadly in their turn. "Generous latitude" in argument is the broad benchmark given by the judiciary to trial lawyers and the outside borders of such a boundary are often difficult to distinguish.[99] Talking out of turn and talking when there is even no turn to take at all is the extra advantage which many trial lawyers carve out from the rules and which are an outgrowth of both their roles as stage directors and their own individual personalities, persons, and styles.

The extra restraints slapped upon those escapees by the judicial system are slight and relatively easy to shake off. Such restraints may come in the form of the "single raised eyebrow" admonishment by the court cautioning the speaker against a comment, outburst, or style that borders on being abusive (whatever that is in the context of each unique case). They may come in the form of the "see me in my chambers" admonishment by the court cautioning the speaker against a style that includes expressing personal beliefs as to the truth or falsity of the evidence or as to which party should prevail (whatever those snippets might sound like as they emanate *sotto voce* from a whispered aside). They may come in the form of the "repeated sustained objection" admonishment cautioning the speaker against a style that traipses on inserting so much irrelevant material into a presentation that the argument ends up straying too far "outside the record" (whatever that process truly encompasses).[100]

Violations are extremely difficult to identify even by experienced judges, and reigning in the miscreants has its own problems. It is a problematic system which empowers the trial lawyer to be fluid with the story in a substantial respect, and then empowers the judge to impose poorly defined limits on them doing so; no solidly outlined court or trial procedures assist the judge to do the heavy lifting when necessary to place some effective constraints on the sketchiest presentations.

In between the timidity of casual admonishments and the severity of issuing a formal order of contempt, one compromise tool that the judge has at trial is the sidebar, the pulling of the agent, the real actor's representative, off the stage and behind the curtains for a brief moment often to demand an equally brief justification of the comment, question, or style which was just presented in front of the footlights.[101] In practice, sidebars can be relatively nerve-wracking moments-of-truth when a trial lawyer is pushed to explain themselves to a judge with no preparation time or warning, and sometimes with quite serious repercussions to the progress of the case itself. It is at sidebar where a trial lawyer is held to think on their feet and to do so efficiently and effectively, and such compacted colloquies can often be the very linchpin upon which the balance of a case's trajectory then rests.

No orator, actor, agent, or author is ever really exempt from the threat of sidebar within any mode of expression, even the most poetic and fantastic, and many traditional works of philosophy and religion have their own versions of sidebars often in the form of follow-up comments to challenge why some important text was offered for public consideration—the Talmud in Jewish law, and Zen koans in Buddhist teachings, for instance, utilize commentaries to not just illuminate, support, or enhance propositions made in the original work but to demand a mandatory justification as well.[102] If attention to any particular style is to be justified as lawful to a jurist specifically, it is possibly at sidebar where the justification then likely is posited and then lives or dies.

A second pliable tool that the judiciary possesses outside of the contempt sanction is plain old disregard. Merely ignoring trial lawyers is not that difficult a job for many judges and they will just rely on infinite patience and the mechanism of judicial review to pass the problem up the ladder (or "down the line" depending on your semantic preference for categorizing hierarchies) to more and more stringent judicial oversight by next level appellate panels. The trial judge ignores the miscreant and into the picture strides the reviewing judges who are charged with evaluating error down below, including error created by litigants through their trial lawyers and by the trial lawyers themselves.

In this process, another lawyer now representing the appellant or respondent is pressed to explain in a far lengthier and more complicated format the recitation of why a different lawyer said what they said, and why them doing so was a legitimate exercise of an advocate's inherent powers to persuade and of a litigant's right to have their representative influence. Review supposedly corrals the errant. Review also brings into a different spotlight those who erred. Appeal to a court of review can be a harsh test to an appellate lawyer of how well they do in the game of "creative reinterpretation," including in explaining why their colleague's proposed connection to the fact finder was a lot more tangential than it was direct, was really "on all ones or twos" versus the "on all fours" which the trial lawyer may have boldly proclaimed to the judge or jury far back in the trial stage.

Validating and Invalidating Exercises in Style

Those confinements and escapes in the context of trial lawyer storymanipulating bring us back to considerations of where style fits in overall. Style in legal argument is mediated by a host of fluctuating factors that can be difficult to even delineate much less totally account for. As noted in the previous chapter, unquestionably important aural qualities of tone of voice, inflection, volume, change in speech pattern, and peculiar timing which are inherent in every speaker's personalized delivery all impact an audience's reception of a trial lawyer's message. *How* one hears what one hears wildly affects what one may then be persuaded of, and live oral argument escapes the limitations of the printed page in that regard. The study of paralinguistics substantiates that numerous vocal effects have an important role to play in the communication of meaning to targeted listeners;[103] to that end, the most concrete way to identify and be swayed by the mimic or the sarcastic nag, for instance, is to hear for oneself the unique intonations of their voice since no amount of adjectives, italics, scare quotes, highlighting or underlining will sufficiently and comprehensively convey those varieties of special message through writing alone.[104]

Additionally, there are as many styles as there are trial lawyers (or that would be truer if trial lawyers weren't so frequently derivative of other lawyers). It should be kept in mind that style in law is not a copyrightable object protected by intellectual property laws, and therefore allows for outright thievery as well as for the fluid "borrowing" of others' techniques with no attribution made—simply "taking a page out of their book" is the most apt description of this common phenomenon among advocates.

Of course, theft doesn't always have to be sensible, and some styles seem at first glance quite undesirable to have ever been borrowed or been used at all—why would a trial lawyer want to argue outdated tropes or insert class-based triggering references for instance? The answer to that question must factor in just how a particular client's interests can best get promoted to influence a particular jury pool composition. Affected by situationally set factors of local forum and type of claim, style choice (including weird style choice) is multi-factorial. What is chosen ascends from a sizing up of the client in the first consult, from a preferred taxonomic arrangement, from impromptu decisions made at *voir dire* and at sidebars, from denials of motions *in limine*, from the looks on the faces of the panel as they are finally sworn in, and as a delicate reflection of the trial lawyer's own personal experience of the human condition, their own individual propensities being on all fours as it is with their styles employed as social creatures, as arguers in their own cases and own lives.

For their part, as they sit in the jury box in the courtroom, jurors are the consumers of all the pontificating and speechifying going on in front of them, the receptacles for all those personalities and styles being purveyed to them, the appreciators of the vaudeville act and the hook as one big show. Stand ins for the community at large, their intellectual autonomy must not be overlooked. They may approve and select one metaphorical scene above another from this metaphorical offering, but they may also reject all choices presented and utilize seat-of-the-pants heuristic devices to just ignore the trial lawyers altogether, to themselves take over from the footlights of the stage to subjectively gauge credibility, liability, and plain old likability of a performer, be it participant *or* representative in the trial. All monologuing villains run the risk of the hero eventually just getting so fed up with listening to the explanatory chatter that they take matters into their own hands.

Their autonomy imparts to them the unusual power to stop the monologue, to close the curtains entirely. This is where they simply "nullify" all that has gone before, that is, not do what they are told but instead do purely as they wish. It can be done either (a) where they acquit a defendant in a criminal case even though they or other members of the jury believe the defendant is guilty,[105] or (b) where they choose to do what they think is "right" in either a criminal or civil case in disregard or spite of what they have been instructed or have heard received in evidence.[106] "Jury nullification" is not only a jury's knowing and deliberate rejection of the evidence presented to them, not only simply their refusal to apply the law as they were instructed by the judge to do, it is more than just that: it is that rejection or refusal levied for the specific reason that they want to send a message about some social issue that is larger than the case itself, or because the result dictated by the law is fundamentally contrary to what they believe is their own sense of justice, morality, or fairness and they refuse to administer such a result.[107]

This exertion of intellectual power is often overlooked and just as often also derided by the judiciary as if it were misconduct hostile or antagonistic to the true course of justice.[108] It is not of course, it is a reflection of the jury's independent role as proxies for the community distinct from being only tools of the litigation system exerted by combatants to get disputes to a bloodless conclusion. And, by the way, not just as *functional* substitutes in the sense that matters of practicality require that we randomly deputize six or twelve token members from the populace due to the obvious fact that courtrooms physically can't hold entire communities. Their "stand in" role intrinsically includes their moral representation of discerned group standards, beliefs, and convictions as a basic source from which their fuller decisional power springs.

Cynically, that imprimatur of community moral authority, which is weighty enough to be allowed to override judicial or statutory authority, is an enticement to be manipulated to advantage by the trial lawyer's words as well. But the trial lawyer must beware of the possibility for jurors' disdain of claims of moral primacy and of operative logic entirely. Intuitive and intensely personal feelings about "fairness" and about "what is right" may override trial operations no matter how insistent advocates and judges may be about obedience to rules and instructions imposed during the trial. In the same way that religion offers an illogical, anti-intellectual comfort to the susceptible parishioner, the lure of simply delivering oneself over to "blind faith" alone can denigrate and devalue external proofs in an instant.

Even in nullifying, of course, the jury panel is fenced in by the practicalities of both courtroom dynamics and the verdict form. Eager though they may be to explain their crisis of conscience or their newly found just and righteous conclusions, no avenue is really available for them to make any actual speech doing so. Checking boxes and putting numbers in blanks on a paper form is about the best it gets for a jury's options for true self expression and for partaking in their own Argument.

And of course should they wish to *not* reject and nullify the proceeding but to adhere to the instructions and issue a decision comporting with the evidence, jurors are influenced by the trial lawyer's words one final time in the jury room during deliberations, only the words are now faint echoes, those reverberations holding fast in the juror's minds even though not currently sounding in their ears. While in the jury room after the evidence has been presented and after they have been formally instructed and physically removed from the courtroom environment, there is a new dual theme of privacy and secrecy, the expression of a strong public policy doctrine employed of protecting jurors by seclusion from all improper influences.[109]

Not, to be sure, from *all* influence itself, just from improper influence, given that the very purpose of having more than one of them is so that the decision reached is by the group; in their own dynamic they are encouraged to quite directly influence each other.[110] Only the irredeemably naïve assume that those in the room are unencumbered by appeals to passion, prejudice, or sympathy since it is in this very locale that the trial lawyer has already anticipated that all sorts of passions, prejudices, and sympathies suggested earlier by the presentation of style will now likely be recalled and confronted head on. The hope is that each now reminisces on the trial lawyer's proclamations and then employs the trial lawyer's evaluations of credibility and liability based on an earlier suggestion that the trial lawyer's taxonomy was the best of the available choices.

This last gasp of manipulation efforts then is all about the struggle for the jury's *memory*—their storage or erasure of words, depending on which process is more sorely needed. Some styles in opening and closing lend themselves well to making certain words and thoughts memorable, others not so much. As the novice trial lawyer soon learns, repetition alone has mostly poor effect; studies show that mere rote reprisals of the same "really important" word or phrase over and over actually end up derailing retention, not enhancing it.[111] Similar appeal and recall problems arise with efforts at utilizing simple volume control to gain an impact; while most trial lawyers don't actually shout or whisper, a regrettable outcome of doing so is usually juror resentment, not alliance. With such rehearsals and exhortations, the goal is to emphasize important over unimportant bits so that jurors will take up the work later and influence each other with reminders of certain notable sound bites. That goal is rarely achieved with those techniques in isolation. Other styles appeal to the disintegration of information, and the goal is to deemphasize in a way that jurors will later influence each other by pointing out absences, small gaps and large holes where truths in the form of expected sound bites and key documents *should* have been provided but weren't.

In each instance, initially held convictions, recalibrations of personal belief, and impairments to objective observations, all become important to manipulate, and throughout it is the tight control of information flow as executed via the tighter implementation of style. A winner's decision gets created, say, from amalgams of well modulated tone and exhortation based on appeals to quasi-religious insights or, alternatively, perhaps from an alluring patter of gerrymandered ignorances based on appeals to base prejudices, or maybe on both in succession. Success is tied to exploiting whatever is at hand right as a witness testifies as much as it is to preparation and exertion before they testify, and stems from anything that a trial lawyer can find or construct, including that which the opponent has overlooked or failed to toy with themselves.[112]

Persuasive techniques of storymanipulating, relative truth handling, and particularly the procedural assistance of covering up the competitor's proposed truisms through objections and exclusions of evidence—all are directives to-and-from attention which need to work in a concert of urgency to push out the desired decision alone onto the verdict form.

So Many Representatives for So Many Others

Consider how we have identified that jurors are proxies for communities and how trial lawyers are proxies for clients. There is some sophistication to acknowledge as we explore why that is so. As to the former pairing, we acknowledge that jurors aren't merely society's "stunt doubles," people who are cleverly employed to look and act similar to the entire community in order to fool others that they really are the entire community for visual or situational purposes; we get it that jurors are far better described as the litigants' and citizenry's "peers" who have been "hand picked" (um, randomly chosen in a lottery, but whatever) out of the entire population for a democratic purpose, supposedly ordinary people who have been generously cloaked with a specific and extraordinary power to make a very specific and extraordinary decision on behalf of the entire community of which they are only a miniscule part.

Clearly that arrangement is far different conceptually than what stunt doubles ever do for their actor counterparts, but it has its parallels in that everyone is complicit in accepting that one social unit is being made equivalent to another social unit for a good reason. The phenomenon of representation is valuable in keeping many institutions functioning, and we acknowledge a need for juries to represent communities in the same fashion that we have a need for trial lawyers to represent clients and for stunt doubles to represent actors—needs with origins in convenience but which culminate in functionality, in more workable systems that obtain more usable and swifter dispute resolution worthy results.

What is distinct about the pairing of lawyer and client in particular? It does not have the same dynamic as jury and community, that's for sure: the lawyer's representative capacity does give them extraordinary power but not the power to make ultimate decisions for the client (indeed the Model Rules of Professional Conduct strictly prohibit that) only to make strategic decisions for them. And as representatives they certainly have not been hand-picked by any community to be so—they are self-selected and self-serving workers making a living off voluntarily inserting themselves into a semi-utilitarian process. No abstract democratic ideal is invoked in constructing the social union known as "lawyer and client," it is a relationship whose genesis and maintenance is in economic, not political, principles. It may be a little brusque to say, but really some pricey schooling and a craving to exert influence funneled into the maw of a capitalist system where the citizenry is constantly battling with each other enables any one to make a buck through "being the authorized representative" of another as long as they earned a state-issued license to do so and have been able to convince the other that representation is needed and that it should be by them in particular.

The one-to-one correspondence between attorney and client is not the one-to-one correspondence between juror and community. While the lawyer is not the stunt double exactly, there is a personal and financial component to the relationship that motivates the lawyer standing up at a table or positioned in front of a bench acting and talking as if they were the other person. Billboards and 1–900 numbers remind us that clients have certainly been known to hire lawyers based almost exclusively on the lawyer's engaging physical appearance, attractive qualities, and charm and suave nature alone—their style subbing in as their main value as it were.

More importantly, it is the client who instigates everything: they have to have a need, they have to find and hire another to address the need, they have to voluntarily select and pay the other, yet form an economically beneficial arrangement to secure an objective, fashion a solution, and figure out practical routes of negotiation and influence malleable enough to attain success on it, including through the weirdness and risk of litigation.

Once that representation game starts, and especially once it moves into the trial system, it exhibits a compulsive force which then escapes the grasp of the represented person fairly quickly. The trial lawyer, as a very special doppelgänger, has substantial work to do in now being someone else (or a host of someone elses) and the client, though the original instigator, only hinders the effort from there. Choosiness comes into play: as this other person, what exactly should be revealed and what generally should be kept private? Distancing comes into play: how "aligned with" the client should it appear that the trial lawyer is personally or publicly? Timing comes into play: as this other person, just when is it advisable to be vocal and when it is more effective to be mute? No client knows, but all lawyers everywhere certainly should.

Without outright mocking the client, the trial lawyer nevertheless adopts the client's "voice." Representation requires some affectation but not too much; it reaches stridently for others' acceptance but has to be reserved in the asking; with every pronouncement that "I am here on behalf of . . . " it points toward the fact that a person has formally replaced another person while scrambling with every other phrase available to point *away* from the replacement as being anything significant. The play is for pay but it is absolute anathema for the replacement to expressly point out either that pay is involved or that play is occurring.

Instead, closer personal relationships are promised. Above all, the representative wants the jury to conflate not just the attorney-client relationship, but the aspirations of each as well. The jury should think that the client's desires are the trial lawyer's desires. The jury should think that this is a collaboration of the highest order in that not only do two people in front of them want something as one but that the jury should be naturally joining in to want that same thing too. The proposed group project might demand that attention is stirred or it might demand that no attention is necessary, that the status quo can be maintained by healthy disregard and inactivity. In either instance, the person doing the demanding is in effect a human cloak placed over another's shoulders. Every sound emanating from the cloak says, in primary effect, "there is no cloak here"—and yet all is deception personified, a walking, talking shroud of relative truths and suppressed data parading around as real truths and real data and eliciting style to do so.

It is superficially a goal for any speaker to want to enable their listener to discover or learn something for themselves; empowering the audience as part and parcel of the "discovery" of the trial lawyer's conclusion from their premises can be particularly effective at times. But that is certainly not a universal principle, and it may well be far more useful to *not* want a juror to care about being invited to participate in doing any actual work. Constantly recalling that they are not there voluntarily aids the trial lawyer in weighing whether jurors might just prefer to have a break from engaging in rational thought (as all people do from time to time in plenty of other aspects of their lives). An effective trial lawyer should cater to a natural proclivity for laziness as well as for industry.

An effective trial lawyer should also pull in help wherever it might be offered and in our theater analogy that means using props. We know that all lawyers use words. We know that all lawyers use other people. It can come as no great shock to acknowledge that all lawyers use objects to manipulate as well. Appreciating object manipulation is indispensable to appreciating another important etiology of Argument and that is where we must head next.

Notes

1 See, Bourne, Kylie. "Commanding and controlling protest crowds." *Critical Horizons* 12, no. 2 (2011): 189–210.
2 Mansbridge, Jane J. *Beyond adversary democracy*. University of Chicago Press, 1983.
3 See, Caplan, David. *Language: Structure, processing, and disorders*. The MIT Press, 1992 at pp. 84–6.
4 See, e.g., Schacter, Daniel L., and Randy L. Buckner. "Priming and the brain." *Neuron* 20, no. 2 (1998): 185–95.
5 See, Hirshman, Elliot, and Robert A. Bjork. "The generation effect: Support for a two-factor theory." *Journal of Experimental Psychology: Learning, Memory, and Cognition* 14, no. 3 (1988): 484.
6 See, e.g., State v. Mannix, 263 Or App 162, 326 P3d 1236 (2014).
7 A concern that arises in the case law almost exclusively due to race, with the rule being that the striking of even one venireperson for a racial reason almost certainly violates the equal protection clause of state and federal constitutions. See, Roberts v. State, 627 So 2d 1114 (Ala Crim App 1993).
8 American Bar Association. House of Delegates, and Center for Professional Responsibility (American Bar Association). *Model rules of professional conduct*. American Bar Association, 2006.
9 Fuller, Lon L. *The law in quest of itself*. The Lawbook Exchange, Ltd., 1999 at p. 86.
10 Irwin, Terence. "The development of ethics: A historical and critical study." In *The philosophical forum*, vol. 42, no. 3. Blackwell Publishing Inc, 2011, pp. 269–335.
11 See, Solan, Lawrence M. "Lawyers as insincere (but truthful) actors." *Journal of Legal Profession* 36 (2011): 487.
12 See, Costanzo, Mark A., and Ellen Gerrity. "The effects and effectiveness of using torture as an interrogation device: Using research to inform the policy debate." *Social Issues and Policy Review* 3, no. 1 (2009): 179–210.

13 On this topic see generally, Garrity v. New Jersey, 385 U.S. 493, 87 S. Ct. 616 (1967) at fn. 5.

14 See, Strack, Hermann Leberecht. *Introduction to the Talmud and Midrash*. Fortress Press, 1996.

15 Courts themselves fare no better than any other public institutions from making such lofty proclamations. See, e.g., In McCreary County v. American Civil Liberties Union, 545 U.S. 844 (2005), where the Supreme Court held 5-4 that Ten Commandment displays in two Kentucky county courthouses violated the establishment clause of the First Amendment.

16 See, e.g., Moir v. Ozeruga, 313 Or App 9, 496 P3d 655 (2021).

17 Law and justice can often present as entirely independent concepts. John Rawls' philosophical work "Justice as Fairness: A Restatement" (2001) does not mention the word "law" anywhere in its 200 plus pages analyzing balances and imbalances of fairness, equilibrium, and cooperation in society.

18 White, James Boyd. *Heracles' bow: Essays on the rhetoric and poetics of the law*. University of Wisconsin Press, 1985 at p. 222.

19 Langevoort, Donald C., and Robert K. Rasmussen. "Skewing the results: The role of lawyers in transmitting legal rules." *Southern California Interdisciplinary Law Journal* 5 (1996): 375.

20 Taken from Posner, Richard A. *The economics of justice*. Harvard University Press, 1983.

21 See, Layard, P. Richard G. *Cost-benefit analysis*. Cambridge University Press, 1994.

22 See, e.g., Green, Leon. "Blindfolding the jury." *Texas Law Review* 33 (1954): 157.

23 See, Herald Ass'n, Inc. v. Ellison, 138 Vt 529, 419 A2d 323 (1980) (holding that even as to trials, the right to access to a judicial proceeding is not an absolute one, but, rather, a right to be weighed against other interests).

24 See, Vaughn v. Progressive Cas. Ins. Co., 907 So 2d 1248, 1252 (Fla Dist Ct App 2005) where an appellate panel was concerned with the "intemperate" remarks by an experienced senior judge under the dual pressure of completing a case before his certification expired while dealing with "obstreperous" lawyers interminably dragging out a witness's examination:

> The function of a . . . trial judge is not that of an umpire or of a moderator at a town meeting. A trial is not a game of sport where umpires engage in heated discussion with players who have allegedly broken the rules, and it is not a town meeting where moderators scold citizens who promote their self-interests or voice their grievances in a manner and with language unbecoming the solemnity of a courtroom. Rather, a trial is a formal proceeding where "every litigant is entitled to nothing less than the cold neutrality of an impartial judge" charged with the duty to ensure that every grievance is fairly resolved in accordance with the rules of evidence and trial procedure.

25 See, e.g., Hovey v. Davis, 120 Or App 425, 852 P2d 929 (1993), rev den, 318 Or 26 (1993).

26 See, Vasek, M. "Lying as a skill: The development of deception in children." In *Deception: Perspectives on human and nonhuman deceit* (Robert W. Mitchell and Nicholas S. Thompson, eds.). State University of New York Press, 1986 at pp. 271–92.

27 See, e.g., Lafferty v. Stevens Mem'l Hosp., 136 Wash App 1027 (2006).
28 Aristodemou, Maria. *Law, psychoanalysis, society: Taking the unconscious seriously.* Routledge, 2014 at p. 26.
29 Truth affirmations have their own special lexicon and manner of presentation: "That is 100% the truth!" "I am absolutely positive that is so!" "I would bet my life on that being so!" Counter to how other pleas for acceptance work, it is interesting that rising inflections, increased volume, and earnest repetitions do not harbor acceptance nearly as well as presentations which take the opposite trajectory—a single staccato sentence in a terse, sotto voice delivered with a lowered head usually garners the closest attention.
30 Daicoff, Susan Swaim. *Lawyer, know thyself: A psychological analysis of personality strengths and weaknesses.* American Psychological Association, 2004 at p. 32.
31 Mahon, James Edwin. "Two definitions of lying." *International Journal of Applied Philosophy* 22, no. 2 (2008): 211–30.
32 See, e.g., Carson, Thomas L. "The definition of lying." *Noûs* 40, no. 2 (2006): 284–306.
33 From "Lies, liars, and lying: An introductory overview." In *Lying, cheating, and carrying on: Developmental, clinical, and sociocultural aspects of dishonesty and deceit* (Salman Akhtar and Henri Parens, eds.). Jason Aronson Inc, 2009 at p. 1.
34 Sterelny, Kim. *The evolved apprentice.* MIT Press, 2012 at p. 111.
35 Schlagel, Richard H. "Contextualistic realism." *Philosophy and Phenomenological Research* 41, no. 4 (1981): 437–51 at pp. 251–2.
36 DeMott, Deborah A. "The lawyer as agent." *Fordham Law Review* 67 (1998): 301.
37 DeMott, Deborah A. "Disloyal agents." *Alabama Law Review* 58 (2006): 1049.
38 Taken from Saarni, C., and M. Lewis. "Deceit and illusion in human affairs." In *Lying and deception in everyday life* (Michael Lewis and Carolyn Saarni, eds.). Guilford Press, 1993 at pp. 26–7.
39 See generally, Yan, Wen-Jing, Qi Wu, Jing Liang, Yu-Hsin Chen, and Xiaolan Fu. "How fast are the leaked facial expressions: The duration of micro-expressions." *Journal of Nonverbal Behavior* 37 (2013): 217–30.
40 See, Edehlson, G.A. "Developmental aspects of lying." In *Lying, cheating, and carrying on: developmental, clinical, and sociocultural aspects of dishonesty and deceit* (Salman Akhtar and Henri Parens, eds.). Jason Aronson Inc, 2009 at p. 34.
41 See, Bates, J.A.V. "The communicative hand." In *The Body as a medium of expression: Essays based on a course of lectures given at the Institute of Contemporary Arts, London* (Jonathan Benthall and Ted Polhemus, eds.). E.P. Dutton and Co., Inc. 1975, at pp. 175–94.
42 See, Riggio, R.E., and R.S. Feldman (eds.). *Applications of nonverbal communication* (1st ed.). Psychology Press, 2005.
43 See, Clément, Fabrice. "To trust or not to trust? Children's social epistemology." *Review of Philosophy and Psychology* 1 (2010): 531–49.
44 See, Hobbs, Pamela. "'Is that what we're here about?': A lawyer's use of impression management in a closing argument at trial." *Discourse & Society* 14, no. 3 (2003): 273–90 (demonstrating how a Black attorney addressing a predominantly Black jury uses the stylistic and rhetorical dimensions of African American vernacular English (AAVE) to construct a shared identity with the jury).
45 Haack, Susan. *Evidence matters: Science, proof, and truth in the law.* Cambridge University Press, 2014 at pp. 30–1.

46 Proctor, Robert N., and Londa Schiebinger. "Agnotology: The making and unmaking of ignorance." (2008) In *Routledge international handbook of ignorance studies* (Matthias Gross and Linsey McGoey, eds.). Routledge, 2015.

47 For the archetypal example, see Robert DeNiro's character's command to the bedeviled head chef in the kitchen of a Las Vegas casino: "From now on, I want you to put an equal amount of blueberries in each muffin." *Casino* (Universal Pictures 1995). The screenwriter likely composed the scene to illustrate DeNiro's character as an obsessive despot, but I listen to the line's delivery as conveying a more subtle message: that the *appearance* of equality—in everyone finding the same number of blueberries in their muffins— actually *is* equality. As the stage manager of his own play, De Niro wants his guests to individually experience a distinct emotion of reassurance and he does so by using a familiar physical object that is the very essence of comfort, a blueberry muffin, yet by manipulating a feature of the object—numerically equal berry numbers compared across a statistical sampling—which doesn't have anything to do with comfort at all. A trial lawyer would easily identify with someone deliberately manufacturing a group's emotional satisfaction with all being fair, not by logic but merely by a prop carrying weighty symbolic content. It is effective stagecraft (and a story, by the way, which has now been layered, first inside the film and second inside this endnote).

48 The example is taken from Windt, Jennifer M. *Dreaming: A conceptual framework for philosophy of mind and empirical research.* MIT press, 2015 at p. 13.

49 Werth, Lucy Fontaine, and Jenny Flaherty. "A phenomenological approach to human deception." In *Deception: Perspectives on human and nonhuman deceit* (Robert W. Mitchell and Nicholas S. Thompson, eds.). State University of New York Press, 1986 at p. 293.

50 Landsman, Stephan. "A brief survey on the development of the adversary system." *Ohio State Journal of Criminal Law* 44 (1983): 713.

51 Cheyney, Edward P. "The court of star chamber." *The American Historical Review* 18, no. 4 (1913): 727–50.

52 Ibid.

53 Ibid.

54 Michael, Helen K. "Role of natural law in early American constitutionalism: Did the founders contemplate judicial enforcement of unwritten individual rights, the." *North Carolina Law Review* 69 (1990): 421.

55 Zande, Daniel L. Vande. "Coercive power and the demise of the star chamber." *American Journal of Legal History* 50, no. 3 (2010): 326–49.

56 See, e.g., Timberlake, William "Constructing animal cognition." In *The cognitive animal: Empirical and theoretical perspectives on animal cognition* (Marc Bekoff, Colin Allen, and Gordon M. Burghardt, eds.). MIT press, 2002 at pp. 105–13.

57 Farnsworth, E. Allan. *An introduction to the legal system of the United States.* Oxford University Press, 2010.

58 Summers, Robert S. "Formal legal truth and substantive truth in judicial fact-finding--their justified divergence in some particular cases." *Law and Philosophy* 18 (1999): 497–511.

59 See, Calabresi, Guido. "The exclusionary rule." *Harvard Journal of Law & Public Policy* 26 (2003): 111.

60 Stuntz, William J. "Virtues and vices of the exclusionary rule, the." *Harvard Journal of Law & Public Policy* 20 (1996): 443.
61 See, Smith v. State, 352 So 3d 1147, 1158 (Miss Ct App 2022) ("In our system of justice it is the role of the jury to determine truth").
62 See generally, Frank, Mitchell J., and Osvaldo F. Morera. "Professionalism and advocacy at trial-real jurors speak in detail about the performance of their advocates." *Baylor Law Review* 64 (2012): 1.
63 The distinctive physical layout of courtroom areas has contextual significance. The spatial division between the actual "bench" and the actual "bar" is a deliberate signal that roles are to be kept distinct with the judge either sequestered in a separate "chamber" or raised up in elevation at a dais (or at least separated from everyone else in a common area by some sort of imposing-looking barrier) and the structural demarcation of a swinging gate signifying where advocates are allowed to roam versus where the public is confined in the "back of the room," the gallery. Other environmental elements emphasize separation and status: counsel must "sit at table," witnesses must "take the stand," juries must be placed in a "box," and everyone must rise and sit as jurists and juries physically enter and leave parts of the room; these are all key aspects of the visual distancing, connections, and imports of furniture and architecture subtly illustrating *imbalances*, not balances, of power distributions. See, Hazard, John N. "Furniture arrangement as a symbol of judicial roles." In *Folk law: Essays in the theory and practice of lex non scripta*. Vol. 1 (Alison Dundes Renteln and Alan Dundes, eds.). University of Wisconsin Press, 1995.
64 See generally, Finkel, Norman J., and Norman J. Finkel. *Commonsense justice: Jurors' notions of the law*. Harvard University Press, 2009.
65 Ibid.
66 See, e.g., Grenier, Addie. "Order in the court: Communication patterns in the courtroom & their effects." *Order* (2024).
67 Shari Seidman Diamond, Jonathan D. Casper, Cami L. Heiert, and Anna-Maria Marshall. "Juror reactions to attorneys at trial." *Journal of Criminal Law and Criminology* 87 (1996): 17.
68 See generally, Hahn, Peter W., and Susan D. Clayton. "The effects of attorney presentation style, attorney gender, and juror gender on juror decisions." *Law and Human Behavior* 20, no. 5 (1996): 533–54.
69 Smith, John W. "An 'informational' perspective on manipulation." In *Deception: Perspectives on human and nonhuman deceit* (Robert W. Mitchell and Nicholas S. Thompson, eds.). State University of New York Press, 1986 at p. 83.
70 Toulmin, Stephen E. *The uses of argument*. Cambridge University Press, 2003.
71 See, Walton, Douglas. *The place of emotion in argument*. Penn State Press, 2010 at pp. 2–6.
72 Impeachment provides a tool to test a witness's perception, credibility, and truthfulness, which is essential because a jury is free to believe any, all, or none of a witness's testimony. See generally, State v. Townsend, 649 SW3d 72 (Mo Ct App 2022), reh'g and/or transfer den (June 13, 2022), transfer den (Aug. 30, 2022). Courts often couch the doctrine in the language of personal attack and personal value. See, e.g., People v. Witt, 227 Ill App 3d 936, 592 NE2d 402 (1992) ("purpose of impeaching evidence is to destroy the credibility of the witness"); State v. Stinson, 43 Kan App 2d 468, 227 P3d 11 (2010) (to "impeach a witness" means to call into

question the veracity of the witness by showing that the witness is "unworthy of belief").

73 Parkin, David. "Political language." *Annual Review of Anthropology* 13, no. 1 (1984): 345–65.

74 The archetypal oratorical device of dogged insistence as a demand for action has to be Cato the Elder's incessant entreaty to the Roman Senate during the Punic Wars of "*Carthago delenda est*" ("Carthage must be destroyed"). His repetition of the phrase at every opportunity folded together elements of compulsion, personal conviction, and a lack of sensible alternatives that eventually achieved the desired effect of war. The filibuster has its uses to be sure, but reiteration when it is relentless with no other incentive added to the mix poses its dangers—sometimes instead of wearing down an audience's resistance, unyielding demands build up defiance.

75 McClain, Emlin. "Classification of the law for lawyers." *American Law Review* 26 (1892): 223. Interestingly, this ancient treatise also refers to the concept of cases being "on all fours" (discussed in the Introduction).

76 Smith, Edward E. "Categorization." In *Thinking: An invitation to cognitive science, Vol. 3.* (Daniel N. Osherson and Edward E. Smith, eds.). The MIT Press, 1990 at pp. 33–53.

77 Pound, Roscoe. "Classification of law." *Harvard Law Review* 37, no. 8 (1924): 933–69.

78 Williams, David M., and Malte C. Ebach. *Cladistics*. Vol. 88. Cambridge University Press, 2020.

79 See generally, Endersby, Jim. "Lumpers and splitters: Darwin, Hooker, and the search for order." *Science* 326, no. 5959 (2009): 1496–9.

80 Grant, Peter R. "Ecology and evolution of Darwin's Finches (Princeton Science Library Edition)." In *Ecology and Evolution of Darwin's Finches (Princeton Science Library Edition)*. Princeton University Press, 2017.

81 Simpson, George Gaylord. *The principles of classification and a classification of mammals*. Vol. 85. American Museum of Natural History, 1945.

82 Rapp, Christof. *Aristotle's rhetoric*. Akademie Verlag, 2002.

83 See, Greene, Jamal. "Pathetic argument in constitutional law." *Columbia Law Review* 113 (2013): 1389 at 1398.

84 Underwood v. City of Portland, 319 Or App 648, 510 P3d 918 (2022).

85 Donohue, William A. "Analyzing negotiation tactics: Development of a negotiation interact system." *Human Communication Research* 7, no. 3 (1981): 273–87.

86 See Walton, Douglas. *The place of emotion in argument*. Penn State Press (2010) at p. 153: "[A]rguing in a way that is threatening to your hearer and actually threatening your hearer—that is, making a specific threat against him—are two different things."

87 See, e.g., Hyman, Neil S. "Strict liability for damage caused by animals." *Loyola Law Review* 21 (1975): 785.

88 Bite cases can create opportunities for excess and exaggeration both dog- and person-related: one of the best examples of litigants detonating a simple "dog bite case" into the most profound mess possible is Bros. v. Lipp, 2004 Mass App Div 21 (Dist Ct 2004), aff'd, 63 Mass App Ct 1112, 825 NE2d 1080 (2005). In Bros, plaintiffs were walking their dog near defendants' residence when defendants' dog attacked plaintiffs' dog, an attack during which their dog and they sustained wounds. While the relatively routine factual disputes were about who owned the attacking dog and

the severity of plaintiffs' injuries, the ensuing trial was an epic of accusation and abuse that made the dog attack itself pale in comparison. At one point, the court noted that "spewing what had become their customary invective, the defendants demanded, *inter alia,* disbarment of the plaintiffs' attorney; perjury, extortion and fraud charges against [plaintiffs] and a change of venue because the court was "being run by gangsters" who were conspiring with the plaintiffs in their "frame up." The appellate opinion concluded that sanctions on defendants were warranted due to "flagrant, antagonistic disrespect for the judicial system . . . [and] affirmative, consistent efforts to undermine its effective and efficient operation."

89 Gould, Stephen Jay. *Wonderful life: the Burgess Shale and the nature of history*. WW Norton & Company, 1989.

90 Through a process called "publishing" to the jury. See, e.g., State v. Clevenger, 289 SW3d 626, 628 (Mo Ct App 2009) (regarding whether publishing certain exhibits to the jury violates a defendant's right to a fair trial).

91 The occasional grimace, squint, or eye roll from the client in the chair at counsel table is tolerated but not much more than just a little; while emotional outbursts from participants are not unusual, neither are they encouraged (behaviors collectively called "testifying from your seat"), and any excess in that regard can create prejudice sufficient to cause a mistrial—thus ruining all the entitled grimacing, squinting, and eye rolling that the lawyer had previously been engaging in on the client's behalf. See, Pier 66 Co. v. Poulos, 542 So 2d 377 (Fla Dist Ct App 1989) (courts have wide latitude in coping with instances of emotional moments in conduct of party or testimony of witness as such are "not unusual occurrences" in the course of trial).

92 See generally, Susskind, Lawrence, and Patrick Field. *Dealing with an angry public: The mutual gains approach to resolving disputes*. Simon and Schuster, 1996.

93 See, e.g., Caldwell, H. Mitchell, L. Timothy Perrin, and Christopher L. Frost. "The art and architecture of closing argument." *Tulane Law Review* 76 (2001): 961.

94 See, Baron, Jane B. "The many promises of storytelling in law: An essay review of narrative and the legal discourse: A reader in storytelling and the law." *Rutgers Law Journal* 23 (1991): 79.

95 Cf., *The Big Cage* (1933), a movie about a circus threatened with bankruptcy staging a lion and tiger fight for the public, and in which a very real, unplanned and brutal fight between a real lion and real tiger actually occurred on set and which the director then selected to actually film and release to the public.

96 Sherman, Josepha. *Storytelling: An encyclopedia of mythology and folklore*. Routledge, 2015.

97 Ong, Walter J. *Orality and literacy*. Routledge, 2013 at p. 34.

98 Hoeken, Hans, and Mario Van Vliet. "Suspense, curiosity, and surprise: How discourse structure influences the affective and cognitive processing of a story." *Poetics* 27, no. 4 (2000): 277–86.

99 See, e.g., Medes v. Geico Corp., 97 Conn App 630, 905 A2d 1249 (2006).

100 State v. Jones, 355 NC 117, 558 SE2d 97 (2002).

101 Trial lawyers can request sidebars but are powerless to compel them; judges can and often do refuse a trial lawyer's request for one, yet no trial lawyer has any option to refuse a judge's demand for the same. Sidebars are distracting to the jury, tend to remind the jury that interesting information is being actively kept from them,

are rarely recorded (thus what is said in them is not made part of the official court record), and often engender appellate concerns that due process and confrontation rights were violated by such secrecy (see, e.g., State v. Kollie, 994 NW2d 367 (ND 2023), reh'g den (Sept. 6, 2023)), so it is hardly a surprise that they are as disfavored by the judiciary as they are.

102 See, e.g., Watts, Alan. *The way of zen*. Vintage, 1999.

103 See generally, Schuller, Björn, Stefan Steidl, Anton Batliner, Felix Burkhardt, Laurence Devillers, Christian Müller, and Shrikanth Narayanan. "Paralinguistics in speech and language—state-of-the-art and the challenge." *Computer Speech & Language* 27, no. 1 (2013): 4–39.

104 Intonation alone can absolutely dictate import. The low growl of a stranger saying "I'm gonna take you out, get you in my car, we're going for a long, long, long drive" can flip from a mobster's intimidating threat to a lover's tender promise depending entirely on the speaker's tonal delivery (see, Van Morrison's "A town called Paradise" from the album *No Guru, No Method, No Teacher* (1986)).

105 People v. Rodriguez, 508 P3d 276 (Colo App 2022).

106 Conaway, Teresa L., Carol L. Mutz, and Joann M. Ross. "Jury nullification: A selective, annotated bibliography." *Valparaiso University Law Review* 39 (2004): 393.

107 See, e.g., Sayles v. State, 245 Md App 128, 226 A3d 349 (2020), rev'd, 472 Md 207 (2021).

108 See, e.g., State v. Martin, 80917-2-I, 2021 WL 2206460, at 3 (Wash Ct App June 1, 2021), rev den, 497 P3d 375 (Wash 2021) (denying that juries have any constitutional or statutory "right" to nullify).

109 See, e.g., Hassard v. DS Retail, LLC, 4-22-0687, 2023 WL 3991095, at 1 (Ill App Ct June 9, 2023), appeal den, 129842, 2023 WL 6444884 (Ill Sept 27, 2023).

110 See, Caldwell v. New York City Transit Auth., 203 AD3d 6, 161 NYS3d 179 (2021) (holding that it is desired that there are "attempts [by each juror] to influence with his or her individual judgment and persuasion the reasoning of the other").

111 Potter, Mary C. "Remembering." In *Thinking: An invitation to cognitive science, Vol. 3*. (Daniel N. Oshersonc and Edward E. Smith, eds.). The MIT Press, 1990 at p. 6.

112 "For be a man's intellectual superiority what it will, it can never assume the practical, available supremacy over other men, without the aid of some sort of external arts and entrenchments, always, in themselves, more or less paltry and base." From Chapter XXXIII in Melville, Herman. "Moby Dick. New York: Modern Library" (First published 1851).

3

The Manipulation of Objects to Advance Personal Interests

In which items both animate and inanimate being employed for evidentiary purposes in a trial are not necessarily handled or arranged as they truly should be, decried how they truly should be, or celebrated as they truly should be, but rather have artificial presentations made of them and biased semantic operations performed on them by trial lawyers solely so that their conceptual appearance can be altered enough to then have a salutary effect on the ultimate decisions of others.

The Tribulations of Trials

All trials preface their theatrical parades of formality with a less theatrical and more private prologue of informality (or rather a set of prologues) composed of a slew of pre-trial scheduling conferences, in-chamber evidentiary discussions, casual settlement negotiations, ceremonious chit-chat, and hot and heavy issue-circumscribing bargaining sessions. These events transpire between the judge and counsel, ofttimes with parties present on the record and the public observing, but just as often behind closed doors with no record kept and no one else invited in at all.

The very start of a trial for the jury is only after that set of informal prologues have concluded, and the very first public act is where the court makes a short public introduction of the players and the case to the audience and then "summarizes" what is at stake in the dispute. With the case summary, judges do their best to craft and then monotonically recite "what this one is about" as a short paragraph to the jury. The case summary is (a) as even-handed, (b) as non-inflammatory, (c) as verbally concise, and (d) as narrowly drafted as is possible under the circumstances.[1] Need it be said by now that they are also artifices?

Every trial, of course has its successes and its failures in that regard and the competing lawyers weigh in on whether those criteria are truly met or not with the case summary version that each side proposes compared to that version which is eventually chosen to be read out loud. At least all participants concede that there needs to be some sort of original "framing" story for the decision-makers to get an initial grip on in order to justify why they are there at all, and case summaries outwardly serve that purpose. No summary, no matter how cautiously crafted, can fully escape attributions of partiality from the first word presented, especially the "expectancy bias" which many jurors have at the front end to want to judge a new case in terms of expectancies they developed from their personal experiences.[2]

To the same extent that trial lawyers fill their hours and days with arguing, judges do not; as receptacles of the arguments of others, judges get invigorated or exhausted as the occasion requires via listening to and considering lawyer argument. Lawyer argument offers a testing ground for addressing the judge's own thoughts, and it is sporadically of assistance to the judge in checking off answers to those thoughts, although there is no question that it can also be just as much a hindrance.

Somewhat akin to lawyers, judges listen, judges reason, and judges opine. Judges have their own particular body language and modes of expression, albeit usually somewhat more subtle than outright eye-rolling and jaw-clenching (although one would be surprised at what can be read in even the slightest of facial tics). In so engaging, judges do *not*, on the other hand, represent individuals along the way; they certainly don't have "clients," and the best that can be found for that category as a counterpart is the local community which the judge's particular jurisdiction encompasses, city, county, state, or nation. Judges don't have proxies or stand-ins or doppelgangers or stunt doubles. Their role in the play is in service of large size social forces comparable to how the lawyer's role is in service of undeniably small size private forces, even though both actors contribute generically to maintenance of the social compact through attending to such service.

The creation and delivery of a case summary to the jury at the start of trial is thus an encapsulated announcement of just how removed judges are from proxies and also supposedly from argumentative acts proffered by self-interested individuals. The judiciary jealously guards its intellectual independence and experiences a constant need to continually distance its members from the litigants, witnesses, advocates, and jurors start to finish, as well as a need to benefit the appropriate jurisdiction where their members are benched in presiding over all the other actors. A case summary then is a type of theatrical shorthand used to trumpet that separation and that benefit at the onset of a trial.

As noted, even *that* presentation, however, is artifice. A newscaster-type broadcast of the salient points of the dispute by an impressively robed authority figure may sound tamper-proof, but it is still a product of earlier manipulations ongoing throughout that set of prologues which the jury barely knew were even occurring. A large goal of an acceptable case summary is brevity, to inform those in the present of an event from the past in the briefest manner possible, yet as every author knows, the best abbreviations are the direct by-product of heavy editing and editorializing processes applied to thoughts as they arrive in bulk.

To that end, recitation of the summary is another piece of mind control of the jury through the manipulation of a seemingly innocuous object—a boring office report—relying on the perception that it was effortless to come by. The case summary is actually a skillful piece of covert propaganda: it hides the desirable and the undesirable in the inoffensive verbiage of the interoffice memo, it cloaks a tableau of bitter fighting behind the façade of gentlemanly cooperation. The message that a grudge match between entrenched combatants is about to bust out is a message which leaks freely through the pores of the paper as the judge reads dryly from it.

From the case summary there then arises a prodigious litany of other objects for the advocates to now organize and remark upon as the accouterments of the fight. The physical objects in the battle are in *person* form, as in litigants and witnesses, and in *paper* form, as in exhibits (along with some related electronic images, videos, photos, and the sort). As those objects are paraded about the courtroom during the trial, they are seen as people speaking from the seat in a witness stand or as printed documents being handed across tables—stapled sets of pages with exhibit stickers at their bottoms, covers in their fronts, and tags on their sides. The nonphysical objects presented are in indirect form, as in the topics that the people happen to be speaking about or that are depicted within the paper documents. Interest in the objects spans the spectrum from eye-closing tedium, with the engineering expert's professional qualifications, for instance, to eye-opening fascination, as frequently accompanies displays of unusual weapons or poisons, or recounts of certain salacious sexual acts.

Interest is also regulated, however, by the advocates filtering the physical presentations through the nonphysical; a skilled examination can act to greatly enhance or greatly minimize the intense sensory impact of viewing burnt clothes inside of an evidence bag.

Where the physical and conceptual objects are animals, especially dogs, jurors are highly susceptible to their interest being piqued by such filtering efforts since our perceptions of dogs are closely accompanied by a complex of emotive attachments and prejudices, all ripe for manipulation. Simply as a general precept, domesticated species of animals will often comprise unique bridges to social interactions among strangers.[3] One, since dogs in particular are intrinsically interesting biological objects, then the people peripherally associated with them tend to become peripherally interesting, and two, people tend to form strong impressions of a perceived personal connection, "dispositional attributions" as it were, concerning others based solely on their peripheral association with dogs.[4] The dog as a physical object being actually present in the courtroom is mostly unavailable as an option,[5] but the dog as a nonphysical, conceptual object being conceptually present in a case is a commonplace in many actions.

The dog as a concept offers a conduit by which jury attention can be uniquely garnered. There are "dog cases" and there are "dog cases" of course, and not each is a study in wide-eyed captivation for its audience simply *because* a dog is involved—cases involving breeder disputes over breeding contracts and cases involving ownership quarrels or boarding kennel negligence may elicit the same sighs of impatience as where the subject of the action is a dented car or broken machine. Dog biting and dog injury cases, dog theft and dog neglect cases, on the other hand, carry enough historical and emotional baggage with their cultural perception to at least have the capacity to raise, not lower, juror interest.

The available facts to consider in a "dog bites person" case, of course, include ten thousand more details than those in the case summary recited to the jury, and both openings and closings are campaigns to vigorously filter perceptions into usable forms, rife not just with callouts to names, dates, places, and circumstances far beyond the summary's abrupt and abbreviated description, but with calls to act on those details and to create a cohesive and valuable result from its scattered bits and pieces.

Dog Handling by Litigants and Dog "Handling" by Lawyers

Little of the interest which eventually might be generated appears at the start of the dog bite case. Indeed, it is hard to identify anything philosophically or emotionally substantial arising from the mundanity of a standard dog-bites-person case when first mentioned, and any randomly selected dispute hardly eclipses any other, dog's name and victim's blood type notwithstanding.

One reason why they are initially dull (as most lawsuit beginnings go anyway) is because we are so unsurprised by the series of obvious common-sense guidelines and common law rules which parcel out responsibility in such cases. We accept with a small yawn that (a) lots of people own and supervise dogs which act as somewhat complex moving objects, (b) those objects have sharp parts which can injure others if someone is not careful with the animals they are attached to, and (c) owning such an object includes being responsible for injuries created by its careless supervision. End of story. Mostly what increases in dog bite cases as the case proceeds is visceral interest, as when the effects of the bite are unusually gory or fatal, but that's about it and it is almost a mathematical proposition that a jury's level of emotional involvement in such a case can be measured as a metric governed by the age of the victim, the size of the dog, and the number of sutures in the wound.

It is also with a small shrug that we accept that because people express themselves through language, we therefore have a good chance of discerning their knowledge of past dog-related conduct and their intentions about ongoing dog-related conduct simply through what they say. Akin to many other types of personal injury cases, dog bite cases center upon dog bite stories, none of which stray too far outside of the expected chronicling of the mundanity of "one day a dog bit a person." As the fact finder listens somewhat indifferently, the litigants' subsequent explanations in the dog bite case operate to set the scene for, relate details of, and then cap the reason for, the tale. It is witness' words which build a shrine to, or dig a grave for, the respective participants. The legal and financial responsibility ultimately imposed on one litigant for the series of control and biting events at issue claimed to have adversely affected the other litigant is along a path of words lain down by both. Again, none of this is surprising.

However, there is an uncommon participant in a dog bite case who is not present in any other type of case, and that is some dog somewhere. The cars in car crash cases, the dwellings in landlord-tenant cases, and the slippery puddles in slip and fall cases don't have personalities or minds, but dogs presumably do.[6] Fact finders cannot ignore this unique distinction and attentive lawyers latch onto it with all their teeth. In no small part, then, it becomes fairly important that as the evidence is adduced, the character and mindset of that particular subject dog also sets the scene for, relates the details of, and then caps the reason for, how and why this particular tale has import.

Again, as with the gun, vial of poison, or burnt clothes, interest in a distinctive object is able to be piqued but adroit filtering also avoids the interest from waning or being quickly mollified since living breathing creatures embodying personalities and minds demand additional explanations of significance which inanimate poisons and tattered clothes do not. Again, a selected style that is tailored to inflame or temper unspoken primal questions about "what really are dogs anyway?" and "just how bad do bites feel anyway?" is essential.

Because dogs *cannot* express themselves through language then there is no actual and direct "discerning" of personality or mind available to engage in and nearly all is an admixture of sideways inference, seat-of-the-pants projections, and pure guesswork—the dog's (literal or figurative) shrine is built, or grave is dug, with guesses alone, and the bulk of them made about the animal's past, present, and likely future behavior are riddled with implicit biases. One bias is plain old fear, and we tend to begrudgingly assign larger weight to a poor prognosis of the dog's anticipated future behavior (anxiety and distrust about who is probably next in line to get injured by those sharp parts) than to an encouraging one. What was potentially banal becomes potentially fascinating due to perceived threat, and the trial lawyer sits up and takes careful note that as fear is a powerful motivating force, so here is an additionally novel and useful way in which to employ a newly selected style to motivate the jury to a client-favorable decision.

Divining dog minds is an immensely creative pastime.[7] Few rules apply. If the specific facts at hand don't necessarily support appeal to a fear bias, then perhaps they might to that of other biases people carry with them regarding love, sympathy, loyalty, physical resemblances, neurotic fixation, or outrage. Entire reservoirs of bias likely sit within each juror waiting to be released, and the right words combined with the right dog just might do it.

Undeniably, the trial lawyer is not the only one playing the interpretation game: the dog in the dog bite case is actually a heavily manipulated object in several senses.[8] It is manipulated by the court system overall by not being allowed to be present in the courtroom at all even though a case may be entirely about it and about its very personal fate.[9] It is manipulated by the litigants by being classified in the pleadings and spoken about in the testimony in a conciliatory or aggrandizing fashion based on the litigant's interest in conveying a particular message to the jury.

The dog is manipulated more directly by the judge as the judgment is reached which can include—in addition to compensation sought or responsibility shed—the animal's reintroduction or distribution back among the general populace. Relocation, training, or humane euthanasia, as it happens, is often the most direct answer to the communal concern "Are we sure an animal is safe?"[10] Not least, it is also manipulated by the community at large as the concerned focus of community apprehension and fear or, alternatively, of community compassion, fondness, protection, and sympathy.

In one view, an object as conceptually curious as someone's pet dog can be seen as a tangible product which people have manufactured through artificial selection in order to deposit their needs and anxieties, a market good with financial, situational, and emotional inputs, outputs, and overflow valves at each end. The commodification and the weaponization of dogs in general is a historical and legal reality;[11] their finite and perishable nature in general is a biological reality,[12] and their transactional and market value in general is a sturdily constructed practical and legal reality.[13]

Of course they are manipulated objects, simply being even more so in courtrooms. The nation's best animal control field officer has nothing on the nation's worst trial lawyer when it comes to the real art of animal "handling." At its best, a handily employed trap, snare, or noose can only limit an animals' locomotory movement through physical space; even a page-worn thesaurus accompanied by some woeful lamentations about "danger" and a half-baked grasp of anthropomorphism, on the other hand, can completely devastate an animal's movement through legal conceptual space. In turn, a commonplace document such as an order or judgment can harshly circumscribe, and even end entirely, an animal's subsequent movement through social and existential space.

With such control in mind, two caveats arise. The first is to recognize that when it comes to manipulation, dogs are also powerful volitional actors in their own right; the sophomoric fictions of animal rights advocates notwithstanding, it is supremely unwise to think of them as simply passive furred receptacles of natural goodness being acted upon by mean or loving people. There is considerable research literature analyzing the ways in which dogs deceive people in addition to being deceived by people; it is not just that intentions to manipulate human behaviors and intentions to manipulate human mental states have been objectively discerned,[14] it is that their complicity in deception is an evolutionarily derived adaptation in place for hundreds of thousands of years which has served canids well in thriving around and within human communities.[15] Dog "lies" for the most part go unrecognized by those around them; sneakily influencing owners to feed them, house them, protect them, and repair them is an aspect of their phenotypical (behavioral) and genotypical (ancestral) repertoire suspended well below the innocent looking surface features topically exhibited in daily activities of face-licking and tail-wagging.

The second is to recognize that since they are potentially and actually quite dangerous objects, then the conceptual control of dogs has its social and emotional boundaries. One, the particulars of a biting case may require that the dog at issue be demonized, not lionized. A vicious attack on the dog which itself viciously attacked another is sometimes the most effective approach to steering the fact finder to a hard but necessary course of action, of destruction perhaps as opposed to preservation:

> [T]he dog was a most worthless cur, a most mischievous animal, not employed in destroying the wild beasts of the forest, but entering into the fields of his master's neighbors, and destroying their sheep; that he was a wolf in the clothing of a dog; a *caput lupinum*, and instead of being of the value of fifty dollars, as the plaintiff states in his writ, he was really of no value beyond the value of his skin. . . . The evidence did not rest on the act of assembly; was not by way of justification; but on common law, by showing the real value of the dog; and if the owner had placed his affections on him, he had placed them, not on the noble animal, a faithful dog, a friend and companion, as the counsel have, in such vivid colors, represented him to us, but on the vilest cur that ever cut the throat of a sheep, or sucked his blood.[16]

Two, the exaggeration pendulum swings in both directions: in the way that familiarity breeds contempt, overdoing puppy love has a serious antithetical risk. We have all encountered those familiar stories about "a boy and his dog," the "heartwarming tales of heroism and adventure in the snowy pass, the summer fields, or the rafting trip."[17] A dog playing with a child is a cloying scene familiar to many from the antiquity of saccharine children's literature all the way to the modernity of saccharine YouTube videos—and certainly is a handy fiction for the trial lawyer to use to spark emotional leniency and financial generosity.

Judges and juries will usually bend an obligatory knee toward sentiments about how much all of us just love dogs so unreservedly and how they wish all in earshot to know that "I have a dog myself." The folksy affect (comprised of an appeal to traditional and familial sentiment surrounding personal pets but often heavily abbreviated and launched in an overly contrived manner) is an analgesic frequently dispensed by trial lawyers scrambling to forge some sort of connection with a disconnected group.[18] As a palliative, however, it should come with a warning label, one alerting the prescriber of a high risk of overdose in the patient—just as nostalgia for the doddering uncle may congeal into suspicion and contempt, the more the proposition "dogs are so loved" is dolloped out the more it may come to stir that all too human inclination to distrust and to scorn, and thus dissolve the intended import.

A (Mis)Remembrance of Things Past

The manipulation of the dog in a case to accomplish mind control over the jury to achieve the favorable result links us back to the "storytelling" (recall "storymanipulating") function which we noted that the trial lawyer needs to cultivate. Anecdote is hardly sufficient; effectively managed stories must have a devoted aim of earning distinct legal repercussions. Dog ownership carries with it an inevitable amount of risk just like with any other human activity. A past recounting of dog experiences necessarily enfolds personal histories, and inside each history sits a bevy of personal opinions and folk theories about the "real" accountability and responsibility for the risk. We don't necessarily want to eliminate all risk since truly doing so means eliminating the activity itself. We mostly want to minimize risks down to socially acceptable levels in order to strike a balance between engaging in the activity yet not paying too high a price in doing so.[19]

This is not a simple process, and it is fraught with all the perils accompanying our maneuvering around other activities that might put us in jeopardy but still seem necessary, nonetheless, to participate in (such as driving cars and getting in elevators). Risk calculation is a simultaneously intuitive and intuition-bewildering activity that balances costs and benefits. Those assessments unique to owning dogs include squaring compassion with frugality, squaring moral standards against predispositions for self-preservation, and squaring the integrity of individuals with that of the groups to which those individuals belong.[20] Entangling philosophies with the need to assess the complicity or excuses of others, the best "dog ownership" storymanipulating efforts are ones intimately related to ultimate attributions of fault and need, since assigning blame usually lines up pretty well with folk psychology inclinations as to how people should "really" be expected to behave around others (qua dogs) as well as what people should "really" be doing for themselves (qua dogs).

The trial lawyer taps us lightly on our shoulder to remind us that this is all done in service of the client. To manipulate the dog as an object across the margins of a jury trial script is to work to place blame or praise wherever the client's interests demand that blame or praise needs to be placed. That means weaving the responsibility of the peripheral person into an argument, lambasting one who refuses to accept accountability for a dog's behavior, mocking that a dog has a right to defend itself against torment, tolerating offenses and aggressions so as to defuse them, and allowing highly selected anecdotes to implicate that sentiment alone is enough. Repetition of harsh words and soft transitions in pronouns and verb forms can allude to a sense of injustice and anger on anyone's behalf, even the dog's, if doing so alters the narrative to redirect fault lines.

Legal argument in a dog case is thus also behavior modification in action; one side calls the assignment of blame for a dog bite an intellectual realization and the other calls it an intellectual trap, and a broken one at that. Given the complexities of prophecies of dog behavior, it is necessarily both: it is a realization and a trap because it is asking a juror to make a decision about responsibility based on status but without telling them that such decision-making doesn't always require a legitimate causal basis. Responsibility can be attributable on the superficial condition that a dangerous object simply *appears* to pose unacceptable risks, as well as on the deeper condition that an innocent object will transform into a dangerous one not only because a person forecasts that it could but also because objectively empirical analyses make it more rather than less likely that it will do so. The goal is to modify a juror's behavior. The way to achieve that goal is to argue (on the surface) about a dog's behavior and (below the surface) about a person's behavior.

Even obvious categorical distinctions between dogs and people can be overridden with story manipulation: a trial lawyer's argument may well invoke the idea that if the juror really thinks about it, the word "person" is merely a linguistic convention reflecting our assignment of subjective value to a particular biological arrangement in one particular species of animal out of the entire animal kingdom to which all animals belong.[21] Simply coming up with such a word to claim that we are immutably distinct from all other animals doesn't magically obliterate the real-world fact that we are not, says the inventive trial lawyer. The argument can extend from there: were we to try to carve out all the ways in which persons are somehow unique when compared to other animals, says the advocate, the synthetic nature of the construct "person" would be revealed. Creative oppositional term use and subtly manufactured taxonomies can enable dog cases to be turned into people cases with the *dogs* being the stand ins, the stunt doubles, the doppelgängers.

What limits, including ethical ones if any, are there to playing with reading dog minds and evidencing dog personalities to make dogs into litigation targets? Well, ethics ultimately involve socially directed behaviors, so distinctions in species arrangements alone are no help to creating ethical "reasons" to distinguish such arrangements. When one thinks about *behaviors* in which animals engage, particularly as to dogs, one quickly thinks of numerous activities where dogs reveal that their cognition manifests in the form of quasi-readable minds: we employ specialty dog trainers, and licensed animal behaviorists, and professionally educated ethologists to work on peering into their heads; we construct agility and obedience courses and put on dog shows and performance events to appreciate how their brains react in tandem with their bodies; and we use whistles and leashes and harnesses and muzzles and sprays and gestures and sounds and commands and instructions and techniques to exploit mind-body connections. Those activities all work due to our suppositions that dogs, as with a few other species, display intentions and purposes and desires and can make decisions to do things as well as to not do things using processing effects which can easily be compared to how human minds work.[22]

The trial lawyer is perfectly okay with correlating minds with other minds—that's exactly their cup of tea. Dog minds don't work in concert like human minds do, of course. There is no such thing as dog group sociality or dog political communities, so there are no dog group agreements or anything even close to *mores* or mutually constructed ethical rules. Yet the social acceptability of phenomena such as dog behaviorists and dog obedience courses reminds the trial lawyer that it shouldn't be that much of an intellectual stretch to at least ask jurors to accept attaching intentionality to the dog as well as attaching more patent interpretations of behaviors. Doing so subtly alludes to the imposition of legal and ethical consequences to dogs' independent conduct without claiming that such exists. At the same time, the trial lawyer can nevertheless demand that dogs, as objects having minds, be complicit in the parceling out of responsibilities, and that a person's mere status as the owner of a dog doesn't necessarily eclipse a dog's own cognitively independent decisions to bite or not bite a person.

A well-made storyline can thus convince a fact finder that they are being tricked into manufacturing an "ethical reason" that ownership status is subsumed to, or overrides, conduct only because someone is pretending that the distinction between "person" and "animal" is fundamental. They can also be led to see the trick for what it is—an attempt to insert "ethics" into a scenario where ethics doesn't particularly belong. An adeptly manipulated storyline might locate the juncture where it is entirely *unethical* to impose a burden on one animal's status and eliminate it for another animal's behavior and to observe that no ethical reason exists as to how we could objectively divide right from wrong in that way. The lawyer's version of "playing" with dogs in this sense makes the owner's version of "fetch and sit" pale woefully in comparison.

One message resulting from all of this about dogs is that in legal argument "ethics" itself can be and is often manipulated as an object at trial as well. Yes, the "responsibility" which dog owners have been invested with historically has been based on what they do, not who they are. Ethics, nevertheless, encompasses a bewildering panoply of social rules and regulations cultivated from historical circumstances and assignments of *status* as well as activity.[23] Anxious to constrain millennia of evolved human behaviors, but equally anxious to identify millennia of human status categories, we end up embracing a generic ethic to not harm each other and our rules reflect the simultaneously exhilarating and staid task of attaching legal and moral responsibility to our bad conduct. Forcing human responsibility on mere status alone, however, as in the status of simply owning a dog, is, and should be, abhorrent to us as some new sort of ethical command. We certainly don't take the status of "owning a car" and then attach to it legal responsibility for anything and everything that the car then autonomously "does" to others.

Ethical precepts being a function of conduct, and conduct being at the heart of human-dog interactions, then we manage to invest nearly every point of contact with dogs with ethical repercussions. "How could you do that to that poor animal?" rings out sharply across dog parks and living room alike to remind us of our own ethical responsibilities, while "He knows exactly what he did" and "She's just playing dumb" (among a thousand other similar admonishments) are handed down daily to spot and assign ethical breaches among the canine populace for *its* complicity. Again, innovative placement of those ethical concerns into taxonomies can transcend species lines and affect the application of legal rules, and the trial lawyer nudges attention toward or away from the client as becomes necessary.

Doing that means that lawyers must use mind control techniques to excuse behavior (of dogs as well as of people) in order to help a client avoid legal accountability. Proposing that noble or vile motives lay behind a participant's actions can evoke sympathy or antipathy accordingly; vague suggestions that the observed conduct reflects a certain personality type—the innuendo of "I think that we all know someone just like that"—can imply justifications for behavioral repertoires without overtly identifying any particular trait.[24]

Truly, there is nothing stopping the trial lawyer from speculating about the genesis or the larger meaning for *any* person's behavior even in the complete absence of any obvious physical action that would buttress the existence of the proposed cause; generalization is a very human weakness that can be pitilessly capitalized upon. Depending on the moment's need, the trial lawyer can float the notion either that we are all similar "under the skin" or are all dissimilar in that everyone has a unique personality, that is, that universals are either obvious or illusory.[25]

Finally, the artistic crafting of implication-rich labels and categories of "archetypes" of people such as the "vulnerable child," "protective mother," "target of the assault," or "perpetrator of the offense" have their emotive uses, monikers employed with quasi-legal terminology and which folk law and folk psychology tacitly approve of, ones which seem on their face to be objective but which at heart mostly just excite base passions.[26]

All these are available tactics a trial lawyer should be employing to manipulate the object of attention in the trial, packeted in dog form or packeted in ethical command form. In the end, the excusing, implying, and labeling is all tied to word play but the words need more than simply their utterance alone—they can't just sit out there intellectually unconnected to their direct objects. Fixing the sentiment to the topic of discussion, such as the specific dog or owner or victim or official governmental unit, is a process carefully rigged through the introduction of exhibits, the examination of witnesses, and the offering of jury instructions, formalized processes which we have seen must be carefully regulated in order to navigate past the hazard of all those wonderful excuses, implications, and labels simply getting dumped from purview at decision time. Notably, we come to find that it isn't just suppressed and unsuppressed evidence which might lead to an unfavorable judgment, it is suppressed and unsuppressed emotive constructs which can create disaster as well.

Mind Reading the Room

It cannot be overemphasized that Argument is managed narrative which is heavily invested with perceptions: perceptions about the speaker (as noted earlier about their own physical appearance and vocal presentations) and perceptions about the unique topic or subject about which the speaker happens to be talking.[27] An audience's perceptions are dependent on the fusion of speaker themselves and speaker's content, including the structure of what is being stated, the import of what is being left unstated, and just how the speaker frames each.

Effective speakers engage in relentless mind control with their audiences, and when their topic involves other people, many speakers invite their audiences to do likewise—to expand their own perceptions by also entering someone else's mind to see what they "really mean" or what they are "really saying," that is, they offer the chance to play along in the game of mind reading. "Let's peek inside the witness's head and uncover what they really mean" is an enticement which the trial lawyer frequently offers to jurors, though not to help them but to control them even further.

Mind reading, of course, is a dangerous activity in part because it is so infectious and immunity is hard to come by. Inviting someone to hypothesize another's true intent entices them to, by instinct and extension, contemplate the requester's intentions in doing so. The invitee has no reason not to also suspect, locate, and draw to the surface the unspoken aims of the speaker as well. While the trial lawyer wants the target of such uncanny perception to only be the witness talking on the stand, an astute juror can accept the invitation to mind read and then overdo it by applying the scheme to everyone in the room who is speaking—including the trial lawyer talking at the box or counsel table. It is worrisome that like mind reading, the casting of distrust is also contagious.

Moreover, because human minds are unfathomable then there is no discernable backstop definitively bringing extraction of the unspoken words to a halt; how many more disguised intentions might exist and what else can be inferred from what has been said is practically limitless. A trial lawyer's rephrasing of a witness' statements which invites interpretations that are too broad is an activity which risks a listener's reception being antagonistic. If the mind is a finite and language-barren one, such as with a dog's mind, there is far less to risk; no words exist to presuppose at all, much less unspoken words to bring to any surface. Everything available to interpret is really a function of conduct alone (including vocalizations).

With dogs it isn't that one needs to "glean clues from nonverbal signals" since nonverbal signals are *all there is to work with in the first place.* Is a dog's averted downward gaze or intensely fixed stare a warning sign? Confirmation can't come from speech, even from an ethologist's proclaimed firm expert opinion, only from more conduct following or preceding the stare. Is a wildly wagging tail or a quivering lifted paw an invitation? Again, there is no way to match the prediction with the mind since the mind is unable to admit or deny the invitation by explaining itself. Decrees of expert authority on animal behavior notwithstanding, at the end of the day dog minds have to be cobbled together from dog actions and dog sounds, full stop.

Where the mind is a human one and thus language-enriched, confirmation is available and no additional conduct required, but a new concern does appear. Can the verbal confirmation of a piece of conduct's meaning be trusted simply because the person *says* it can be? Reliance on words as being supportive of intent is a notoriously hard case philosophically. Human minds are opaque, deceptive expressions are easy to come by, and inquirers become understandably anxious over the sincerity of expressed intent as well as the likelihood of hidden intent. We recognize trust issues aplenty over the unspoken, over the limitations of realistic expectations about another's authenticity, and the game of matching conduct signals and matching words of assurance is a game which everyone, Tinder dates and international diplomats alike, all nervously play.

In that light, we often are compelled to concede outside limits to word-hearing projects being reliable mind-reading projects, that is, requisitely accept that human minds may be partly controlled but cannot truly be *fully* read. In comparison, we note that dog minds are very poor analogues to human minds and if behaviors are all we get to work with, then there is some comfort in the knowledge that as the behaviors can be controlled so too the minds might be as well.

With the dog as an object at trial, anyone can be an authority on their "real" intent—the dog cannot refute. Spoken assurances by experts and owners can be pronounced. Behavioral control can be described, promised, and demanded. With plausible proposals, avenues of interpretation can thereby open so that even the absence of any conduct at all (by the dog which sits stock still) or complete silence (by the owner who keeps their mouth fully shut) can be exploited to reinforce an accountability theme or to dismantle it. Sometimes both a noteworthy silence and an acceptable interpretation of that silence is what the trial lawyer seeks to control, and the fact that it is an animal's silence may be just another strength, not a weakness. The forensic psychologist presupposes that assessing nonverbal conduct, body language, and expression of jurors has its importance and restrictions in jury selection, but the trial lawyer recognizes its effects at every moment of the trial, beginning to end, when those attributes are paralleled or modeled through the animal's mind as an object of discussion in front of the jury.[28]

We also recognize that there is a well-worn lexicon attached to discussions about dogs, and it revolves in part around references to canine-specific (and breed-specific) behavioral suites and in part around references to canine-generic (and breed-generic) physical accoutrements.[29] It is a lexicon, moreover, which is wonderfully handy for the trial lawyer to use and adjust to fit whatever rhetorical need that particular moment requires.

It is a familiar language—most jurors own dogs and no one truly needs to have dog-owner-adjacent terms explained to them. Its brightest promise for the advocate involves its colorful terminology. Hopefully steering clear of the outright pun and the tired cliché, abundant jargon is available to the speaker about the paraphernalia of fur coats, paws, snouts, tails, and the associated activities of wagging, barking, biting, heeling, sniffing, and so on. It is also highly extensible language—abundant thematic referents are available to link case issues to animalistic imagery implicit within legal institutions, such as the batons and handcuffs of the policing authority, the confinement, bars, and locks of courtrooms and prisons, and the punishment and exoneration features of the judiciary.

Mostly, it is a dramatic language—notable alignments between people and dogs work dramatically in both directions. Anthropomorphisms abound to refer to dogs in person terms, and references from literature and popular culture make themselves available at every turn to transform verbally a person in their juridical form as plaintiff, defendant, or witness into an illustrative form as a beast, companion, or guardian, or as some manner of begging, aggressive, or obedient entity.[30]

The opportunity is frequently seized because comparisons between the practical and the illustrative are necessary components of a particular mode of persuasion in oratory, the call for the listener to use mental imagery. Human brains enlist internally constructed images all the time to explore parallels, retrieve memories, and solve perceptually confusing problems, among other tasks.[31] Resemblances between people and dogs are ripe with promise in all those respects. Subsurface concerns about insecurity and disorder can be heightened through using suggestive language regarding dogs by offering images of them as functional stand-ins for other worrisome dangers or risks. Biting and being bitten may seem on their face to be relatively position-neutral events determinable objectively through description and detached from personal opinion, but that is only if the trial lawyer wants them to be.

A person being hurt by an animal is a ripe area for feelings cloaked as facts, and is an event intimately connected under the surface to the implication that animal traits and human behaviors must be significantly linked. Dogs are gateways to emotion: *animus* in that sense can be exploited as some of the most predatory and powerful of metaphorical invitations a trial lawyer can hand to a juror:

> Awareness of the snarling police dog, of the sniffer, not only helps unearth the importance of repression and fear in fabricating order, but starkly reveals the predatory animus of liberal order. If ferocious dogs have long been symbolic of legal rituals, then images of pearly white, beastly fangs have been central to this imaginary . . . [In] both human and non-human animals the teeth are the most striking natural instrument of power and the very first manifestation of order. Teeth influenced the development of stone weapons, and later the sword, and even the structure of military formations . . . [A] common way of describing the force of law is often to equate the law with "teeth" or a "bite"—"the law has teeth"—or similarly how "the law doesn't have a bite", due to having "no teeth". The figurative powers of teeth, then, point towards the ways terror, law and animal monstrosity undergird the sovereign principle of order. As a "threat to the world outside", the violence of teeth . . . becomes most visible whenever the mouth opens. The teeth of power are at once a power to order through the act of devouring whatever or

> whoever exists external to the conventions of social order. The struggle between beast and sovereign is often the struggle over who will devour the other. This is to say that the sovereign fear of being devoured by beasts calls forth the sovereign's own appetite, its own cravings for devouring the beast which threatens to upend "good order".[32]

Not all attributions are appropriate of course but the trial lawyer knows that as well—and uses that misstep as a persuasive device if necessary. Calling out the other side for its seemingly *improper* diversions is a classic manipulative tool. The trial lawyer questions, for instance, why so much attention is being paid to what is going on in a person's mind—about their distress or suffering for instance—yet the poor animal's mind is disdained (or vice versa). In short, impressions of mental and motivational bases of a dog's behavior can be played in either direction—as the most inappropriate of reckless speculations or as the most callous of misjudgments. Both directions influence, both directions attribute value to human and animal comparisons and exchanges, both directions lay claim to the authority of assigning psychological factors as crucial, and both directions place a leash on the listener and walk them toward distrust or commitment as the case may be.

None of this, by the way, is so that the juror actually learns something about animal cognition, quite the opposite. The empirical question of whether animals have minds is not just one reserved for ethologists and cognitive scientists but spans the disciplines and tends to bewilder each new inquirer, true. Yet *trial is not school*: when the trial lawyer asks the question, they do so with an agenda notably distinct from that of the teacher, zoo visitor, or field biologist. They do not wish the query to lead to anything analytic but instead desire far more that the question is asked than that it is ever answered. They want *more* questions to rise in the listener's mind, not less, and to the extent that a conclusion is reached, they want to direct the listener to a *non*-empirical conclusion.

That means that the specific way questions about animal minds are phrased is paramount, carefully constructed so that the listener is prompted to take a personal interest, to become involved at an intensely personal, not analytic, level. The scientist asks, "Have individuals of a certain species evolved cognition?" whereas the trial lawyer asks, "Don't you think that dog X must have its own thoughts and feelings about Y?" No answer necessary, just some mental imagery and fanciful meditation. For the trial lawyer, there is real mileage to get out of the targeted listener, that is, each individual juror on the panel, engaging entirely subjectively. The truths, distortions, or exaggerations which result will be theirs alone, and they won't be irked to have accepted the invitation to fantasize since they get it that it is not a topic where anything is verifiable—in pondering about what goes on inside of a dog's head, getting a visceral or emotive jolt out of the activity isn't just *enough*, it is the very *point* of the entire exercise.

All this potency is also a matter of balance. Kept in the back of the trial lawyer's own mind at all times is the largest goal of obtaining the benefit which the client has posited, and that goal can be badly disserved by an actual science lesson in the same way that it can be well served by the hesitation and measured reserve which science often brings to the art of inquiry. Professional obligations entrenched in the very heart of attorney-client relationships demand that tribute be paid not to non-clients actually learning anything educational at all, but only to the client's particular interest being satisfied and being satisfied effectively and without undue distraction or delay.

The Canon of Canines as Persuasion Devices

This leads us to deliberate on what dog-related criteria in particular might be uniquely exploitable about presenting dogs on the courtroom stage in their role as litigation objects controlled in order to garner decisions by people about people. There is a lot of costuming and props to choose from, certainly. In terms of what fascinates us as potential prey items—the paraphernalia which predators employ to predate—across their bodies, dogs have all the right tools in the morphological toolbox to be of high interest to us, traits in the form of strength, speed, ferocity, endurance, intelligence, and vocalization. At the business end of every individual dog we also are quick to note that they also possess those effective resource-acquisition items in the anatomical toolbox of superior stereoscopic vision, keen olfactory capabilities, strong sites for large jaw muscle attachments, and good carnassial dentition with substantial crushing teeth.[33]

All of these features and factors are ones required evolutionarily to be a successful wolf, and all are ones that, prehistorically, human communities intimate with wolves could not ignore without risking injury or death. We are adapted by natural selection forces to have both feared and needed those tools in our own evolutionary trajectory, and that means we have little trouble switching viewpoints back and forth between feeling like their prey to feeling like their masters. Add to that mix that dogs also have a recognizable variety of facial expressions, while both they and we are also evolutionarily adapted to derive meaning from faces, and the coalition of mutual curiosity makes interpretation nearly mandatory in every encounter.[34] In sum, dog bodies and dog actions offer up an advantageous part of the menu to trial lawyers from which to select relatable or unrelatable features so that they in turn may expand their menu of styles to offer up to the jury to consume.

Since the dog is used as a distraction to get to the juror's embracement of the client, such interpretations portend the opportunity for dog-person incidents to initiate human behavioral changes—not just to treat a dog differently or to change a routine in places where dogs are normally handled (in homes and yards and public spaces outside of a courtroom), but also to alter how one "handles" a dog thematically in more removed environments (such as courtrooms), including as part of the analysis of what might transform future interactions. Stigmatizing dogs is often a reflection of a person's general fear of the overall environment one happens to live in or find themselves in at the moment, so resolving dog-related legal issues is a channel by which to exert power to transform such environments. The trial lawyer seizes on the potential for those environmental transformations to apply not just to the participants but to the supposedly removed observers, the jury.

For instance, the trial lawyer can take a page out of Melville's book and layer a basic story about a dog on top of a leveled-up story about a person (the client or litigant) telling their story about the dog, and then once more on top of a capping story about the lawyer telling that person's story for them as their representative. Doing so sets out a route inviting a juror to fold into their deliberation the twinned components of implied authority and change in their own lives stemming from express authority and the wish to change which seems necessary in the lives of the litigants and their stories. An open call for a small group to rouse a shift in the public dynamic—even in the context of a seemingly trivial dispute involving what to do about someone's dog—is a powerful influential device to galvanize action. It is a phenomenon occurring no differently in the courtroom than it does on stage, in battle, or in the civic election process.

We all strive to locate useful explanations for how the larger world works and then to impact that world using those explanations. Dovetailing animals' experiences—especially of a species as familiar and connected to us as domestic canines—with our own experiences in order to forge such explanations matches well with what people already earnestly desire. Whether or not the world has any reason objectively embedded in it, people will look to uncover what that reason might be subjectively to them. The apparatus may well be fragmented and of course no one has the wherewithal, time, and energy to identify every last moving part, but a jury trial seems uniquely positioned to compose a model of the larger world by which reason can be squeezed out of a storyline and contained in the four corners of a verdict form. Artificially arranging and positioning two citizens to make them play out their contest to a weirdly selected contingent of other citizens comprises a microcosm of all manner of fights that we often wish we could not just observe, but stick our noses into, control, and then decide the outcome on. Jury trials hand us that option and place the true power to be wielded in fashioning the outcome in the hands of substitutes, a self-selected delegation of professional manipulators.

Again, it is crucial to remember that trial lawyers specifically have not been involuntarily thrust into the fray—they have intentionally waded into it and get their own personal advantage out of doing so. It is crucial to remember that the trial lawyers are not just handed tools enabling them to control desired outcomes but are also handed tools enabling them to restrict and curtail undesired ones. If the outcome is short and disjointed, or lengthy and predictable, it doesn't matter, what matters is that it is achieved. The tool use is part of the lofty profession of lawyering but it is also part of the nitty gritty of representing and it is done for pay.

The tools purchased and utilized may be unpleasant ones. They may be as minor as false ire, the "urgh" of sideways jaw and lifted lip. They may include slight annoyances, false sympathy, the "tsk tsk" of a clucking tongue and tilted head. Lawyers, in pursuit of their goal, may on a small scale pander to frustration even while it is their language use that initially created the frustration.

On the larger end, however, lawyers, in pursuit of their goal, may take the climatic and absolutely devastate it by transforming it into the anticlimactic, that is they may stop their own case and trial if doing so is what best serves the client's core interests—

regardless of the dramatic disaster which any play director would try to avoid at all costs of ringing the curtain down on the actors prematurely before the big denouement. To that end, little is more frustrating to a juror than learning that there is no outcome to a trial at all but, too bad, the trial lawyer's aims simply may have shifted away from "pleasing the jury" to "creating a mistrial" or something similar.

Judges will frequently take pains to go back to jury rooms to explain to jurors why a case was dismissed or a claim abandoned mid-stream, making their services not further required. The recent hot button term "closure" is colloquially synonymous with "explanation" and in some form has always been favored by human nature; the juror yearns for explanation, aches to *assemble*, not disassemble, a storyline even while the trial lawyer may insist on doing only the latter. Still, the trial lawyer may use false signals of support to invest one avenue toward an answer with the strength of reason and promise and divest the opponent's avenue with the fragility of criticism and obscurity. The requirement that explanation be had or a decision be made demands that one storyline must yield to the other, but satisfying the client's interest may not require an explanation or decision at all. "Closure" is at the trial lawyer's sole discretion to distribute or withhold.

That tool use also informs us that the demarcation between an objective analysis and a subjective one is notoriously fuzzy. Consider the dog bite case where the competing pretenses are these: for plaintiff, that objective analysis of what the dog did rules the day, and for defendant, that subjective feelings about the dog should take precedence. Both parties know that dog bites cannot be studied experimentally (especially given that exposing a volunteer to a bite or provoking a dog to bite would be unethical).[35] Since collecting data through controlled real-time observations isn't feasible, both understand that data has to be gathered indirectly through surveys, anecdote, veterinary cases, emergency room admissions, and interviews with bite victims.[36] Both also get it that those sources are beset by statistical and analytic problems of convenience sampling, self-selection bias, and small sample sizes.[37]

Moreover, it must be accepted, assessments are notoriously ineffable: it seems an open question as to whether it constitutes a "bite" (a) whenever a dog holds a person's body part in their mouth and applies pressure, (b) as long as a dog's tooth at least abrades, although perhaps not punctures, the skin, or (c) even where an article of clothing has been pierced in spite of the absence of bodily contact.[38] Both combatants would like to have the jury consider if anyone can accurately "measure" phenomena such as expressions indicative of pain, bite duration, distinctions between predation and appeasement gestures, or locomotory-related or posture-related behavioral effects. Neither want the jury to know the answer.

The defense notes that human behavior preceding bites has its own causal significance, such as macro-movements made very near a dog or subtle forms of well-intentioned tactile contact with a dog, such as excessive petting or hugging. The plaintiff knows that punctures can be counted, larger numbers are more impressive, and thus the more holes the better. Add to that confounding factor the wide range of human non-linguistic vocalizations we engage in specific to dogs—from tongue clicking to hissing or whistling—behaviors which are easy to describe as to the effect they are meant to elicit, but as to which it is nearly impossible to ascertain what final message is actually being received by the animal, and subjectivity on both sides seems unavoidable.

The plaintiff has to work with the reality that association between bite severity and the plethora of human and dog characteristics identified above suggests that modeling can be done but that the elements of the model are going to be unavoidably fluid.[39] Factors ranging from age to size can be inserted or removed with justification and a hierarchal model can result from employing parameters that are all context dependent. In sum, objective assessments are uncertain assessments even when couched in the language of empiricism—and defense lawyers in particular latch onto uncertainty like lampreys. The plaintiff wants a good part of the trial to sound like the machinations of animal science grinding its way to an objective conclusion but not *too* much like animal science where the victim is also just another affected animal. The plaintiff wants the jurors to themselves play animal scientists but only up to a point and no further, since at a certain level there is a risk of alienation by the dog lovers in the group (which there almost certainly are as defense counsel well knows since he or she made sure to place them there). The plaintiff wants to compel reason in the same way that the defendant wants to compel passion and neither wants the thing to turn into a research project about teeth or a love letter about pets.

For each trial lawyer, it is a boon, not a burden that there is a lot of misinformation abounding not just in the courtroom, but in the culture too about human-canine interactions, about the real significance of breed and breed characteristics, and about the actual frequency of dog bite-related injuries. Nothing in either trial lawyer's job description includes being a statistician or dutifully correcting the inaccurate beliefs of others. Indeed, an emotion-laden topic such as the human-animal bond is ripe for doing just the opposite—massaging empirically weak and uneducated views on how small dogs behave around children, say, into strengthened personal convictions which track with the client's need to have the viewpoint's holder align with their interests in a small dog/small child-related dispute.

There is a wealth of misinformation on animals to use in that regard: what can be played with includes clear-cut factual errors, misinterpretations, omissions, emotionally loaded language, and exaggerations based on misunderstood or inaccurate statistics or based on reliance on the interpretation by third parties of other authors' meanings about domestic animals.

Effective tool use by the trial lawyer includes seeking out topics and objects that stimulate others. People are evolutionarily adapted to pay attention to novel "supernormal" stimuli, especially when it comes to animals; daily, the hyperbole we engage in about animals exerts a massive pull on the inclinations people have to overreact about what is already feared or admired.[40] These usable errors cluster around, and can be expressed by, impassioned rhetorical devices including plain old generalizations, positive and negative. By drawing out hazy issues as if they comprised social problems demanding a legal solution (says plaintiff) or legal problems demanding a social solution (says defendant), each trial lawyer as advocate in the dispute studies and embraces each distortion or error that arises as a new invitation for which a new rhetorical device might support attaining each client's litigation-related goal.

Overreaching the Verdict

Whether it is desirable or not, at least it is certainly possible to traverse the path from complaint to verdict by pure demagoguery no differently than with other social or political institutions.[41] A trial lawyer's positions throughout an entire case start to finish can be semantically outrageous, no doubt—most defense lawyers in most wrongful death cases, for instance, will confirm that plaintiff's counsel in such cases veer toward hyperbole at every reasonable opportunity. Nothing truly stops advocates from using rhetoric in intellectually reckless ways; even the most recalcitrant can still baldly misdefine and devalue rights, responsibilities, persons, and victims, and all who argue motions have had the experience of hearing an opponent stretch and twist meaning away from the proposition at hand, sometimes within the space of a single testimonial exchange or sentence.[42]

Jurors are pulled along that path, sometimes willingly and sometimes with silent yet seething frustration, as we have seen. The fact that the end decision is theirs doesn't ease the knowledge that they have no control over getting to that end—sit and listen, sit and listen, sit and listen some more, is their assigned duty, like it or not. By the time that the announcements of the jury instructions finally roll around, it is almost inevitable that some resentment may have built up along those lines, but there is also a growing awareness that a shift in control has now arrived with it. Jurors are commanded by the court in the instructions that they have no power to simply choose whom to blame without identifying the existence of some evidence somewhere enabling them to do so, and they are equally commanded to heed the fact that no authority has been conferred on them, directly or indirectly, to choose a champion in the absence of evidentiary support. They are always informed, but may not always privately appreciate, that they are limited by the instructed law. They are always discouraged by, but may not always privately comply with, admonitions to not rule from their hearts but to instead rule from their heads.

Once the informational dynamic has shifted post-instruction, where does the trial lawyer sit in this altered situation? The likelihood of a jury's growing awareness of a clandestine ability to just ignore judicial command is not lost on the trial lawyer—they aren't new to the trick of recognizing dissension in others and exploiting it. Among the six or twelve in the box, small signals may arise—the light of some growing comprehension leaking and filtering amidst the cracks of all those stoic faces—right before or during closing. It is an illumination which suggests that the jury instruction phase was or just might about to be an enormous waste of time. Trial lawyers are on the lookout for those flashes of rebellion, those subtle disclosures of a personal decision having already been made and the solemnity of the court's instruction about to be damned.

Of course, the cynical folk beliefs of long-married spouses notwithstanding, there really is no objectively solid way to know if a person's mind has truly been switched or made up simply by looking at their face alone. But fantastic bets have been made, won, and lost on even less than a stranger's grimace—and trial lawyers are nothing if not fantastic bettors. Given that the trial lawyer has no legal obligation to parrot or wholeheartedly support every jury instruction specifically (much less every pre- or post-instruction judicial admonition, encouragement, or discouragement in general), the trial lawyer finds in themselves some new power to be the gadfly and not the Boy Scout, to egg on or inflame potential dissent as opposed to discouraging it.

Much of the tension at the end of the trial between the bench and the bar stems from an undercurrent of who will win the tug of war for the jury's attention to, or rejection of, their somber civic duty. The craftiest trial lawyer can even play both parts of the script at the same time by insisting that the jury solemnly attend to duty while simultaneously inciting a very clear rebellion from being bound by it if contrary to their own consciences. Daniel Webster famously exhibited a talent for working the end of a speech away from its start within the shift of a single sentence:

> Gentlemen, your whole concern should be to do your duty, and leave consequences to take care of themselves. You will receive the law from the Court. Your verdict, it is true, may endanger the prisoner's life; but then, it is to save other lives. If the prisoner's guilt has been shown and proved beyond all reasonable doubt, you will convict him. You are the judges of the whole case. You owe a duty to the public as well as to the prisoner at the bar. You cannot presume to be wiser than the law... With consciences satisfied with the discharge of duty, no consequences can harm you. There is no evil that we cannot either face or fly from, but the consciousness of duty disregarded.[43]

One major element affecting that tug of war of allegiance is the specific topic of the case at bar. A drunk driving case, for instance, necessarily invokes quite sensitive topics of shame, intoxication, sobriety, and of the cloaking or shucking of social responsibilities by people in public and private life regarding the misuse of alcohol.[44] Some jurors may have such intense feelings about those fundamental aspects of human behavior such as drinking, that even though they deny in *voir dire* that having them would eliminate them from the panel sufficient to get them into the box, the tempering of alcohol use is such a massively pervasive aspect of theirs and of communal life that certain aspects of those feelings are quite likely to have bubbled up by the time that the first witness has taken the stand. When the witness feels it, they at least get the chance to blurt out something in response to a question in examination, even if inappropriate, but the juror fields no such opportunity. Court cases, as we well know from public and popular expression in the media, can spark lots of outrage and personal opinions; the more volatile the topic, the more flagrant the urge to express oneself may be displayed.[45] Jurors feel, but have no direct verbal outlet for expressing their feelings for, that pinch.

And topics involving animals, and particularly those centering around dogs specifically, tend to engender just those concentrated types of sentiments doubled. Akin to as with alcohol use, when asked in *voir dire* about if strong emotions about dogs would make it too hard for them to be fair and impartial decisionmakers, nearly every potential juror in an animal case nods assuredly that they can hold emotion in check and rule unimpaired. They are dead wrong. They know it and the participants know it too, but there is frequently a shared ruse that everyone is going to ignore the deception in part because exposing it would decimate the entire pool's ability to participate.

Every one of us have far too many messy cultural, economic, and personal entanglements with animals to completely divorce ourselves emotionally in an animal case—even the most urbanized, pigeon-hating, rat-averse, cockroach-repulsed, and meat-eating non-pet-owner has sensitivity issues about the furred and fluffy. None can compartmentalize so well that their decision-making acts are somehow entirely unaffected by their private experiences. Both sociologist and evolutionary biologist will listen to all those remonstrations and commiserate that it is an impossible thing to do with animals, to stay intellectually distant from them.[46]

Mighty Power Arrangers

So, we can now connect some dots between bias and animals, and we can see where argument fits into the image that gets constructed by drawing lines between those dots. We will come back to animals specifically in a little bit but at this point we can readily note that just as every trial lawyer in *voir dire* will publicly announce that they also wholeheartedly wish those ultimately selected to be fair and impartial, we can start to appreciate that every one of them privately would accede to the admission that they want no such thing whatsoever. Partiality wins cases. Constructing partiality is a key component of the trial lawyer's job. Since it is harder to construct partiality from those who are truly impartial to begin with, then the *voir dire* exchange is a mutual fraud. Not only does the potential juror misspeak when they claim impartiality, the trial lawyer misspeaks when they applaud it. Not only does the potential juror mislead when they declare an emotional divorce from deciding a case about animal abuse or neglect or ownership or death, the trial lawyer nods sagely but patiently waits for any opportunity in argument to trigger every emotion that is possible to be triggered when the time is ripe to do so. People misleading people is a staple of most trials on both sides of the bar.

In an animal case such as our Smith v. Jones example, human-dog relationships are in turn crucial components of extending the mutual fraud occurring at *voir dire*; decisions made along the path are maelstroms of emotional overlay. Those decisions are not just the final decision where the magic words or the sums awarded are placed on the blanks in the verdict form itself. They include decisions that are silent and agonized over as to whether to believe a percipient witness, whether to trust the opposing lawyer's words, or whether to listen or adhere to the details of a judge's picky instruction on determining liability. In the similar manner to how dogs are able to interpret and misinterpret human emotional states and regulate their behavior accordingly, so too people are more than adept at the same as the trial unfolds and the jury's true role comes into sharper and sharper focus.

The anxiety or frustration a juror can experience can be hidden since like any person they can (and quickly learn to) modulate their expression while in the courtroom. It is a hard reality in the world of the trial lawyer that they must sniff out the best they can those emotional overlays and work diligently to irritate or, alternatively, at times to restore the emotional homeostasis, really in whichever manner the objective of a favorable verdict gets aligned. The work at hand entails locating and fostering a web of connections between what people feel and what the law allows them to do with those feelings in a legal setting. And it is dangerous work, fraught with the vocational peril of pure unlucky fortuity. No juror is obligated to justify a swing from affection to disaffection—it can happen with the flimsiest of instigating forces (or none at all) and can happen slowly over the course of a long court day or in a cognitive instant. As the poet Edward Sill observed, when minds change, irrationality can just as easily be the genesis of the new attitude as can rationality:

> At noon he wakened from his trance
> Mended; was well! They looked askance;
> Took his hand coldly; loved him not,
> Though they had wept him; quite forgot
> His virtues; lent an easy ear
> To slanderous tongues; professed a fear
> He was not what he seemed to be;
> Thanked God they were not such as he;
> Gave to his hunger stones for bread,
> And made him, living, wish him dead.[47]

The Trial as Marriage Ceremony

Manipulating the active dynamic is part and parcel of the trial lawyer's larger creative use of classification schemes, and we are reminded about what different roles each participant plays, not just in pleadings, discovery, and pre-trial motion practice throughout the case, but in the courtroom all during trial processes as well. Folded into all legal classification schemes is a reminder that everyone in the case and in the courtroom is tasked with a different job, the majority of which do not overlap.

In every civil or criminal case in which a jury is used, there is a sharp division of labor. The judge is the only authority on the law, that is, on what rules apply to the dispute. The jury is the only authority on the facts, that is, on deciding what actually and finally happened in the dispute between the parties.[48] A conceptual "marriage" of sorts then must occur at the close of the case in which the judge must inform the jury what law applies to the facts which were found in order to have a decision occur. Since this is a very odd sort of marriage ceremony in which (a) people are not getting married, concepts are; and (b) there is not one, but instead are four officiants conducting the marriage proceedings, then the jury instructions are the vows which the first two officiants (the trial lawyers) subtly force the third officiant (the court) to direct the fourth officiant (the jury) how to actually move along the ceremony and unite the concepts in holy matrimony.

The first three officiants (lawyers and judge) compete, not cooperate, and have some discretion but not very much since they are all tussling over and hampered by what the particular law of the jurisdiction actually states must be applied, regardless of what any might wish the law to be. The fourth officiant (the jury) competes and cooperates internally and has a bit more discretion but is nevertheless constrained as well by having to exercise their discretion only within the confines of what the first set of officiants told them they must stay within. In short, they must pay attention to, and lawfully abide by, what they are being told. Juries tend to have far more respect for what a judge is telling them to do than what a trial lawyer is telling them to do, but still it is important to recognize that by the time they finally get to the jury instruction part of the ceremony at the end of what can be a lengthy and irritating trial process, they have been told numerous times by both judge and trial lawyers about any number of things they "have to do" or "should do" or should "really not do" and, being mere people, can get not just a little testy and rebellious as to being commanded so much for so long about the "ultimately, who really cares" problems of complete strangers.

Jurors certainly will grasp at the very inception of the trial that there is some sort of ceremony of which they appear to be an integral piece. Like all ceremonies, there is a public part and a private part, there are pronouncements made, there is a lot of sitting and standing and sitting again as well as a somewhat familiar and traditional order of presentation of events, with some of the participants in front of everyone else and in formal attire and much of it couched in the language of formality using honorifics and polite attributions of respect. It is serious. It is annoying. It is moving. It is necessary. It is longer than it should be. Many wish they were elsewhere. Until you squint at it from just the right angle, you may not realize just how much a trial can feel an awful lot like your second cousin's wedding.

And, wedding-like, there is so much talking. The stages which the jurors identify when the trial lawyers are the ones talking appear the most prominent, the most endless, and the most overlapping: the persistence of *voir dire* inquiry seems to slide into plaintiff's and defendant's openings which themselves have barely finished when the interminable ping pong match of examination ensues, and which in turn is so closely followed by closings that there may be some confusion about just exactly whose words had been whose. Jurors note that conceptually the entire event is buttressed by lawyers preening and presenting, their speechifying as the bookends and their questioning as the main event. It all clearly has something to do with the most honored guest at the affair, "evidence," which everyone is offering, rebutting, or commenting on, and there is no question that all sorts of interruptions are inserted in between every stage that seem frightfully important as well as that it is hard to discern a real resolution to any one of them.[49]

All this talking takes its toll, especially on weary attention spans. Like many wedding officiants (and guests) who have come before them, jurors have to make some hard selections as to what to really pay attention to and what to let slide. Taking an actual nap is not really an option but taking a "mental health break" by glossing over the eyes and thoughtfully reflecting on the other guests and surrounding architecture during lulls might suffice. Distractions lurk all around trials as they do weddings. Additionally, *when* things occur is of import: any psychologist will tell you that attitudes and perceptions can be heavily affected by the order of events, ceremonial or otherwise, wedding or trial, including "recency effects" and "primacy effects" where a stronger influence may be exerted at the beginning or the end of the ritual, and jurors are no more immune from such effects than are fathers of the bride.[50]

Jurors will also recognize that for all their talking the trial lawyers are not the *primary* officiants of this strange ceremony but are at least given some leeway to try to influence the two others more in command, themselves and the judge. Jurors learn that trial lawyers are allowed to try to do so as to the former via making opening statements and closing arguments, but do not get expressly told that trial lawyers are also allowed to try to do so as to the latter in a different fashion via proposing and arguing for which jury instructions that officiant is going to utilize as final vows.

It is an old adage that "juries decide the facts and judges decide the law," but the adage gets it wrong in both directions: juries only get to decide the facts from the menu of facts which the trial lawyers have first selected to place in front of them. Judges only get to decide the law from a menu of laws which the trial lawyers have arranged via the initial pleadings, honed via the motions process, and which have then been proposed and demanded to be applied from a far larger buffet of laws that have been taken out of consideration by other motions, by the selective presentation of evidence, and by how witnesses have been examined and cross-examined.

For example, the trial lawyer who alleges three alternative claims for relief in their initial complaint controls what law will ultimately be used at the very end; the trial lawyer who then jettisons one of those three claims by a pre-trial stipulation or by winning a pre-trial motion again redirects and controls the law to be used at the end; the trial lawyer who then declines to elicit an element about one of the remaining claims in direct examination, or who perhaps elicits a concession on the element in cross-examination, again redirects and controls the law to be used at the end; and the trial lawyer who then offers or objects to the use of a particular jury instruction regarding the remaining claim redirects and controls the law used at the end even once again.

In short, trial lawyers have far more influence in the marriage of facts to law than the other two officiants might comfortably acknowledge, including by deciding at the outset and even during the ceremony who the groom and bride are even going to be, where the loving couple is going to stand, and how much and how little of the vows each other officiant can even have tucked in their vest pocket as well as actually administer at hand to the soon to be wedded couple. The lawyers' power to begin, interrupt, reform, and conclude the ceremony stems from the power of discourse granted them by the power conferred in their profession and experience as social influencers, a power and experience which walk hand in hand down an aisle festooned on all sides with bouquets of procedural and evidentiary codes hemming in the walkway to the podium.

All weddings have speeches, of course, and as we have seen, this wedding is no different. As the best man and maid of honor will tell you later at the reception, speech as discourse in turn comes out of not just personal experience but out of *all* experience. As we make our pronouncements to others sometimes we verbalize our most impressionable experiences in real time, as with the outburst or excited utterance, a phenomenon so well recognized that the evidence code accepts it as having special credibility.[51] Sometimes we set out semi-objective retrospective accounts of our more mundane experiences, as with the follow up narrative or the monthly report. Sometimes we explore our more wistful experiences with an internally weighted subjective recounting of their self-selected details, as in personal diaries and historical memoirs. It is hard to tell just where the line becomes blurred between those utterances, retellings, and flights of pure fiction because imaginative explanations can come out of any one of those routes but can also be concocted whole cloth and disconnected utterly from actual history.

People certainly can and do verbalize fantasy experiences as if they were utterances or reports, even though their basis has no connection to any event that ever transpired in the world, or to any conceivable timeline, or even to the passage of time at all.[52] Storytelling can incorporate aspects of both discourse and fantasy, and storylines develop in either direction: with the flow of time through which experience is processed and with the non-event as if it had been an experience processed in conjunction in spite of time.

It cannot be overemphasized that Argument with a capital "A" is therefore a special form of officiant discourse in ceremonial garb and that it not just allows for, but truly demands, both objective retrospective accounts *and* highly subjective recounting in tandem with each other. It also allows fully for the two types of accounts to be swirled together so closely that the recipient is perhaps even led to confuse them as ever having been separate accounts in the first place. Advocacy, being preference for one chosen storyline above a competing line, serves its purpose through clarity, certainly, but it also serves its purpose through confusion equally well.

Arguments are invented things. Like mechanical novelties they may have never been constructed before in the history of the world or they may have been amalgams of previous devices ripped off or repurposed for some new use. Like physical machinery, they can operate with an ordered and observable set of mechanisms working in tight conjunction to suit the manufacturer's design. As Rube Goldberg demonstrated, mechanical novelties and physical machinery can be in the form of bizarre assemblies the parts of which purely astonish, and the purpose of which may be unknown, untenable, or plain impossible—and so too can be arguments.

The trial lawyer's argument to the jury is not a narrative or a report—or if it turns out to be only that alone, it is a disastrous misuse of what it could have and should have been. The trial lawyer's argument to the jury is also not a science fiction short story nor an intensely personal memoir either. It is both and it is neither. It is a transmission of proposals to decide, admixed with highly selective and highly biased "factual" reasons to do so. It is a transmission, moreover, as a monologue drafted as if it were a dialogue attentive to, but trying to wriggle out from under, some of the pickiest rules ever constructed, rules proclaimed both by historical documents as well as by a physically present supervisory authority who is really only the third officiant. The documents and the supervisor partly, but not entirely, dictate some of what can be said and what cannot be said, all while the monologue rolls resolutely forward to an uncertain end. It is speech both internal and external and it connects minds to other minds in the most regimented and also in the most plastic way that communication can ever and has ever occurred:

> To speak, I have to be somehow already in communication with the mind I am to address before I start speaking. I can be in touch perhaps through past relationships, by an exchange of glances, by an understanding with a third person who has brought me and my interlocutor together, or in any of countless other ways. (Words are modifications of a more-than-verbal situation.) I have to sense something in the other's mind to which my own utterance can relate. Human communication is never one-way. Always, it not only calls for response but is shaped in its very form and content by anticipated response. This is not to say that I am sure how the other will respond to what I say. But I have to be able to conjecture a possible range of responses at least in some vague way. I have to be somehow inside the mind of the other in advance in order to enter with my message, and he or she must be inside my mind. To formulate anything I must have another person or other persons already 'in mind'. This is the paradox of human communication.[53]

A Correspondence Course

As the wedding advances through its complicated ceremonial stages, the trial lawyer's manipulations of language, people, and objects combine to assemble the necessary apparatus to best advance the client's interests as a direct function of the formality of the proceedings. A style must be inserted. Never forget that the trial lawyer always speaks in the service of someone else and that their efforts at persuasion is in order to serve that someone's personal interests, nothing more. A key part of the project involves using a prepared style to convince the jury that the facts and law beneficial to the client's position are on all fours. Imaginative links must be constructed between certain realities—what witnesses said and what exhibits showed during examination—and hypothetical universes existing only inside of people's minds. To build such links one must find places where realities and fantasies connect, and that is in descriptive relationships.

So much of law is already about relationships—formal and informal connections weaving through the dynamics of contract, tort, property, crimes, probate, and family law disputes—that it is unsurprising to the juror to have another relationship floated for consideration, that of the match between what happened between the parties here and what must be decided in the verdict there. Matching is a variety of correlation which most mathematicians and logicians are easily familiar with, and the acceptance of a satisfactory correlation requires the acceptance of satisfactory links and parallels between two seemingly disparate categories, lists, or sets of items.[54]

At every moment that a match is offered, the wedding ceremony pauses for a moment for reflective contemplation: these are also junctures at which the trial lawyers and the scientist can find some common ground. Analyzing relationships to glean understanding is an activity that both professions engage in, albeit that the trial lawyer's goals are certainly not the scientist's goals as each does so. Still, grasping the epistemology of relationship analysis is a shared concern for both. Both trial lawyer and evolutionary biologist, for instance, acknowledge that trial practice and scientific study enjoin a constant search for links, and that the search for helpful ones is not always easy and is jeopardized by the risk of falling for false connections or missing true ones. Both are intrigued and hampered in equal parts by what objects sit in front of them to be studied and what goals are in mind to be attained.

The trial lawyer has a small size problem in being confronted on all sides with others' *words*—those of legislators, judges, clients, witnesses, officers, neighbors, strangers, relatives, professionals, and busybodies—and words are notoriously chaotic and cluttered reflections of actual events having taken place. The trial lawyer pieces together a relationship from nets fashioned by other's words alone and hopes that the net holds sufficiently to derive value out of the relationship formed. Sometimes the project is a success and the law enforcement officer's handwritten report, say, jives well with the state statute's prohibitory language, with the defendant's directly observed act, and with the lawyer's creative proposal of imagining "people who put themselves in harm's way." Other times the gaps are way too large between the observed and the required such that no whisper or blast of artistic flights of fancy can ever span them.

For their part, the scientist encounters passably comparable successes and failures in the venture to establish rational connections. Relying far more on observation and experiment than on words, each specific scientific discipline presents its own challenges in that regard. For instance, the zoologist can study animal behaviors associated with animal bodies through direct observational links, but the paleontologist enjoys no such luxury. Unable to determine behaviors directly from calipered measurements of fossilized bones and teeth, the paleontologist is pressed to consider modern-day analogues instead and attempts to posit the likely past behaviors of specimens from modeling present behaviors of animals which seem physically comparable.

In such an instance, the paleontologist notices perhaps that the fossilized skull of a *Smilidon fatalis*, the sabertooth cat from the Pleistocene, contains a large sagittal crest for the insertion of large jaw muscles along with massive carnassials in its posterior dentition, and then also notices the same structures in *Panthera leo*, the modern lion.[55] Because those features enable the lion to create sufficient force to crush bone, an inference is made that like structures probably have like actions and that 25,000 years ago *Smilodon* therefore crushed bone in a manner comparable to the way lions do today.[56] The search is really for *homologies*, the shared features of organisms which form the basis for all evolutionary comparisons.[57] The paleontologist may see likely candidates but still employs caution; additional features of *Smilodon*, such as its extraordinarily lengthened front sabers, signal that it likely engaged in other behaviors substantially distinct from how lions act, but at least facially the inferred bone crushing behavior is still apt.

Both the use of homologies and of analogous reasoning is not lost on trial lawyers. They and scientists alike reason in general that organisms and structures in one place can nevertheless likely inform an observer about those patently similar but situated in a different place or time. The compared "organisms" and the compared "places" may be separated by culture, substantial physical distance, or even epochs—both investigators get it that the large past is (cautiously) revealed by the small present not from observation alone but from the use of logic as well, in the form of the reasonable inferences which can be distilled from reasonable observations. The trial lawyer borrows from the paleontologist toolbox and utilizes the inference forceps, wielding it to claim that like factual structures probably have like legal conclusions. It is with those forceps that the trial lawyer forces two nearby structures together, suggesting that citation to Jones v. Smith, a case about a man being bit by a dog while on a run, is not just informative but perhaps even dispositive of the case at bar, Smith v. Jones, about the plaintiff being bit by defendant's dog while out on a walk. The inference is that the cases correspond in enough material detail to be valuable analogues for the other to the extent that their legal outcomes should then be deemed to match as well.

We note at the start that the scientist uses their inference forceps simply to be *descriptive* about the gripped together structures, identifying what is, not what ought to be, while the trial lawyer uses inference to also be *prescriptive*, proposing the imposition and enforcement of a rule as a result of its use. Those distinct uses don't necessarily make the former valid and the latter invalid, they just raise concerns about what consequences might arise from their respective uses, given how each might impact future human conduct. Science describes and law prescribes but both can envision value being generated from the present being on all fours with the past. Two challenges, however, tend to stem from the trial lawyer's prescriptive use.

The first challenge lies in determining just what "enough detail" is in making the match and which details are the ones which should be attended to so that prescription is justified. Relevance for the trial lawyer is necessarily different than relevance for the paleontologist because the trial lawyer's measurement devices, being the words legislators wrote down in codes and which judges wrote down in case reporters, are far less reliable and far more pliable than calipers. Is it necessary to compare the names and addresses of the respective participants in both cases or will simply their conduct do? As to conduct, is the fact that one person walked but the other person ran significant or insignificant? Trial lawyers particularly care about those types of picayune questions since prescriptive use may result in a very real penalty or loss impacting a person (read, client) if used improperly as opposed to simply the body of general knowledge about a topic being made more or less helpful.

The second challenge lies in the use of the inference tool being proper to grip with at all. The logician questions whether fact patterns can have analogues in the same way that animal skulls can have analogues sufficient to support projected physical correspondences. This concern is an empirical one: skulls as objects can be objectively measured and weighed but recitations of events cannot. Spoken and written recitations are unreliable indicators of objective truth given that they are the function of human observers, actors who are notoriously unreliable by defects in their powers of observation and their proclivity to insert subjective opinion into nearly every descriptive gap which someone's observations might create.

As to the second challenge, the historian and sociologist tender counterarguments. Plenty of factual recitations by plenty of subjective reporters have been satisfactory enough, they say, to have people base decisions of the greatest importance to human affairs on them, justifying analogues made between strategies used in past and present military campaigns, for instance, or analogues made between the economic treatment of large social groups as was used in past and may be used in present political movements. We are used to making eventful decisions on an acceptance of the argument that the past usefully informs the present. A verdict or judicial opinion seems like a smaller version of weightier matters we have already sanctioned as allowable from old inferences and older explanations; the words of others from the past are commonly the acceptable antecedents of present-day group decisions.

The trial lawyer steps in with both invitation and warning. We know that strict one-to-one matches between past legal cases and present legal cases cannot exist since, simply by definition alone, the dates of the events and the very names of the litigants must be different even if nothing else. Disassociations only extend from there, not reduce. We also know how selective and partial an advocate can be in sifting through the buffet of available facts in Jones v. Smith to choose those which seem apropos and to eject those which seem of no consequence.

The phenomenon of advocacy strikes deep at the heart of matching efforts. Pondering the dog case, we ask: Were both dogs pit bulls? That correlation, says one advocate, is critical. Were both bites to the left as opposed to the right hand? That, says another competing advocate, is of no matter whatsoever. As the fact finder inquires, "Who is to say?", the system responds: well, it is a mix. Two trial lawyers as battling advocates will present competing opinions and an independent decision-maker will then weigh them and (in large part emotionally), choose the best. The fact finder inquires as to the process by which this happens and the system responds: through the analysis of connections formed by past and present words, through the presentation of argument regarding those previous words and those proposed connections, and through the envisioning of a universe of possible relationships. Weirdly, since relationships are fluid mental concepts, then emotion and subjectivity are not sorted out of the analytical apparatus but are instead made integral parts of it.

The Past as Command, Not Commentary

At this juncture in our reverie from the wedding ceremony, our paleontologist insists on inserting a methodologically based complaint. It seems like an inherently unjust way to obtain consensus in a present case, they say, which allows one to argue analogies to past cases where there may be little or no actual correspondence between the facts of the past and the facts of the present. In other words, analogies which are as free-floating as the mammoth lexicon of human language allows are simply not helpful analogies at all and should not be used to make determinations.

The trial lawyer defends: We actually *disserve* justice as a principle, responds the lawyer, by not using analogy and inference from past cases, regardless of the seeming disconnects between past and present. The legal system would be useless if every case was assumed to be *sui generis*, a novel occurrence, in which an applicable rule had to be newly minted each time, a disposition of a dispute constructed independent of, and oblivious to, all dispositions and disputes that had ever come before it. The very existence of judicial opinions and the case reporters in which those opinions are compiled demands that decisions in past cases have some importance to decisions in present ones.[58]

And of course they do: the doctrine of precedent supports the use of analogue in law to found decisions in private disputes. The human element of arbitrariness and bias which the paleontologist identified in their scientific studies is supposedly addressed in law by safeguards built into the legal system by court procedures and evidence rules. For instance, it is a classic human grievance that an authority figure is suspected of imposing a personal filter on an important decision which materially affects a citizen. From patrol officers issuing traffic tickets to election officials issuing voting results, the suspicion is a constant one that either an element of import is missing or has been added to the calculation being made by some biased authority and must be reinserted or removed as required by fundamental fairness. That grievance is softened somewhat when all participants have access to the same factual predicates for the calculation. In arguing motions to judges, for instance, all three interested parties—the movant, the opponent, and the judge—can read for themselves the operative words of Jones v. Smith and note which may have been inadvertently omitted or intentionally ignored and bring attention to the matching problem created.

In arguing cases to the jury, on the other hand, no such equitable access exists. One, the jury has only heard the facts of the pending case through the tight filter of two (or more) trial lawyers each sifting and removing plenty of facts that might otherwise have been part of the mix. Two, they have no handle or control over the example or parallel that the trial lawyers may offer up for them to accept. Is that true? Did that really happen in that way? Is that consistent with what is already known or with common sense? Three, they are confined in an artificial, informationally closed off environment, more testing laboratory than hotel room.

We are all familiar with incredulity stemming from the unexpected narrative but at least in other interactions outside the courtroom, such as in casual conversations, we have buffers and backstops of balancing information on which to rely. We can check phones, run computer searches, or pick up a book or article to confirm or deny proposed sources. But jurors are stuck—they are prisoners in an artificially comfortable cell denied access to the outside world by the sheer force of social pressure generated by a judge's admonition. Words imprison them and words can set them free. More than as with many other small social groups, jury panels feel firsthand the power of words to control conduct, especially their own. From when they are first *voir dired*, to when the trial lawyers argue to them, to when they argue among themselves in deliberation, they see important decisions balance on a single sentence and outcomes shift with the careful enunciation of a particular phrase, and yet no outside source of information to double check the veracity of any such words or phrases.

An adversarial system demands this be so. Inquisition is not allowed. Inference and analogy by adversaries are employed in order to try to tie the client's fate to the fate of other clients long before them. As <u>Smith</u> goes, so may go Smith. If in a pre-trial motion the judge accepts <u>Smith</u> and ignores Smith, and the case is thus won on the law by the motion being granted and discarding the jury, fine. If, after such a motion is denied, the case is heard and the jury accepts Smith and cares not a whit for *Smith*, and the case is thus won on the facts, fine as well.

In the largest sense, even the favorable verdict is not always the end sought to be achieved—the client's particular interests being served is the true goal. A client's directive may well be "buy as much time as possible by dragging the case out as long as possible," or "make it as costly as you can for the other side to defend the case," or "make the opponent as miserable as possible," or "expose the opponent to public scrutiny as much as possible." A win at verdict may secure part of those things, true, but many client goals may be incompatible with getting to a verdict at all, and a "loss" at verdict so that an appeal can begin or so that a settlement can be reached immediately after a verdict may ironically accomplish the real objective. To that end, as precedent to tie the past and the present together fails, as in the ploy is rejected or is unavailable, the trial lawyer's work toward trying to get the client benefited nevertheless continues.

Homology and analogy, although serious pieces of logic for trial lawyers and scientists in their roles as analysts and evaluators to utilize, are just useful tricks of discourse in the actual practice of law and especially in trial practice; other tricks can sub in to take their place if necessary. The flexibility required to discern the existence of the tricks from what the "law," in all its majesty, allows to be used, is a trial lawyer qualification. The flexibility required to select the best of the tricks or the most efficacious from the bunch available, is a trial lawyer qualification. The flexibility required to present the tricks as something other than tricks, is a trial lawyer qualification as well. The trial lawyer does not necessarily need to be a logician, or a scientist, or even a "good talker," and many practitioners are not any of those things by a long shot yet still succeed at arguing in a manner sufficient to be an effective representative of another person.

When we finally rejoin our wedding ceremony, we are keen to appreciate the first two officiants special role and responsibility in the process: trial lawyers must be persons intently devoted to the pursuit of "relative truths" not "absolute truths," and have commands issuing to them from all sides to sift through vast fields of facts and law in search of the relative versions most useful to their client's goal. Acting on that other's behalf, they are players is a ceremonial game who are manipulative in the best sense of that term, skilled at using the power of spoken and unspoken language to invite and suppress bias, to identify and ignore relationships, to trigger and to decry emotion, and to maneuver laws and argument in doing so all in order to influence another player in their route to a decision.

But they are the most crucial of the officiants. The only possible way that this odd marriage ceremony can be completed is with their firm hand guiding the others in forging a particularly desired union of "truths" about the world so that the blissfully wedded couple, the artificially and carefully selected law, and the artificially and carefully selected facts can now go make a home together and become one, as a judgment, a case's end, an opinion, a verdict. The jurors are metaphysically transcended and by this union new "law" is thus born to inform the next prenuptial conflict when, with the next day's case, a novel yet familiar marital process starts all over once again.

Notes

1 See, e.g., Nolan v. Dillon, 261 Md 516, 276 A2d 36 (1971).
2 See, Kerr, Norbert L. and Robert M. Bray. *The psychology of the courtroom: An introduction*. Academic Press, 1982 at p. 20.
3 Lockwood, Randall. "The influence of animals on social perception." In *New perspectives on our lives with companion animals* (Aaron Honori Katcher and Alan M. Beck, eds.). University of Pennsylvania Press, 1983 at p. 64.
4 Ibid.
5 There are only two reported appellate cases of a judge allowing a dog in a courtroom: one well over a century ago in 1904 in New York where doing so was apparently allowed as a "reasonable" means of enabling a series of witnesses to show who was best "acquainted" with a certain dog (Ross v. Healy et. ux., 45 Misc. 371, 90 N.Y.S. 391 (N.Y. Sup. 1904)), and the other somewhat more recently in Washington state in Arnold v. Laird, 94 Wash.2d 867, 621 P.2d 138 (Wash. 1980) where a dog was allowed into the courtroom as evidence where the dog's condition was in dispute and the court found that "the observation of [the dog as] an object" was required where the object itself could not be admitted in evidence in the normal way. The vast majority of courts, in contrast, exclude dogs as being impermissible distractions to the jury and unnecessary in that human witnesses can readily testify as to any dog's likeness, nature, or behavior. See, e.g., People v. Tomlin, Not Reported in Cal.Rptr.3d, 2004 WL 1368368 (Cal. App. 5 Dist. 2004) Not Officially Published (Cal. Rules of Court, Rules 976, 977); Stewart v. Warren, Not Reported in N.E.2d, 1988 WL 45132 (Ohio App. 2 Dist. 1988); Commonwealth v. Carl, 87 Pa. Super. 110, 1925 WL 5157 (Pa. Super. 1925).
6 Of course, only in small part. We certainly do not think of dogs as "deliberative thinkers," that is considering whether some proposition is true or not sufficient to then rationally evaluate whether there are reasons for or against taking action in light of the proposition's truth. See, Millar, Alan. *Understanding people: Normativity and rationalizing explanation*. Clarendon Press, 2004.
7 For a Sunday stroll through the garden of novelties to be enjoyed where people pretend to know what dogs are really "thinking," consider perusing Bergler, Reinhold. *Man and dog: The psychology of a relationship*. Blackwell Scientific Publications, 1988; Griffin, Donald R. *Animal minds: Beyond cognition to consciousness*. University of Chicago Press, 2001; and Coren, Stanley. *How to speak dog: Mastering the art of dog-human communication*. Simon and Schuster, 2001 to sample just a few random entries in this wild and free form area of creative interpretation.
8 No differently, really, than the dog is and has been in a dozen other respects as well, including in selective breeding, specialized skills training, and genetic engineering. See, e.g., Rollin, Bernard E. *The Frankenstein syndrome: Ethical and social issues in the genetic engineering of animals*. Cambridge University Press, 1995.
9 But cf. Arnold v. Laird, 94 Wash.2d 867, 621 P.2d 138 (Wash. 1980) (dog allowed into courtroom as evidence where dog's condition was in dispute and court found that "the observation of [the dog as] an object" was required); People v. Tomlin, Not Reported in Cal. Rptr. 3d, 2004 WL 1368368 (Cal. App. 5 Dist. 2004) Not Officially Published (Cal. Rules of Court, Rules 976, 977) (dog not "able to testify"

so not allowed in court since "human witnesses could testify as to the dog's nature"); Stewart v. Warren, Not Reported in N.E.2d, 1988 WL 45132 (Ohio App. 2 Dist. 1988) (introduction of dog to jury as a witness deemed "highly questionable" where "without some straining of the imagination, the introduction of the dog itself did not have any tendency to make the existence of any fact in issue more or less probable than it would have been without such evidence"); Commonwealth v. Carl, 87 Pa. Super. 110, 1925 WL 5157 (Pa. Super. 1925) (dog not permitted to be offered in evidence as an exhibit especially when defendant fondled and petted it in the presence of the jury); Gay v. Commonwealth, 231 Ky. 396, 21 S.W.2d 480 (Ky. App. 1929) (dog ordered to be produced in court but solely in order for it to then be killed); Ross v. Healy et. ux., 45 Misc. 371, 90 N.Y.S. 391 (N.Y. Sup. 1904) (dog allowed to be present in courtroom).

10 Contrary to what most animal rights advocates yearn to be so, the field of animal law is chock full of death, dismemberment, and destruction. The daily practice of an animal law lawyer involves death more than does any other specialty, even wrongful death, and animal law cases are mandatorily sustained on a steady diet of dogs killed by cars, cats killed by dogs, horses killed by veterinarians, livestock killed by ranchers, game killed by hunters, and pests and vermin killed by farmers, among other smaller and larger slaughters, with deaths of living organisms in the thousands being the mundane and consistent staple necessarily dealt with in each normal work week.

11 See, e.g., State v. Hoeldt, 139 Wash App 225, 227, 160 P3d 55, 56 (2007) (dog as a deadly weapon).

12 See generally, Fredericks, Anthony D. *How long things live: And how they live as long as they do*. Stackpole Books, 2010.

13 See, e.g., Sawh v. City of Lino Lakes, 823 NW2d 627 (Minn 2012) (dog as a market good).

14 See, Mitchell, Robert W. and Nicholas S. Thompson. "Deception in Play Between Dogs and People." In *Deception: Perspectives on human and nonhuman deceit* (Robert W. Mitchell and Nicholas S. Thompson, eds.). State University of New York Press, 1986 at pp. 193–204.

15 Miklósi, Ádám. *Dog behaviour, evolution, and cognition*. Oxford University Press, 2014.

16 Lentz v. Stroh, 1820 WL 1808:6 (Pa. 1820).

17 See generally, Vesey-FitzGerald, Brian. *The book of the dog*. Borden Publishing Company, 1948.

18 Were there to be a "Field Guide To Lawyers," there is no question that *Homo folksieus* would be one of the most ubiquitous and common species listed and which an enthusiast could readily identify in the wild. Distinguishing features include drab brown coloration regardless of season, a rumpled coat, impaired vision usually corrected by bifocals or horn-rimmed glasses but always with twinkling eyes behind them, and a raspy call. Inexplicably, there are no females or young of this species, and all members of the population are invariably males of a rather advanced age who look uncannily a lot like the observer's own grandfather.

19 See generally, Fischhoff, Baruch. *Acceptable risk*. Cambridge University Press, 1981.

20 See, e.g., Zilcha-Mano, Sigal, Mario Mikulincer, and Phillip R. Shaver. "An attachment perspective on human–pet relationships: Conceptualization and

assessment of pet attachment orientations." *Journal of Research in Personality* 45, no. 4 (2011): 345–57.

21 Frankfurt, Harry G. *Freedom of the will and the concept of a person*. Humana Press, 1988.

22 See, Horowitz, Alexandra. "Theory of mind in dogs? Examining method and concept." *Learning & Behavior* 39 (2011): 314–17.

23 See generally, Dewey, John, and James Hayden Tufts. *Ethics*. Good Press, 2019.

24 Innuendo is a classic rhetorical device, an implied message in the form of an allegation whose content raises the specter of an unwanted ascription of qualities regarding the subject. See generally, Shuy, Roger W. *The language of defamation cases*. Oxford University Press, 2010 at p. 115.

25 The Spanish physician Benigno Risueno de Amador famously wrote "*L'homme moyen n'existe pas*" (the average human does not exist), a proposal with which the juror as armchair statistician and the juror as armchair psychologist may be in sharp disagreement.

26 See, Minow, Martha. *Making all the difference: Inclusion, exclusion, and American law*. Cornell University Press, 1990.

27 See generally, Abbott, H. Porter. *The Cambridge introduction to narrative*. Cambridge University Press, 2020.

28 Walker, Lenore E., David Shapiro, Stephanie Akl, Lenore E. Walker, David Shapiro, and Stephanie Akl. "Jury selection and psychology of the trial." *Introduction to Forensic Psychology: Clinical and Social Psychological Perspectives* (2020): 337–48.

29 Sundman, A.-S., Martin Johnsson, Dominic Wright, and Per Jensen. "Similar recent selection criteria associated with different behavioural effects in two dog breeds." *Genes, Brain and Behavior* 15, no. 8 (2016): 750–6.

30 See generally, Hoage, Robert J. *Perceptions of animals in American culture*. Smithsonian Press, 1989.

31 Kosslyn, Stephen M., William L. Thompson, and Giorgio Ganis. *The case for mental imagery*. Oxford University Press, 2006.

32 Wall, Tyler. "Legal terror and the police dog." *Radical Philosophy* 188, no. 2 (2014): 2–7.

33 Miller, Malcolm E., George C. Christensen, and Howard E. Evans. "Anatomy of the dog." *Academic Medicine* 40, no. 4 (1965): 400.

34 See, e.g., Waller, Bridget M., Kate Peirce, Cátia C. Caeiro, Linda Scheider, Anne M. Burrows, Sandra McCune, and Juliane Kaminski. "Paedomorphic facial expressions give dogs a selective advantage." *PLoS one* 8, no. 12 (2013): e82686.

35 Sharp, Lesley A. *Animal ethos: The morality of human-animal encounters in experimental lab science*. University of California Press, 2018.

36 Morgan, Marina, and John Palmer. "Dog bites." *Bmj* 334, no. 7590 (2007): 413–17.

37 Shuler, Carrie M., Emilio E. DeBess, Jodi A. Lapidus, and Katrina Hedberg. "Canine and human factors related to dog bite injuries." *Journal of the American Veterinary Medical Association* 232, no. 4 (2008): 542–6.

38 Stavrianos, C., D. Tatsis, P. Stavrianou, A. Karamouzi, G. Mihail, and D. Mihailidou. "Intercanine distance as a recognition method of bite marks." *Research Journal of Biological Sciences* 6, no. 1 (2011): 25–9.

39 Gershman, Kenneth A., Jeffrey J. Sacks, and John C. Wright. "Which dogs bite? A case-control study of risk factors." *Pediatrics* 93, no. 6 (1994): 913–17.

40 Barrett, Deirdre. *Supernormal stimuli: How primal urges overran their evolutionary purpose*. WW Norton & Company, 2010.
41 Neumann, Sigmund. "The rule of the demagogue." *American Sociological Review* 3, no. 4 (1938): 487–98.
42 As the sharp legal scholar and even sharper wit Barry Goldman ruefully observed:

> Raising an overabundance of arguments has the effect of cheapening your good ones. It dilutes them. It inflates the currency of persuasion. It's redundant and superfluous, extraneous and duplicative. It's supererogatory and it is pleonastic. It is prolix. My friends, it is otiose.

From Israel, S. and B. Goldman, "Opinions: Essays on lawyering, litigation and arbitration, the placebo effect, *Chutzpah*, and Related Matters." (2016) (self-published) at p. 12.
43 From Daniel Webster's prosecution speech in the 1830 jury trial of John Francis Knapp. See, Farrell, James M. "Classical rhetoric at Salem: Daniel webster and the murder of captain white." *International Journal of the Classical Tradition* 25, no. 1 (2018): 36–56.
44 See, e.g., Grasmick, Harold G., Robert J. Bursik Jr, and Bruce J. Arneklev. "Reduction in drunk driving as a response to increased threats of shame, embarrassment, and legal sanctions." *Criminology* 31, no. 1 (1993): 41–67.
45 See, LaMay, Craig L. "Covering the notorious case: Narrative and the need for sensationalism done well." In *Institutional failures*. Routledge, 2016, pp. 167–86.
46 See, Walsh, Froma. "Human-animal bonds I: The relational significance of companion animals." *Family process* 48, no. 4 (2009): 462–80.
47 Sill, Edward. *Hypocrisy*. Houghton, Mifflin and Company, 1887.
48 Bob Dylan, on point about so many other types of relationships, regularly confused this one: "Judge said to the jury, plain as a thing can be, a woman shot her lover down, murder in the second degree." (from the song "Frankie and Albert" on the album *Good As I Been To You* (1992)); "The judge and the jury they took their stand, the judge had the papers in his right hand, forty-one days, forty-one nights; forty-one years to wear the ball and the stripes." (from the song "In Search of Little Sadie" on the album *Self Portrait* (1970)).
49 This includes the confusion engendered by trying to comprehend when witness questioning will ever end, given re-direct examination, re-cross examinations, rebuttal examinations, and sometimes even surrebuttal examinations when those (more rarely) occur. Trial lawyers generally want their questions to be deemed the most significant and the opposition's questions to be ignored, so seizing opportunities to get one more word in, or the last word in, words which might have a tendency to highlight evidence as something "special" or as having heightened emphasis (as surrebuttal evidence tends to do), is a much sought after effect. See, e.g., State v. Reynolds, 324 Or 550, 556, 931 P2d 94, 96 (1997).
50 See, Kerr, Norbert L., and Robert M. Bray. *The psychology of the courtroom: An introduction*. Academic Press, 1982 at p. 25.
51 Defined generally as those types of statements made right while one is under the stress of excitement of a startling event or condition. See, DeVogel v. Padilla, 22 Wash App 2d 39, 509 P3d 832 (2022).

52 Smith, Sidonie, and Julia Watson. "Witness or false witness?: Metrics of authenticity, collective I-formations, and the ethic of verification in first-person testimony." *Biography* 35, no. 4 (2012): 590–626.
53 Ong, Walter J. *Orality and literacy*. Routledge, 2013 at p. 99.
54 See generally, Lovász, László, and Michael D. Plummer. *Matching theory*. Vol. 367. American Mathematical Soc., 2009.
55 See, e.g., Duckler, Geordie L. "Parietal depressions in skulls of the extinct saber-toothed felid *Smilodon fatalis*: evidence of mechanical strain." *Journal of Vertebrate Paleontology* 17, no. 3 (1997): 600–9.
56 Valkenburgh, B. van, Mark F. Teaford, and Alan Walker. "Molar microwear and diet in large carnivores: inferences concerning diet in the sabretooth cat, Smilodon fatalis." *Journal of Zoology* 222, no. 2 (1990): 319–40.
57 See, Raff, Rudolf A. *The shape of life: Genes, development, and the evolution of animal form*. University of Chicago Press, 2012, at pp. 34–8.
58 See, e.g., Am. Nat'l Ins. Co. v. Arce, 21-0843, 2023 WL 3134718 (Tex Apr 28, 2023) ("Adherence to precedent remains the touchstone of a neutral legal system that provides stability and reliability").

4

Cell Evolution as Metaphor for the Common Law's Evolution through Argument

In which a model of how cells have evolved (as proposed by cell and microbiologists) is ruthlessly hijacked by the author as a concept to help discern if there is a larger significance assignable to the repetitive transport, by trial lawyers, of arguments back and forth across the lanes of time and space. The model is proffered as a means of illuminating how minute, transient, self-interested exploits at the individual level may spontaneously produce larger-unit, semi-permanent, globally impactful consequences without the need to posit any "architect" governing the process or any joint aim by the participants.

A Short But Necessary Science Lesson

Recall the observations back at the end of Chapter 1 that the common law only grows and grows quantitatively over time with very little culling and even less oversight. In a very clear sense, we accept that there is nobody at all in charge or or in control of "cases" as a category, no unifying, supervising authority commanding that a cohesive plan be implemented to which each case filed and decided must adhere in order to achieve a targeted result. There are low- and mid-level procedural blueprints generically followed, to be sure, which work out how all cases march along a technical path of docket filing, service of summons, pleading motion, discovery hearing, and scheduled disposition. Any courthouse clerk, judicial assistant, or legislative aide will affirm those obligations in spades. But there is no grand scheme—no "big point" to having cases exist outside of the social necessity that a working judicial system be available to facilitate getting "justice" (here the trial lawyer coughs) dispensed throughout a participating community.

While this isn't necessarily a problem demanding an immediate explanation, it does beg the philosophical questions of "does law grow?" and "if it does, is law over time getting better, worse, or remaining in stasis?" The day-to-day trial lawyers have no time for such esoterica, and simply shrug and continue to file their individual cases, assert their individual client's interests, make their individual arguments, craft and rely on their individual styles, and hope to attain their individual marital outcomes. Litigators as individuals are busy, busy people who can hardly be bothered by global propositions regarding social progress.

The broader group called Lawyers, however, would be remiss to not pause to ask if they are getting anywhere worthwhile by each contributor contributing. To examine what cases *in toto* might lead to, we can employ the ideas touched upon in Chapter 3 regarding the value of looking for homologous structures to locate significance in shared relationships. There is value to be gleaned in casting for insights by looking around at how the process of growth transpires and consequently displays effects in other systems. As one candidate of "developmental models" among many, let's consider organismal cellular evolution as a possible template.[1]

Modeling between those two different systems, common law and cell biology, requires that we recognize the systems' intersections and separations, and the precursor to doing *that* competently is getting a good handle on how cell evolution works in the first place. For our purposes, we don't really need the full college level biology course explanation, and can reduce things to some more lay-accessible, universal principles.

One, we will accept that a cell is a complex dynamic system of biochemical agents and organic structures forming a microscopic basic unit of life; as tiny membrane-enclosed packets of fluids and organelles, cells best exemplify just how "the complex tends to arise from the simple."[2] Two, we note that cells utilize long chain acids, RNA and DNA, engage in "transcribing" and "translating" one set to the other in order to construct and transfer proteins among themselves, and thereby replicate into other cells. In their primordial form, then, they almost certainly arose in some sort of "RNA-world" context where imprecise primitive translation processes drove small proteins to become larger, more complex proteins through more and more refined replication methods.[3] Three, we recognize that over immense spans of geologic time, the "poor" (i.e., crummy) transcription and translation of informational messages as with RNA eventually led to "better" (i.e., slightly more effective) transcription and translation of informational messages.

In short, adaptive pressures in ancient environments didn't just result in the banality of some cells begetting more cells, it resulted in the austerity of cell replication mechanisms themselves begetting stronger replication mechanisms as well: "Translation [was] the leading edge of a wave of cellular evolution in which proteins evolve[d] to greater and greater levels of complexity and specificity."[4] Yes, new cells form and have formed the templates for new species, but what is most important to note here is that where the classical Darwinian approach had always been to see all evolution as a "procession of forms" with a focus on *species* as the object of interest, the modern cell biologist's approach is to focus instead on the process that produces the forms, focus, as the microbiologist Carl Woese poetically puts it, "on the gem, not the reflections from its facets."[5] It is the *processes inside and outside the cells*, not the cells themselves as they undergo the processes, that provide the strongest explanatory forces for the majesty and wonder that is cell evolution.

Moreover, the processes involved are not just multi-generational (embracing lengthy successions of generations of cells) but multi-environmental as well (embracing broad spans of lineages and locations of cells); that is, true cellular evolution can be accomplished only by a collective evolution in which many diverse cell designs evolve simultaneously and share their novelties with one another. In other words, we can assume that the componentry of primitive cells needed to be cosmopolitan in nature, for only by passing through a number of diverse cellular environments could new generations be significantly altered and refined. Finally, for cellular evolution to occur, mechanisms must exist whereby novelty can be globally disseminated (horizontally exchanged), which in turn demands a universal genetic code (a *lingua franca*) carried by a standard, generic translation apparatus, one readily exchanged among the various cell types.

Strange Liaisons

Now with all that basic biology in hand, we can return to this chapter's task of considering the significance of any curious "on all fours" type parallels hypothetically arising between cell evolution and law's evolved trajectory of litigated cases. In our metaphor, one cell is not necessarily one case alone but may also be a line of cases or a recurring mode or theme among cases (such as with "dog bite cases"). The most basic shared feature is that both systems can be described in terms of dependent generational lineages; as time moves forward, law derives from previous law somewhat as cells derive from previous cells.[6]

In other words, there is a fairly apparent "chain of descent" operating in both systems where descendant cells have split off from and arise from ancestor cells (through divisional events called mitosis and meiosis) and where descendant cases (through divisional events called judgments, review for error, appellate opinions, the publication of opinions in case reporters, and new filings) split off from and arise from ancestor cases. "Dog bite cases" fit comfortably into a standard mold that varies little in basic theme from case to case—we get it that some dog somewhere bites some person each and every instance—and which rely on earlier cases having come to conclusion to help establish laws to use in the subsequent ones for them to get to their conclusions. Being similar yet different over time, dog bite cases evolve in an ancestor-descendant lineage roughly akin to how cell lineages evolve.

The way that generational lines actually develop is, of course, not *that* parallel since with cells it is an actual physical transfer of biological and chemical materials from one to the next, while with cases, Able v. Baker does not transfer any informational content directly over to then "become" Smith v. Jones. At the concept level, however, it is fair to say that Smith v. Jones would likely never have come into existence (i.e., been filed, litigated, and resolved) had it not been for the law that Able v. Baker created enabling it to do so. The two cases are successive "generations" of law in time and in the dependence on one "leading" to the other, simply not in the particular bits and pieces of the actual case information being shared (although even that may happen when appeals result in remand and a new trial level case arises directly from the previous one's ashes).

Suffice it to say that at least the essential *apparatus* of each cell—the fact that the ancestor and the descendant both have long chain acids, membranes, constructed proteins, and usable biochemical agents in place in order to be deemed cells at all and to replicate—mimics the essential *apparatus* of each case—the fact that the ancestor and the descendant both have parties, venues, allegations, and legal theories in place in order to be deemed cases at all and to replicate, and that the apparatus in both instances is a mandatory feature that enables old cohorts to give rise to new ones through relatively mechanical processes occurring in branching patterns over time.

Moreover, case evolution, like cellular evolution, is roughly an unplanned and fortuitous march toward greater and greater complexity. Every lawyer would likely agree with the observation that as time has progressed throughout litigation and appeal, the complex has arisen from the simple in more than one way and not because anyone desired it or directed it to. In general, it is not unfair to suggest that the legal disputes of the 2020s are overall more intricate and more law-bound than the legal disputes of the 1820s or even the 1920s even if no concerted effort was exerted to create such a result. At the same time, we can also see that case evolution, like cellular evolution, is ultimately a self-limiting process. As a feature (a certain type of porous membrane in a cell, perhaps, or a certain type of motion in a hearing) evolves in its next iteration to some greater complexity, the possible ways in and extent to which that feature's design can be altered necessarily diminish and continue to diminish in recognition of processes that have occurred in previous generations.

That statement is as true of membranes in cells as it is of motions in cases in that both require more and more complex processes to survive and propagate in their respective dynamically changing environments. While no one "wants" it to be so, increased integration and complexity in changing environments thus in turn tends to buy specificity—but at the cost of flexibility. What novelty and pliancy there clearly remain in the mechanics of arguing cases today is still necessarily a greatly reduced version of what trial lawyers had been able to do when presenting arguments in the past, in no small part because the legal ecosystem where cases wither and thrive is a greatly expanded one. Gripe about it or laud about it as lawyers and jurists may, still, as procedural rules proliferate, procedural boundaries clearly shrink.

Two, we can note the next interesting shared feature of the two systems which is that some manner of evolution is certainly occurring in both components of our model. Here, we will give "evolution" its most rudimentary definition of simply "any change occurring over time" and for our purposes in this metaphorical exercise will not refine it to mean only biological evolution,that is, evolution by natural selection, which is a far more detailed and intricate mechanism requiring the actual inheritance of characteristics and significant changes in allele frequencies.

The parallel of note in this feature is that characteristics in individuals tend to be both accurately and inaccurately copied in the next go-round's "lineup." The next generation's version of cell or of case might be very faithful to a progenitor as to some feature yet might exhibit a slight or major difference as to another. The children are like their parents but not quite like their parents. The questions which are then begged are "in what ways are they different?" and "what, if anything, is significant about the differences?"

In meiotically dividing cells, the different feature in the descendant cell that is distinct from the parent or grandparent cell has to arise at the genetic level to become transmitted forward at all. Noticing it is challenging: the change in genotype might be revealed in the cell's appearance, that is, its phenotype, or it might remain concealed in the genotype without getting expressed. Comparatively, in legal cases, the different feature in the descendant case distinct from the prior generation's case may arise in any aspect of the case from caption to verdict and an awareness of it might stem from a change in issues revealed via a court's decision but which may remain concealed and not expressed until well into the appellate phase or beyond. In cells, genotypes become altered by transcription and translation deformation-related phenomena such as mutation, crossing over, and linkage, whereas in cases legal issues become altered by such "transcription and translation deformation-related phenomena" as judicial interpretation, conflict of laws doctrines, law of the forum rules, preemption doctrines, and legislative repeal.

In sum, a cell's offspring may look nearly identical to, or deviate wildly from, its parents. So too with a case's offspring in relation to the next case "down the generational line." At any given snapshot in time, cells will look, morphologically, *like* each other, again each presenting structurally with membranes, walls, mitochondria, organelles, Golgi apparatus and the like. Similarly, at any given snapshot in time, cases will look, morphologically, like each other, again each presenting structurally with captions identifying the named parties and the forum, pleading forms identifying the factual allegations and legal claims for relief, discovery documents identifying the evidentiary basis for the pleadings, and the briefs and motions identifying the issues to be determined. As to their function, it becomes apparent that both cells and cases express a mixture of inconsequential and highly consequential functional distinctions from parent to offspring, distinctions which are sometimes but not always revealed in their overt physical forms or structures, yet the larger "significance" of which becomes transparent over time in witnessing their effects in and across their communities.

Expressing Preferences

The information in cases, by the way, is obviously transmitted by language use in general, though not just by *any* old language use but most specifically via the peculiar code in which trial lawyers speak as discussed above, including in the format of motions, advice, asides, and of course argument. Just as with cellular evolution, case evolution demands that mechanisms must exist in the law whereby novelty can be "globally" disseminated (horizontally exchanged), which include the implementation of a universal lawyer's code (a legalistic *lingua franca*) carried by a standard, generic translation apparatus of lawyer-speak directed to the client, to the lay public, to the jury, and to the decision-makers as the occasion requires.

The trial lawyer's code is definitely not boundless but rather has some "lex-ical" and lexical boundaries: it is composed of a terminology derivative of legal definitions which can't be ignored or dodged completely. No one rational, for example, would contest that an animal has a "body," and that depiction (and its stylistic associations and connections) may be and have been freely toyed with. Plenty of rational people, including judges and legislators, on the other hand, would vehemently deny that an animal's *dead* body is a "corpse." It is not[7]—it is at best "the remains" and at worst "a carcass" and the legal fact that statutory definitions circumscribe the terminology surrounding "corpses" to the remains of persons alone illustrate how words act as constraints on case evolution which cannot be circumvented by even the most creative of legal speakers. Akin to what the chemical composition of amino acids limits them to transmit to the next generation of cells, a legalistic *lingua franca* similarly imposes transmission parameters on its users.

A brief warning about the overextension of our model is appropriate here. It is true that informational content changes in subsequent generations are events that occur in case "reproduction" as they do in cell reproduction. It is also undeniable, however, that there is no one-to-one correspondence at all in our analogue about such changes since it is abundantly clear that the compared mechanics are wildly distinct: the transmission mechanism for cells is biochemical whereas the transmission mechanism for cases is via written scripts. Not just transfer in those disparate processes, but patterns of growth as well operate wildly differently from each other—a "mismatched concept comparison" problem that academics before me have recognized and tried to overcome:

> When I came to the point of describing the genesis of multicellular animals and plants from unicellular organisms, I was inspired to use Legos as a metaphor: the bricks represent the cells, and the most elaborate models, made up of hundreds of different pieces, represent complex animals and plants. For a biologist, this idea is preposterous. First of all, cells are so familiar to him or her that there is no need to describe them with metaphors. Further, the metaphor is peculiar because the elaboration of a living form is dynamic. The initial cell divides in two, the daughter cells then divide, and so forth. All the cells divide as an embryo grown into an individual. But the Lego bricks are static; they do not divide. To build a Lego model is to assemble preformed pieces according to a preconceived plan. This is true, but I also grant great importance to the didactic aspect of metaphors, to their power to aid understanding of abstract concepts.[8]

Nevertheless, in my metaphor and in spite of whether it is lengthy amino acid chains or it is lengthy typewritten pages that are being transferred from one lineage to the next, at least here both transmitter and receiver rely on effective conduits of valuable data regardless; they are not the static blocks of non-information which Legos embody. Both employ copying processes, none of which are fault-free. Both are interconnected with predecessors and ancestors in transfers across time and space. Both have the resulting generation's structure and functions impacted by the preceding generation's behaviors. The activities of transcription and translation of the chain acids happening within the core of a cell in order to produce a new cell is mimicked only conceptually by the transcription and translation of the relevant issues happening within the core of a case in order to produce useful legal issues and thus a decision in a new case. Messenger RNA is responsible for the former process and judges and juries are responsible for the latter process—yet existentially, information in both *is* transcribed and then translated in a complicated set of copying procedures among each to create new functioning organisms, in law or in life.

One more point with a comparison at the deeper, genotype level is worth noting in our model. Consider the replication of errors. In cell reproduction, where mutation or environmental effects cause RNA to miscode and production of the protein is thereby deformed, the standard outcome is simply death of the daughter cell.[9] Rarely, the miscoded data will survive into the next generation and impact the reproductive mechanisms of those which inherit it. Error is a source of variation and (unusually) speciation may be its result. So too, mistakes or local influences may cause a jury panel or judge to "misjudge" a claim and "deform" an issue, and the consequences of that manner of miscoding are by definition without significance if the case ends there (i.e., by not being appealed, aka the new protein is then never replicated). The effects, either small or large, of a novel proposition's propagation into an appellate opinion have the potential to impact descendant populations; other cases may follow the precedent and thereby be realigned or misaligned on some crucial legal point. Error is thus also a source of variation and (unusually) *entirely* new law may result. The entire phenomenon of "dissents" in judicial opinions in a sense reflects components of the case reproduction system trying to adjust (or at least memorialize) this manner of miscoding.[10]

Again, that sort of change is rare and requires propagation into a future generation: a clear mistake made in one case almost certainly will not be propounded in the regular course, and it is only where the appeal process empowers the novelty to be repeated may it then continue to reemerge in a line of cases, that is, may then spread across jurisdictions. The death (sometimes) of an old common law rule or the evolution (sometimes) of a new common law rule is thus ensconced in the evolving body of law as a function of both chance and of appeal and error, of larger scale genotypical changes across not just single case "ancestors" and single "descendants" but across generational waves of litigants. The result is that modified lineages are created in both parts of the model. The point is that each individual case's outcome has at least the capacity to warp or distort a rule of law such that law transforms as a consequence.

Again, we don't need our metaphor to be an exact homology or analogy in every respect to still be instructive and helpful: again, yes, cells employ the biochemistry of DNA and RNA to replicate and of course no clear exact correspondence can be envisioned there with the wildly disparate timing (millennia for cells versus years or decades for cases) and wildly disparate physical environments (bodies and populations for cells versus verdicts and reporters for cases) as to when and where cases "replicate." But scouring the model to postulate exact complements (demanding an exact match of functional ribosomes, say, with exasperated judicial clerks) misses the bigger venture of trying to identify useful insights into the nature of process itself in order to fashion large picture significance for the fundamental change occurring in either system. As trial lawyers, we should be most interested in trying to build an answer to "is anything valuable happening" to law over all these centuries of litigated and appealed cases. This inquiry is (or at least should be) interesting to us in large part because we are so intimately connected to procedures as motivating agents and because our vocation compels us to be existentially interested in trying to understand available answers to "is anything valuable happening" in sensitivity to our own clients' interests at this very moment.

Means Masquerading as Ends

That should bring us to our third and most interesting shared feature in line, which has to do with where the concept of teleology fits in with both systems, that is, if it is possible to explain each phenomenon in terms of the purposes they serve rather than of the mechanical methods and causes by which they arise.[11]

Note that with systems as to which there is a designer, it is the designer's purpose which (at least initially) drives the system toward its intended goal. Automobiles clearly have human designers and the express reason that cars look and operate the way they do is because car appearance and car handling are direct functions of human automobile designers intentionally wanting those phenomena to transpire. Actions taken along the way from a concept on a sketch pad to a test run on a track are all actions engaged in "on purpose," where the end product is adjudged to be a good or bad fit with the design insofar in as what resulted then accomplished or failed a certain goal of what completed automobiles are "supposed" to look like and do.

The scare quotes used on the words "purpose" and "supposed" are there because we recognize that designers put conscious effort into designs and designing. We can say, colloquially, that cars have "evolved" since their designs have changed over time, but those changes arose from two sources: human imagination and human conduct, and they "evolved" through a combination of the prior plans of humans and the subsequent selection by humans of different forms of cars based on trial and error.[12] Cells, without question, are not automobiles in that respect at all. There is no designer of cells. The reason that cells look and operate the way they do is not because any external supervisory power "wants" those things to transpire, and no entity's conscious effort into designs and designing exists in any manner. Actions taken along the way from membrane-entrapped mitochondria to meiotic divisions and beyond are actions driven by the blind, non-random, but also non-purposeful, process of evolution by natural selection, not by design. Cellular evolution has no plan.

Cases are in that way far, far more like cells than they are like cars. Every state certainly has a legislative body to propose and enact laws for cases to rely on. Every state certainly has a bar association to which lawyers must belong in order to practice law and pursue cases within that state. Across the country, there are plenty of professional organizations and legal associations purposely created, organized, and implemented to have lawyers discuss and apply law to clients and communities so that cases may perhaps better progress to their conclusions. In short, yes, there are many broad, unifying, "locally designed" forces at work in law as it goes about its business. But as to Law overall, there is no Designer. There is no grand overarching scheme to have all law "go" in any particular direction, to have all lawsuits and appeals as a cohesive unit express some core, jointly shared endpoint or common purpose.[13] Each separate case certainly incorporates rules that are very explicitly designed by legislators and jurists to have litigants reach certain goals within the case itself, but that "purposefulness" ends when the parties' dispute ends, at the verdict. The rules employed along the way are utilized to serve only internal ends, not external ones:

> The development of our law has gone on for nearly a thousand years, like the development of a plant, each generation taking the inevitable next step, mind, like matter, simply obeying a law of spontaneous growth. . . . In regard to the law, it is true, no doubt, that an evolutionist will hesitate to affirm universal validity for his social ideals, or for the principles which he thinks should be embodied in legislation. He is content if he can prove them best for here and now. He may be ready to admit that he knows nothing about an absolute best in the cosmos, and even that he knows next to nothing about a permanent best for men. Still it is true that a body of law is more rational and more civilized when every rule it contains is referred articulately and definitely to an end which it subserves, and when the grounds for desiring that end are stated or are ready to be stated in words.[14]

The absence of any design in that respect is not a hiccup in the system, is not because we just haven't gotten around to agreeing on one yet—to the contrary, we have seen already why this couldn't ever be in the first place. Any global, cross-community, or nation-wide project to have a shared legal goal would by definition require that cases, and thus lawyers, then align shoulder to shoulder with each other in fashioning and pursuing the identified common interest. But the core nature of the attorney-client relationship flatly and profoundly prohibits all that. There are no common interests in law possible which transcend self-interests. There are no common interests in representing clients possible which transcend the clients' interests. Self-interest by the client and the representative and interest protection are forces which must be directed individually, not collectively. Self-interest is "What is good for this particular client in this particular instance?" not "What is good for everybody all the time?" Self-interest in that respect is an acid, a socially healthy acid but viciously corrosive acid nonetheless, one that dissolves all attempts by any appointed cell designer to try to take hold of groups, to try to dictate the cells to join forces and march forward to a chosen end of justice or fairness or righteousness.[15] Case evolution has no plan because self-interest prevents cases as a whole from having a planner.

Protection of the client's individual interests through the case-by-case use of persuasion, argument, lying, and manipulation is what leads us to the key observation that neither system embodies any teleological explanations, that both are non-teleological and without any purpose or goal, that both enable large-scale effects to manifest without any drive or desire or purpose to have such exist.[16] There is real value in the metaphorical proposal that intellectual processes can run on the same track as biomechanical processes, a track devoted to serial informational exchanges and modifications, and that the track doesn't necessarily have to have an intended end station. Yet something immensely valuable develops, or rather emerges, out of it nonetheless. True for cells as it is true for cases.

Now we can appreciate that if the actual "biological" process by which *cases* replicate and evolve over time is by trial lawyer's argument, then tracing an argument's path from consult to pleading to motion to opening to examination to closing to trial opinion to appellate opinion can explain why cases grow in number and complexity but don't have a designed endpoint in the manner that cells grow in number and complexity but don't have a designed endpoint. (Any reader who might blanche at this interval and retort that in fact cells *do* have directed endpoints, that they *are* "supposed" to create tissues which lead to organs which lead to organisms—that is, who believe that some larger plan commands cells to have to ultimately become entire animals and plants—is a reader who simply seriously miscomprehends how evolution by natural selection in fact works.)

Again, evolutionary change does not occur in response to any particular need at all, but instead involves entirely undirected mutations which, when combined with a non-random difference in reproductive output among replicating entities (often due to differences in survival in a particular environment) happen to result in an increase in the proportion of beneficial, heritable characteristics within a population from one generation to the next.[17] Planning isn't part of it, nor is anything getting "better" or "worse" overall. In organismal biology changes occur to organisms not because there is any need or reason to have them occur but simply because a confluence of a small number of basic conditions of ecology and heredity, acting inside of a dynamically changing biotic and abiotic environment, naturally *make* them occur. *There is no direction.* In litigation, and similarly, changes occur not because there is any need or reason to have them occur but simply because a confluence of a small number of basic conditions of jurisdiction and appellate transmission, acting inside of a dynamically changing social and political environment, naturally make them occur. No force pushes Smith v. Jones forward to "lead" to Jones v. Smith coming into existence and either may stop or continue as the client interests within them stop or continue. *There is no direction.*

Signs and Portents

Let's look at this metaphor from a short distance as a helpful or unhelpful "narrative of correlation." Is the story of cell evolution truly on all fours with the story of case evolution? No, not by a long shot. Do they even share the same fact patterns or the same analytic themes allowing us to characterize them as functionally equivalent stories? Not really. But can a useful correspondence be located between their respective processes sufficient to viably compare their trajectories? Perhaps. If we simply and generically envision the underlying structures at work and the processes both undergo, then certain correspondences become disclosed which have some merit as comparisons. Accept that with both:

1. We can identify a progenitor unit enclosed by a barrier with clear contours where data outside the unit is brought across a threshold into the unit to be assembled.
2. During the assembly, the data inside the unit is then copied by a mechanism which utilizes a special language in order to do so.
3. The copying is done by writing down certain elements and converting them into a new data set which is then transferred back across the threshold so that a companion entity is constructed. Two or more entities exist where there was only one before.

4. Sometimes the copying to the new entity is faithful and sometimes it is less than faithful and the new data set inside the newly replicated entity reflects any similarities or transformations.
5. The new entity looks similar to but somewhat different from the first, and it repeats the assembly and copying processes. All of that is repeated again and again, creating subsequent generations of derived data sets.
6. Complexity grows with each new generation of entities and each generation is limited by that complexity to a narrower set of features.
7. The quantity of new data sets increases as opposed to decreases, and there is no end to the generations nor is there any overall design that any follow or any plan to fulfill.
8. Consequently, large-scale qualitative changes to the entire system emerge over time.

Note that the changes observed happening at stage 4 above is crucial in both systems: if all cases were truly on all fours, then the common law would grow *mitotically* and each case would be structurally identical to the next so there would be no change in proposition or in precedent. But we recognize that of course cases all have to have some distinctions among them, small and large, so growth is really *meiotically,* where new cases are only roughly the same and frequently quite different from their predecessors. Just as cell replication has no teleology, no purpose, so too cases brought and fought have no larger "purpose" toward which all are aimed, no designed mutually agreed upon goal they must seek as a cohesive unit to reach some consensus as an endpoint.

Forums for disputes, that is, jurisdictions, do not coordinate with each other to synchronize cases so that each case's progress and conclusions mesh with each other. Jurists, that is, the decision-makers inside of jurisdictions, do not coordinate with each other to fashion national or global objectives so that their decisions mesh. And lawyers do not coordinate with each other in composing some grand scheme of representing clients and pursuing client interests as a cohesive network of joint lawyering; they just each bring their own cases as a function of individual lawyering as a paid profession, one being engaged in by countless individuals driven by social and economic forces to make a living busy with learning about laws, deploying laws, and changing laws while doing so. Politics impinge. Social networks impinge. Market changes impinge. Personal lives impinge. Each lawyer is battered on all sides by unrelenting influences acting to form and deform their lawyerly trajectory through jurisprudential space. And each doggedly "lawyers on" as an individual, not as a group, project.

That all their cases share very common structural elements, such as the insertion of case captions and the use of pleading paper and the payment of filing fees, for lawyers those are all artefacts of simply how court rules and legislated procedures impose organizational requirements on them as they promote their projects. That their cases share common intellectual elements, such as factual allegations and legal theories and evidence needing to be formally admitted into the court record through offered exhibits, those are all artefacts of a judicial system in general that must account for contests to be decided in a regimented and formalistic fashion so the projects have some structure to them. That their cases share common institutional elements, such as reported decisions and money judgments and case precedent, those are artefacts of a judicial system as well, but are also, in a sense, merely accidental by-products that aren't mandatory elements of law at all. It isn't really required for a case to be concluded by judgment; every trial lawyer will tell you that for every case that gets to a final judgment, a hundred quite similar cases never made it nearly that far but instead resolved privately through settlement or were dismissed or abandoned for one reason or another. Even without a judgment in hand, law was still employed, application of law still directly controlled the outcome, and legal issues still affected both the client and the trajectory of the next subsequent case.

"For The Sake Of Argument" and Arguments Forsaken

The combined effect of all those phenomena—of the captions and fees and allegations and judgments—of all those individual efforts by individual actors with their own individual agendas, are efforts which result in a larger consequence of the law reaching back and itself transforming and reflecting social and economic change. The whole is greater than the sum of its parts and Argument makes that greater whole happen. So: the trial lawyer's opening and closing, though not deliberately directed to achieving any large-scale change (and in fact many of which warn directly *against* large-scale change), nevertheless still creates large-scale change—just as the cells replicating and joining together into tissues and then organs and then organ systems and then organisms are not deliberately directed to "achieving" organisms and species at all, yet nevertheless still produce an immensely powerful effect of constructing organisms and species and populations and ecosystems, that is, some of the largest scale environmental changes that there are in the world.

Don't disregard that it is not just rigorous or effective argument which accomplishes this magical transformation, it is also bad argument and *meh* argument and entirely forgotten or ignored argument as well. As there is no editor for case reporters, there is no stage director for cases or trials, no orchestration is engaged in, no debate or Olympic judges assign scores to presentations, no quality control manager weighs in with a quarterly report with a list of suggestions on how to fine-tune next session's arguments to be stronger. Yet the music and drama of persuasion leading to the development and evolution of law nonetheless ultimately issues. In other words, it isn't really that "bad cases make bad law," it's simply that "bad cases make law" just as good and mid cases do also.

All the manipulation we have been talking about is at the microscopic level and is relatively chaos-driven by the self-interest of a million different people who, as they manipulate words and objects and people, seek client goals important only to that particular client. As with cells however, blind forces in law have large-scale macroscopic effects and impacts sufficient to make entire new legal organisms—in our instance new legal propositions and principles. More important, however, is the observation that Argument is a process and as such generates detailed forms called new lawyers and new laws as it unfolds. But it is the *process* of argument, not the lawyers themselves as they undergo the argumentation process, that must be highlighted as the explanatory force for case evolution.

With cases envisioned akin to cells, then Argument ripples through cellular and intercellular spaces alike. Persuasion in the form of style propagates outward through the cytoplasm pushing cases along with it. Words call forth effects and are the universal means of influencing human beings everywhere. Inside the realm of law where words cascade endlessly as attempts to influence particular groups of human beings, stand lawyers using style to further their cases. Style affects rules, it affects the application of rules, it affects the effectiveness of rules, it affects the proliferation of rules. None of its effects are planned. The legal representatives in the mix—the purveyors of style questioning the jury pool, examining the witnesses, delivering opening and closing arguments, moving the court, and angling for decisions—they are only refractions in the propagating waves of styles. Their effects are secular and peculiar to advancing clients' interests individually and alone, and the process transcends them.

Is what is new *better*? No. While judgments cannot exist without arguments to found them (and judges to use them as controlled by trial lawyers who offer up cases to judges in order to hear and consider them) the link between the quality of the argument and the quality of the corresponding judgment is tenuous to say the least. The accretion of arguments forms the foundation for the accretion of judgments but a mere change in quantity is of course not always accompanied by a corresponding change in quality.[18] A plethora of opinions in the 70s on civil rights, all lawyer argument inspired, didn't transform civil rights law as some sort of progression from bad to better—it just increased complexity and expanded boundaries without necessarily making the content inside those boundaries purposeful. Spoiler for idealists: civil rights law is not a cohesive and well-organized project by committed participants toward a committed endpoint all devoted to enshrining rigorous civil rights principles in all of society; it is far, far messier than that.[19] All of that nobility is an artificial construct. Many decisions were poor, or selfish, or mundane—the main result was that there were a lot and that new cases and new arguments arose and evolved from them as the source, and some (though many would say not nearly enough) social enlightenment effects ensued as consequential reverberations.

Trial lawyers choose. Trial lawyers argue *facts* by selection and by emphasis. Trial lawyers argue *law* by selection and by emphasis. From the environmental primordial soup of facts and law floating freely outside of the case's "membrane," which adaptive pressures compel trial lawyers to pick from, attend to, or disregard, issues for determination then form. Internally the issues are transcribed and translated for the juror to assimilate and themselves transform into a decision. The juror is presumed to be interested in choosing between two offerings by opposing "organelles" but of course there is nothing (including in the unfolding and folding of those other message-transmitting instruments called jury instructions) that compel the choice; it may be that jurors build their own protein, or combine the offerings, or decline to accept the offerings (nullify) and instead produce decisions from their own desires and beliefs.

There is some small transparency—we can review verdicts and can ask jurors afterward how they "reasoned to their conclusion," that is, how they came to reach that verdict, through logic or emotion or common sense or otherwise. But much is still necessarily opaque in such a complex system—with no formal mechanism or legal obligation to *have* to explain the basis for their decision, the other elements in the process, the litigants, lawyers, and court, are as blind as to how the jury truly got there as they are blind to its true impact: what the effect might be tomorrow, or to the other guy down the hall, or at a larger socially significant scale to everyone in a specific community.

The high-level observable properties of multicellular organisms can be discerned as *emergent* properties in that what is being observed are features both determined by, yet at the same time distinct from, lower-level features, the astronomical number of cells and cellular coalitions transpiring inside of them.[20] Individual cell level events and interactions lead to cell wall rigidity, elasticity, permeability, energy transport, waste disposal, and so on, which in turn lead to cell growth, cell differentiation, and cell associations which in turn lead to tissues and organs which in turn lead to whole organisms. But the distinctive nature of what a whole organism *is* and how it *behaves* only arises when its fundamental components combine in a certain fashion; significance sourced at the microscopic level becomes a quite different significance at the macroscopic level.

In the way that we can explain the existence of organisms as emergent phenomena, we can then also try to explain the existence of Law as emergent from its compositional pieces: the upper-level behavior of case law is contingent on, arises out of, yet differs from the lower-level behaviors of the various individual cases. Like organisms, case law behavior has an etiology but is unique unto itself, conjoining dependence (on the microscopic core operative facts and initiated legal theories) and autonomy (its decisions and precedents transcending each individual case). The emergence phenomenon arises from all the complexity created by the energy transporting and waste disposing of the individual laws by lawyer organelles scurrying about pushing and pulling all their individual filings and motions so that a decision-maker will pay attention to them.

That is one reason why the significance of a verdict obtained at the close of a jury trial can take on a whole new life beyond the peculiar value it had to the participants to whom it was first delivered. Non-parties marvel at the million-dollar award to the customer litigant scalded by hot coffee at the diner in large part simply because of the sum awarded being such a large one. Yet to lawyers the sum's larger meaning may be as a diffraction of what is known about far smaller verdicts issued before it, what is believed verdicts in general are supposed to essentially reflect as to sensible impositions of liability and sensible calculations of damages, and what models of social interaction it is felt that jury trials and their resultant verdicts are supposed to universally reflect. The large sum might encourage another lawyer to pursue a similar sounding claim. It might instigate a legislative body to enact a new statute restricting damages awards. It might be vaguely recalled by a juror in another case as they ponder in deliberation on some suit they sit on. It might be inserted by an appellate panel in a reviewed case as a cautionary tale or guidepost for valuation. The influence is as far-reaching as it is unpredictable.

Because of their emergent nature, however, individual verdicts can only be "explained" as much or as little as the combined effect of the components leading up to them can be "explained," an intensely difficult task. Any trial lawyer with a pretty good handle on the machinations of how the civil procedure rules work in light of a particular judge's proclivities can predict (mostly) what will happen to a specific pleading issue that is challenged via a specific motion in a specific case. The predictability quotient of small-scale events occurring in a lawsuit is not that difficult to calculate and is a function of legal knowledge and principled rule applications—small level bits of information used to solidly pin down the wind-blown outer edges of small level processes.

In contrast, no trial lawyer anywhere can exactly predict a jury verdict regardless of the amount of knowledge or experience they might hold, or how well they think they know people or law.[21] Verdicts, like tornados and presidential elections, are large-scale events affected by too many data points and outside influences, the emergence of complexity whose components include (for verdicts anyway) both the employment as well as the reception of style, that truly indefinable quality we have examined above and which cannot truly be accurately estimated, measured, or weighed. What will the trial lawyer arguing in closing "do" with the outrageously *recherche* answer provided by the star witness? What will each juror "do" with what the trial lawyer chooses to say or not say about that answer? What will the jurors as a group "do" with what the other jurors think about each trial lawyer's take on, or failure to address, the answer? There is no equation to implement, there is no analytic framework to apply to ballast such types of predictions to even a likelihood much less a moral certainty.

When case law is viewed as the product of Argument creating and being created by laws applied to a host of individuals over the broad span of time and across jurisdictions, even less prediction is available. At our moment in jurisprudential time as we stand right now, we cannot really know what is essential and what is accessory to the evolution of the law. Time may bring a total revision of legal concepts such as then reveal our present outlook as unnecessary, our present questions as misdirected, or our present difficulties as entirely illusory. We can at least recognize that the forces at work are far more than "blind chance" alone—there is *some* non-designed rhyme and reason to law's evolution. It is almost certainly not that which mirrors a pursuit of justice, nor is it likely out of some grand scheme of social good that the community as a whole has planned out to be constructed. It is more the fruition of patterns observed in the scramble of personal interests being pursued, it is more the expressions of style from individual lawyers as they manipulate and promote private interests doing so by blending arguments across their own personal time and space.

Notes

1 I am certainly not the first author to propose modeling a socio-political system off a bio-physical one:

> [T]he curious pattern which (social atomism) traces of unrelated human units milling around in a social vacuum echoes very closely the equally strange pattern of unrelated Democritean atoms spinning in the void.

Midgley, Mary. *Science and poetry*. Routledge, 2013 at p. 69.

2 Woese, Carl R. "On the evolution of cells." *Proceedings of the National Academy of Sciences* 99, no. 13 (2002): 8742–7.
3 Ibid.
4 Ibid.
5 Ibid.
6 As the pathologist Rudolph Virchow observed, "*Omnis cellula e cellula*" (all cells only arise from pre-existing cells).
7 The term "corpse" is universally defined in law dictionaries as "[t]he dead body of a human being." See, *Ballentine's Law Dictionary* (3d ed.1969); State v. Hill, 333 SW3d 106, 135 (Tenn Crim App 2010).
8 Meinesz, Alexandre. *How life began: evolution's three geneses*. University of Chicago Press, 2019 at pp. 143–4.
9 See, e.g., Yan, Liewei L., and Hani S. Zaher. "How do cells cope with RNA damage and its consequences?" *Journal of Biological Chemistry* 294, no. 41 (2019): 15158–71.
10 See, Ginsburg, Ruth Bader. "The role of dissenting opinions." *Minnesota Law Review* 95 (2010): 1.
11 See generally, Woodfield, Andrew. *Teleology*. Cambridge University Press, 1976.
12 See, Williams, George C. *Plan and purpose in nature*. Weidenfeld and Nicholson, 1996.
13 In fairness, there are a few institutions and proponents which put considerable effort into certain limited types of attempts, such as with the "Restatements of the Law" produced by the American Law Institute, "model codes" propounded by the ABA, and several legal treatises on the topic published by academics. The uniformity to which those authors aim, however, is primarily to counter the unfairness of provinciality, a wish to apply law regularly across a confusing patchwork of jurisdictional boundaries; the homogeneity of rules alone is their goal, not the attainment of some grand decisional endpoint for all lawyers and their cases.
14 Holmes, Oliver Wendell. "The path of the law." *Harvard Law Review* 110, no. 5 (1897) at pp. 51–2, reprinted in Beth, Loren P. *Landmarks of law. Highlights of legal opinion* (R.D. Henson, ed.). Harper & Brothers, 1960.
15 As Holmes further noted, with court cases "the means do not exist for determinations that shall be good for all time [and] the decision can do no more than embody the preference of a given body in a given time and place." Ibid., at p. 47.
16 See generally, Nagel, Ernest. *Teleology revisited and other essays in the philosophy and history of science*. Columbia University Press, 1979.
17 Gregory, T. Ryan. "Understanding natural selection: essential concepts and common misconceptions." *Evolution: Education and Outreach* 2, no. 2 (2009): 156–75.
18 Cf., Carlson, David Gray. "Hegel's Theory of Quantity." *Cardozo Law Review* 22, no. 2 (January 2001) at pp. 425–594.
19 See, e.g., Halpern, Stephen C. *On the limits of the law: The ironic legacy of Title VI of the 1964 Civil Rights Act*. JHU Press, 1995.
20 This section is taken in part from O'Connor, D.J. "Emergent properties." In *Old and new questions in physics, cosmology, philosophy, and theoretical biology: Essays in honor of Wolfgang Yourgrau*. Springer US, 2015, at pp. 719–32.
21 Cf. Miller, Michael Owen, and Thomas A. Mauet. "The psychology of jury persuasion." *American Journal of Trial Advocacy* 22 (1998): 549.

Conclusion

In spite of still perhaps being recorded on some reporter's transcript somewhere, the large majority of trial lawyers' arguments are all effectively long gone, words that were at one time critically important to speaker and audience in the heat of their transmission, yet which have slowly cooled of noteworthiness and import by the inexorable passage of the cases of which they were a part. A minute few have been preserved as part of the literature of history,[1] but all others are ignobly discarded, persuasions deposited into the dustbins of the past by time and smothered into extinction by indifference.

Each individual argument is necessarily transient since each is a product of a very specific private dispute between combatants who have since moved onto other conflicts. Once the court day is over and the lights to the courtroom turned off, there is no good reason for the arguments made on another's behalf to have survived past a dispute that eventually was resolved to someone's satisfaction. Individual cases necessarily have their ends sooner or later, and thus so do the individual arguments which drove and were driven by those individual cases. Since the remaining value of those ends is as legal precedent for the next case (if even that), their attendant impassioned arguments—if preserved at all—persist at best as fragmented extracts mentioned in the footnotes and asides of later judicial opinions.[2]

But in *toto*, they have all become Argument and as such are not just well preserved but well installed as a fundamental feature of the legal landscape. As the critic Scott Romine said of the poetry of Ella Wheeler Wilcox, "If her poetry has not survived as art, it retains for the cultural historian its value as artifact."[3] So too could the same be said as to every opening and closing ever made—individually none are uniquely recalled, but collectively all combine to manifest one of the strongest expressions of intellectual and social freedom our society has ever constructed. While the famous ones have a modest cultural value as templates for future proposals and models of past ideas, the doctrine of Argument itself being a conduit for manipulating beliefs through the selfish management of words, rules, people, and objects is absolutely transformative.

It is in this respect that cases *in toto* and lawyers *in toto* do not have their end at all even as individual instances terminate—participants retire or die but both Cases and Lawyers continue to be produced. The operation of our legal system continues to not just allow them, but to require them. As the highlight for the cell biologist committed to grasping cell evolution is on the processes, not on the particular cells engaging in those processes, so too the highlight for the Lawyer as legal philosopher committed to grasping case evolution is on the processes, not on the particular lawyers and cases engaged in those processes.

Legal argument is speech at once both raw and refined, people speaking freely but not freely, whether in versions notable or versions forgotten. Its evolution tracks the way speech in general has evolved, and integral to the appreciation of legal argument is its "free yet not free" aspect. In the movie *The Contender*, Joan Allen's character defends to Jeff Bridges' character her obstinacy in protecting private information about herself at the crucial point of the plot's political conflict, saying "Principles only mean something when you stick to them when it is inconvenient."[4] Her comment resonates with the larger notion that the First Amendment to the US Constitution embodies several core principles, not the least of which expresses our profound respect for the freedom to speak (or in Allen's case, refrain from speaking) including about one's past, one's present, or one's mind. As her character infers, that freedom is usually made most concrete and real when the message presented is one that (a) carries with it attendant costs to the speaker for making it, (b) is inconvenient and uncomfortable for others to hear, and (c) contains assertions that may be outrageous, ridiculous, or downright horrid. When it comes to presenting messages, none of those conditions are foreign to trial lawyers.

Freedoms tend to be extremely messy things. For the most part, they don't fit neatly into easily consumable packets and don't get expressed well in prepared sound bites, in thoughtful judicial comments, in cleverly constructed movie quotes, or in formal legal language on complicated documents.[5] A good mental image of the free speech right, for instance, is much more an awkward patchwork of vivid, discomforting whisperings, of lurid, wincing outbursts. In the animal law world, it might be expressed through a client's conspiratorial hiss of a fervent wish that their own dog were dead; a back-of-the-courtroom observer's offhand mouthing of spite about a mentally ill defendant's neglect of his sick horse; a witness's tearful recrimination after leaving the stand that her friend lied about the pet's purchase; an activist's irrational diatribe that a cattle owner should suffer the same as his cattle; or through a veterinarian's gleeful phone message promising to kill a client's cat should the spay bill not be paid by noon.

None of these words are easy to hear, nor are really productive, nor very informative, nor certainly noble in any sense, yet all are protected and given their own intrinsic value by the First Amendment. Moreover, every one of those despicable emanations (and worse and better) can be and are parroted by the advocate—and not just parroted, but of course also reformed, reimagined, and reworked to prove a self-interested point or convince an uninterested decision-maker to become interested in arriving at a decision.

In parallel, Argument is an extremely messy thing which also doesn't fit neatly into the frame of an easily consumable concept. The standout among those speech expressions is the trial lawyer's argument to the jury in opening and closing and their arguments to the court within the interstices of a litigated case. Equally protected and given intrinsic value by the First Amendment, lawyer arguments accomplish an unplanned but powerful social objective—communal mind control by communally approved mind controllers called legal representatives to produce communal versions of individual justice. The "good" that such controllers accomplish is not the facile and sophomoric good which the schoolchild is taught or which the legislator stumps for. It is a more complex and sophisticated good that folds justice in on itself and marks self-interest as something other than simply pejorative. It is a good that carries with it attendant costs to the speaker for constructing it. It is a good which was inconvenient and uncomfortable for others to hear. It is a good embellished by outrageous, ridiculous, or downright horrid assertions.

Freedom, in order to work effectively as a social construct, thus also requires manipulation. For real freedoms to have effect, language must be manipulated, as must people, and as must the universe of objects with which people construct and surround themselves. Comparable to money, cars, food, and homes, we have readily observed that dogs are heavily manipulated objects which people willfully insert into their daily lives. Emotions are wrapped up in them, resources are expended on them, and relationships are transformed by them. We have noted that with dogs and people, the *creation* of tension is more often the largest effect as opposed to the *release* of tension. Both species are impacted. Expression is impacted. Freedoms of all varieties are impacted as well. There is no question that innumerable dog-lovers wish grave ill to dog-haters (or at least people who do not control their dogs) and will proudly proclaim so on a plethora of websites, e-mail strings, editorials, and online blogs. There is also no question that their right to so proclaim is protected and made real by the First Amendment, and that the hammer that strikes at the off-leash owner brings its head down uncomfortably close to the proclaimers' own pens and keyboards sufficient to jostle them as they write and type.

In turn, a fluctuation of behavioral suites tying dogs to people transpires: As goes the owner of the dog who bites, so goes the owner of the dog who *almost* bites, or *wants* to bite but has not bitten yet, or for whom biting is simply a far away future wish currently unfulfilled. As goes the lawyer for the owner of the dog who bites, so goes the lawyer for the owner of the dog who almost bites, or wants to bite but has not bitten yet, or for whom biting is simply a far away future wish currently unfulfilled. As the manipulations propagate, respective freedoms to act and not act, to expose truths and to hide truths, become constructed. In expressing themselves to the world, dogs and dog owners experience a conceptual pressure on their lives of far greater import than any physical pressure either owner or victim may have experienced in the bite incident itself.

"Principles only mean something when you stick to them when it is inconvenient." It is extremely "inconvenient" for all sorts of people—in the immediate and harsh sense that being found responsible for a dog's behavior happens to be a major inconvenience—to ponder whether a litigant is at fault. It is nearly impossible to recognize any "principle" involved in actually making dogs behave poorly, but it is not that difficult at all to recognize serious principles involved in possessing and being responsible for poorly behaving dogs. Socrates' plea of "Know thyself" encapsulates the innate human drive to observe all that goes on in the world, to try to understand what one can of the world's myriad complexities, and to grapple with unweaving the tangles and consequences of the deviant and aberrant behavior of other people (or of oneself). In order to gain some insight into integral facets of that complexity, we will almost certainly make ourselves uncomfortable as we confront realities of human behavior and human evolution. Person-dog interactions bring into sharp focus the discomfort and importance of knowing that people have been hurt and might again be hurt by what other people do, and bring into even sharper focus the need for effective advocacy to advance the personal interests of those who hurt others and who are themselves hurt.

Argument is as crucially important to the way we express ourselves in law as the First Amendment is to the way we express ourselves in general. Both legal speech and free speech are communal phenomena. Both require a social context, neither exist outside of their social context, and each in a sense *create* new social contexts as well. As the legal scholar Professor James Boyd White observed: "The law is an art of persuasion that creates the objects of its persuasion, for it constitutes both the community and the culture it commends."[6] Argument in law, and the manipulation required to give it life (especially in a jury trial), has its inconveniences, its supreme frustrations, and its defects. None of those override the freedom it gives to the key participants in legal disputes, the trial lawyers, to try to control public outcomes in the service of representing and protecting private individuals.

As freedom consists in the ability and opportunity to act in conformity with one's wishes, desires, and preferences, the trial lawyer as representative on a public stage must not be denied both ability and opportunity to exercise every semantic tool imagined. Deception is an important one, and it is tyranny to shame, proscribe, or eliminate its use. Were the inconvenience and the purportedly moral concerns about lying leveraged to dismantle the trial lawyer's power to argue and manipulate, the consequences would cause a destructive impact to how knowledge works, how information ebbs and flows among the members of a democracy, and also to how individual interests are imparted value as key components of how the public mind expresses itself in resolving the disputes of its members.

Legal argument also tracks the way "doing science" in general has evolved, and equally integral to the appreciation of legal argument is its "scientific yet not scientific" aspect. Lawyers postulate, like scientists. Lawyers offer tentative or provisional explanations to explain a set of observed facts, like scientists. Lawyers propose intelligent guesses, grounded in past knowledge, to forecast the results of manipulating variables about those facts, like scientists. Most comparably, lawyers will float ideas for possibly meaningful relationships which might exist between those variables, pondering out loud if perhaps one thing is on all fours with another thing, just like scientists. Walter Probert, a law professor who wrote regularly on lawyer communication, mused carefully over the notion that law, like science, has its own special semantics, its own "language." In his admonition that lawyers need to be "aware of the complexities and subtleties of language," he illuminated how adherents in the respective disciplines both construct explanations of the world through their use of special dialects:

> [H]umans do not react simply to sentences. Rather they react to sentences in context, not only the immediate verbal context of the sentence but the larger environmental context, as well as the predispositional context of the person reacting. [T]he lawyer as advocate is not looking for emotions but for patterns of organization, for orientations . . . the trick is to master language itself to the point that the language structures which are built correlate with the structures of the nonverbal world environment to make for maximal predictability and adaptation.[7]

Yet doing *true* science also requires much more. Conducting experiments, testing data, falsifying theories, and conducting peer review of published results (among many other things), are all activities which no lawyer even thinks about since there is no need to. The "science" which trial lawyers engage in at the threshold of a case when they first model, formulate, and announce their postulate stops shifts to the "art" of manipulating others' minds in order to have others simply *accept* a postulate flat out as a subjective belief. Argument doesn't test for objective truth since empirical proof is extraneous to the goal.

The use of reason, on the other hand, isn't extraneous. Lawyers whose cases involve animals in particular tend to find scientific reasoning highly advantageous to attaining their persuasion goals. For instance, the Covid-19 pandemic revealed how a zoonosis could create extreme legal and political discomfort for us about interpersonal exchanges—not just exchanges of organic materials in transmitting the disease *between* us and animals, but exchanges of informational power *among ourselves* about our biological status in relation to animals.[8] Covid awareness efforts were met with significant backlash across a variety of social spectra by many insinuating that scientific reasoning might somehow harm rather than help policy decisions to be made about those exchanges. That backlash was an offshoot of a much broader effort by the ignorant to denounce science in general and evolutionary relationships specifically.

It is a denunciation which can find a foothold wherever there is the rejection of reason, including in law.[9] It wasn't just that organic and power exchanges occurring in the recent pandemic levied threats to our physical well-being. It was that our reactions to those exchanges levied threats to our democratic and jurisprudential well-being as well—by threatening to derail the use of scientific reasoning and legal mechanisms in combating, in controlling, those exchanges.

It is, all of it, a combat between influence and intellect. Hidden behind and between the words which legislators and jurists employ in statutes, ordinances, court cases, and appellate opinions, are existential dangers. They might come in the form of deliberate or inadvertent neglect, poor reasoning, definitional distortion, promotion of folk law beliefs, or religious myopia as to just what animals are. All have the potential to advance anti-scientific attitudes and irrational legal precedents as to both people and animals into the future. Some of the most immediate dangers arise simply from the common citizen's unfamiliarity with scientific reasoning in the first place:

> [There] seems to be a significant disconnect between the nature of the world as reflected in everyday experience and the one revealed by systematic scientific investigation. . . . Intuitive interpretations of the world, though sufficient for navigating daily life, are usually fundamentally at odds with scientific principles.[10]

Revealing epistemological and ontological flaws in the artificial human/animal distinctions which many laws promote, in light of what evolution informs us is actually the case, is one of the remarkable benefits yet undirected effects of Argument. At a basic level, without individual lawyers even knowing or planning to do so, the true and untrue and partially true words with which all trial lawyers manipulate others in the courtroom environment are words that assist in *allaying* further uncertainty and confusion in applying biological principles to animals and ourselves as biological objects.

Anti-science is (a) the rejection of mainstream scientific views and methods and (b) replacement of the same with unproven or deliberately misleading theories, both actions often being taken for political gain.[11] Although anti-science proponents primarily target scientists and attempt to discredit scientific projects, neither lawyers nor law are somehow exempt from such attacks. Anti-science has emerged as a dominant and highly lethal force, and one that threatens global security, as much as does terrorism or nuclear proliferation. It is a force directed against ways of knowing; it seeks to eviscerate knowledge.

The practice of law is a classic way in which social groups learn about themselves through publicizing conflicts among their members. Legal knowledge, and thus social knowledge, is intimately entangled within the mechanisms we have developed to present and resolve those disputes. Because the presentments and the resolutions are accomplished by speech, then an anti-science attack on knowledge operates as an attack on speech itself. Allen's character from *The Contender* would easily recognize such a threat. A good trial lawyer should themselves recognize the threat as they propose not just an inconvenient principle, but a downright awful one as they maneuver to sway their jury panel. The meaningfulness inherent in sticking to principles when it is inconvenient to do so is a staple of nearly every trial.

And since we know that trial is speech (even if of an intricately engineered sort), then any counteroffensive against anti-science must include trial lawyers. One way to mount such a counteroffensive and build new infrastructure to combat anti-science, is to support the peculiar forms of free speech bubbling up from the messy froth of trials. In the sense that anti-science is a movement directed against empiricism and logic as analytical tools in specific disciplines, the trial lawyer may likely maintain a sympathetic but removed disinterest. To the extent that it is a movement directed against empiricism and logic as tools of public expression and individual problem solving, however, those sympathies should transform into opprobrium and challenge since the movement's destructive force then directly impacts legal practices, and in turn communal interests.

Cultural perceptions about lawyers shift back and forth from regaling them as highly respected guardians of the public trust, to scorning them as charlatans and cheap con artists of the lowest degree, as well as to all points in between. The child's lie might be attributable to, and excused on account of, a labeling mistake or an error in basic comprehension—not so for the trial lawyer. The clergyman's baseless promise might be attributable to, and excused on account of, the fervor of raw belief or being possessed by an institutionally acceptable passion about eradicating perceived social evils—but the trial lawyer gets no such absolution. Trial lawyers are full on adults, are in full control of their own faculties, are fully responsible for their own words, and via state-regulated licenses are granted extensive power, incentive, and inclination to assist others unique in comparison to all other professions and industries.

It's just that their laser beam gaze happens to be persistently directed toward a minute but special subset of the public, the client, and their laser beam goal-directed behavior happens to be persistently aligned, not with large ideals such as Truth, but with small pedestrian realities such as prevailing party awards, and motions for judgment of acquittal, and signed but not yet officially entered court orders. In the odd stage/ecosystem that is the courtroom, their influence exerts itself by using argument to manipulate a public subgroup, the jury, and to employ cascading magnitudes of rules and procedures to locate, pursue, and obtain a remedy for one citizen as that remedy sits clutched in the hands of other citizens. Lawyers are a convergence of persuaders whose self-interested and client-directed persuasions arise from old social compacts to evolve new ones. They are powerful social forces, whether they know it or not. As actors, stagehands, directors, and playwrights, the styles they adopt and express not only is, but needs to be, their expression and their existence "roled" into one. The law that they manage individually and which manages them collectively in turn is an emerging and evolving resource for the community to protect.

One litmus test for an effective closing is whether the speaker calls back to any grand promises they might have made in opening to address how the evidence adduced during the proceeding then ended up fulfilling their predictions (or at least leaving their opponent's predictions wanting). My very first claims comprised a set of bold implications that capitalization distinctions about "lawyers" and "argument" and "law" would all be given their proper significance. So, what exactly unfolded in that regard? Well, consider that I provided you considerable authority for cultivating a few new definitions:

Lowercase "lawyers" refers to this: individual citizens who are licensed and authorized to represent other citizens in public disputes.

Uppercase "Lawyers," in high contrast, refers to this: large cohorts of complex social devices all machined by competing influences of self-interest, the interests of others, profit motives, and professional aspirations to use techniques sourced from specialized education and experience in order to design peculiarly tailored modes of persuasion which will hopefully alternately raise or bury a series of relative "truths," and to talk through a filter of various styles where they pretend to be others, all in order to achieve discrete goals for both others and for themselves in spite of whether society-wide goals happen to be benefited or harmed in the process.

Lowercase "argument" refers to this: A (some person) and B (some other person) each trying to convince the other that each is right about topic X.

Uppercase "Argument," in high contrast, refers to this: A (a Lawyer), while pretending to be B (a client), trying to convince C (a jury) via style that B is right about topic X and that D (another Lawyer) is wrong about topic X, while D, pretending to be E (another client), is trying to convince C via style that E is right about topic X and that A is wrong about topic X, all while F (a judge) supervises all of A through E.

Lowercase "law" refers to this: an ever-changing collective of rules of grammar and syntax; rules of professional responsibility and ethics; local rules; codified city ordinances, county codes, state and federal administrative regulations, state and federal statutes, evidence codes, and state and federal constitutions; legislative proclamations;

reported and recorded common law; unwritten hometown courtroom policies; and published learned treatises and review articles.

Upper case "Law," in high contrast, refers to this: The cumulative social effect of generations of A's, B's, C's D's, E's, and F's (and higher echelons of F's) engaged in uppercase "Argument" about millions of X's in which the curbing of each participant by the content and boundaries of lowercase "law" results in dramatic changes to both content and boundaries over time.

The X in *this* book is that Argument requires deceit by Lawyers and that Law in turn derives its force and its value from Lawyers in Argument employing that deceit. And seriously now, I really mean it, no more joking, I will swear on a stack of bibles that you've absolutely got to believe me because without a doubt I am totally telling you 110 percent candidly, as God is my witness, that here is the actual, honest, and real deal truth: X is so.

Notes

1 Among these are William Wirt's prosecution of Aaron Burr in Burr's 1814 trial for high treason. When defense counsel advanced the theory that Burr was simply a victim of a co-defendant's scheme, Wirt decimated the proposal by painting for the jury a heartbreaking portrait of the co-defendant's life having been cruelly coopted by Burr instead:

> In a short time, the whole man is changed, and every object of his former delight is relinquished. No more he enjoys the tranquil scene; it has become flat and insipid to his taste. His books are abandoned. His retort and crucible are thrown aside. His shrubbery blooms and breathes its fragrance upon the air in vain; he likes it not. His ear no longer drinks the rich melody of music; it longs for the trumpet's clangor and the cannon's roar. Even the prattle of his babes, once so sweet, no longer affects him; and the angel smile of his wife, which hitherto touched his bosom with ecstasy so unspeakable, is now unseen and unfelt . . . [W]e find her shivering at midnight on the wintry banks of the Ohio and mingling her tears with the torrents that froze as they fell.

From Morris, Charles. *Famous orators of the world and their best orations*. WE Scull, 1902 at p. 72.

2 For example, see Guertin v. Town of Hudson, 71 NH 505, 53 A 736, 737–38 (1902) where the Supreme Court of New Hampshire quoted the following from the closing argument of counsel for defendants and held that it was proper in being warranted by the evidence and in being within the bounds of legitimate advocacy upon the issue of the plaintiff's contributory negligence:

> Married women, ready for a debauch, ready for the purpose that these young men have in their hearts when they start out that night! And the four, filled with liquor and lust, start on their dirty purpose almost at dead of night, with the wind blowing twelve miles an hour, upon a rough, hard, and terrible road; and before they get to the place of their destination the party is broken up by

> an accident, when, according to their own confession, one of the two men had drunk four times of beer and whisky, and the other four times of beer, and as we have proved, a fifth time of whisky; filled themselves with whisky and beer, whisky and beer, and nobody knows what else, and how much else.

3 Bain, Robert A., ed. *Whitman's & Dickinson's contemporaries: an anthology of their verse*. SIU Press, 1996 at pp. 379–80.

4 *The Contender*. Paramount Pictures, 2000.

5 "The only problem with unrestricted choice, however, is that it tends not to lie so far from unrestricted chaos." De Botton, Alain. *The architecture of happiness*. Vintage, 2008 at p. 44.

6 White, James Boyd. *Heracles' bow: Essays on the rhetoric and poetics of the law*. University of Wisconsin Press, 1985 at p. 35.

7 Probert, Walter. "Law and persuasion: The language-behavior of lawyers." *University of Pennsylvania Law Review* 108, no. 1 (1959): 35–58, at pp. 41, 44, and 49. See also, Probert, Walter. "Words consciousness: Law and the control of language." *Case Western Reserve Law Review* 23 (1971): 374.

8 See, Everard, Mark, Paul Johnston, David Santillo, and Chad Staddon. "The role of ecosystems in mitigation and management of Covid-19 and other zoonoses." *Environmental Science & Policy* 111 (2020): 7–17.

9 One should truly blanche to learn that, in the 165 years since the *Origin of Species* was written, Darwin's influence on the common law has been literally nonexistent. Only three published cases even cite to Darwin as a source of authority to support a scientific proposition, all three after 2004. One of the cases begrudges Darwin's work as support for the idea that behavioral, genetic, and phenotypic differences occur between hatchery and natural fish (Trout Unlimited v. Lohn, 2007 WL 1795036 (W.D. Wash. 2007)); a second case acknowledges that "disease, degeneration and death" are "normal," and "may even benefit some species" (In re Union Pacific R.R. Employment Practices Litigation, 378 F.Supp.2d 1139 (D. Neb. 2005)); and the third case accepts that many "life forms" are threatened by loss of ozone since "all species apparently evolved with ozone cover" (Covington v. Jefferson County, 358 F.3d 626 (9th Cir. 2004)). No case, however, from centuries of legal pronouncements, has troubled to acknowledge even fundamental aspects of natural selection, or note shared features between people and animals, or grasp even basic tenets about evolutionary relationships. Law has remained mired in an archaic insistence that "humans" are not "animals" at all and has even to the present day forced legal distinctions far more contrary to, than consistent with, well recognized evolutionary and biological principles.

10 Gregory, T. Ryan. "Understanding natural selection: Essential concepts and common misconceptions." *Evolution: Education and Outreach* 2, no. 2 (2009): 156–75.

11 Holton, Gerald James. *Science and anti-science*. Harvard University Press, 1993.

Envoi

In this book, I have raised at least four metaphors for the reader to reflect on.[1] One is *Theater*, where I equate lawyers with actors in a play, courtrooms with stages, and juries with audiences sitting in the hall. A second is *Transportation* where I equate the publication of opinions with trucks driving about on a crowded roadway, jurists and lawyers as drivers and loaders, and juries and the public as the scrambling pedestrians about to be run over or worse. A third is *The Marriage Ceremony*, where I equate a bride and groom with law and facts respectively, the lawyers, judge, and jury as ceremonial officiants, and the public face of law as the wedding guests. The fourth and most intricate one is *Cell Evolution*, where I equate law cases with generations of living cells, participants in the cases with cell organelles, and the published opinions of those cases with organisms composed of those cells.

But why all that metaphorical fuss? What additional value to an analysis in legal philosophy does even *one* metaphor impart, much less four? Why not just be direct, just talk about a lawyer as a lawyer and a case as a case? To me, the answer to that seemingly hard question is an easy one. The job I have assigned myself as author is not to be descriptive, to simply explain the "what" of what lawyers are or what cases are. I noted right at the beginning of my opening that this is not a technical writing. I aimed away from the lowercase and sought instead to be prescriptive and write in the uppercase, to *persuade*, and specifically to persuade the reader that style and argument and deceit "should be" a distinctive and exceptional component of a trial lawyer's work especially given where law practice historically stems from and where it might be headed toward. Hopefully, this book is filled to the brim with express and implied "shoulds." Persuasion, to me, demands active involvement by the listener to be persuaded, specifically, by being enticed to engage in the mental activity of drawing promising connections between supposedly unrelated concepts. Metaphors link complex concepts by complex imagery and the better that the listener can pictorially envision how two conceptual paths might have intersecting branches, that is, join in thought at identifying an important tangent, then the stronger the listener's chances of comprehending the salient points of the promoted concepts. Hence, metaphors enable all those "shoulds" to produce enriched comparisons and eventually to produce a greater understanding of an intended message.

To persuade in the particular way that I desired, and comparable to thousands of trial lawyers before me, I deliberately selected a unique style by which to do so. Let's call it *Nudging*, a derivation of the Yiddish/English word "nudzh" exquisitely defined by author Leo Rosten as "surreptitious, a kick under the table, a widening-of-the-eyes-accompanied-by-a-slight-tilt-of-the-head to indicate that the recipient . . . is being reminded: of a job to be done, or a nicety that has been overlooked, or a gaucherie committed by a third party, or the impossibility of swallowing what was just said."[2] An effective nudge cobbles together suggestion and conscience in a single pastiche, and floats options of desirable behavioral change conjoined with an insistence that the listener adopt the speaker's preference: "You want to go home and rethink your life."[3] The term's intimation of combining "nagging" and "judging" is deliberate; a critic's firm nudging, pushing, will have the most robust effect when the message has a compelling principle recognizable behind it—perhaps, for example, where important events from normal lives such as plays and weddings and driving cars are tendered as attractive models to urge listeners to favor one side of an important decision which they might be on the cusp of forming.

In my nudging, I urged your attention but also wished to avoid your alienation, and I recognized that writing, like closing, is not a dialogue—the reader doesn't get to talk back but can only listen and listen and listen, very much like a juror. Thus, I talked to myself as if I were you, I asked myself questions and answered my own questions, I interrupted myself, I inflamed and calmed, and I played to what I personally assessed are real human desires and real human worries, including the very pointed worry about whether the intentional deceiving of others, especially of uninformed laity by informed and licensed professionals, is something horribly, inexcusably wrong, or perhaps isn't as bad as it sounds.

I proposed not just one pattern in the world to be "on all fours" with another pattern but doubled down on that proposal by suggesting that patterns might correlate even across disciplines, spanning multiple fields of knowledge within science and out. In honor of my predecessors, I tried to imagine several tasks of capturing several imaginary lions in several types of imaginary cages but instead of using mathematical equations like Ording, or literary devices like Queneau, I used metaphors.

In other words, throughout my argument my especial kick under the table was offering choices of some familiar images and symbols commonly associated with familiar themes and insisting on their consideration as correlates as a way to draw attention to the power of style itself. So, the real question is this: as the reader, as the intended recipient of my carefully cited authorities, my carefully employed language choices, my carefully arranged layering and postulates of fantasy scenarios, and my carefully selected relative truths, just how impossible is it for you to "swallow what was just said"? Have my relative lies convinced you of my relative truths? What verdict are you ready to deliver?

Notes

1 Clearly there are other metaphors liberally sprinkled across these pages, including (a) associating arguments with arrows and targets, (b) comparing proof with fashioning a horse corral, (c) relating law to gameplaying, (d) proposing lawyers to be akin to architects, (e) suggesting that egos act similarly to growing plants, and (f) even a "nested," internal one where within the *Theater* metaphor I describe trial processes in terms of cargo-carrying ships floating from port to port. As is my prerogative, however, I have decided to lump, not split, the balance.

2 Rosten, Leo. *The new joys of Yiddish: Completely updated*. Three Rivers Press, 2001 at p. 273.

3 Obi-Wan Kenobi's instantaneously effective nudge uttered in *Star Wars: Episode II - Attack of the Clones*. 20th Century Studios, 2002.

Bibliography

Abbott, H. Porter. *The Cambridge introduction to narrative*. Cambridge University Press, 2020.

Akhtar, Salman, and Henri Parens. *Lying, cheating, and carrying on: Developmental, clinical, and sociocultural aspects of dishonesty and deceit*. Jason Aronson Inc, 2009.

Aristodemou, Maria. *Law, psychoanalysis, society: Taking the unconscious seriously*. Routledge, 2014.

Baron, Jane B. "The many promises of storytelling in law: An essay review of narrative and the legal discourse: A reader in storytelling and the law." *Rutgers Law Journal* 23 (1991): 79.

Barrett, Deirdre. *Supernormal stimuli: How primal urges overran their evolutionary purpose*. WW Norton & Company, 2010.

Beth, Loren P. *Landmarks of law. Highlights of legal opinion* (R.D. Henson, ed.). Harper & Brothers, 1960.

Bourne, Kylie. "Commanding and controlling protest crowds." *Critical Horizons* 12, no. 2 (2011): 189.

Calabresi, Guido. "The exclusionary rule." *Harvard Journal of Law & Public Policy* 26 (2003): 111.

Caldwell, H. Mitchell, L. Timothy Perrin, and Christopher L. Frost. "The art and architecture of closing argument." *Tulane Law Review* 76 (2001): 961.

Caplan, David. *Language: Structure, processing, and disorders*. The MIT Press, 1992.

Case, Ermine Cowles. *The dilemma of the paleontologist*. University of Michigan Press, 1951.

Cheyney, Edward P. "The court of star chamber." *The American Historical Review* 18, no. 4 (1913): 727.

Conaway, Teresa L., Carol L. Mutz, and Joann M. Ross. "Jury nullification: A selective, annotated bibliography." *Valparaiso University Law Review* 39 (2004): 393.

Cutler, Anne. "The perception of rhythm in spoken and written language." In *Cognition on cognition* (Jacques Mehler and Susana Franck, eds.). MIT Press, 1995, pp. 283–8.

Daicoff, Susan Swaim. *Lawyer, know thyself: A psychological analysis of personality strengths and weaknesses*. American Psychological Association, 2004.

Dawkins, Richard, and J.R. Krebs. "Animal signals: information or manipulation?" In *Behavioural ecology: An evolutionary approach* (J.R. Krebs and N.B. Davies, eds.). Sinauer, 1987, pp. 380–402.

Dewey, John, and James Hayden Tufts. *Ethics*. Good Press, 2019.

Donohue, William A. "Analyzing negotiation tactics: Development of a negotiation interact system." *Human Communication Research* 7, no. 3 (1981): 273.

Duckler, Geordie. *Juris zoology: A dissection of animals as legal objects*. Rowman & Littlefield, 2022.

Endersby, Jim. "Lumpers and splitters: Darwin, Hooker, and the search for order." *Science* 326, no. 5959 (2009): 1496.

Everard, Mark, Paul Johnston, David Santillo, and Chad Staddon. "The role of ecosystems in mitigation and management of Covid-19 and other zoonoses." *Environmental Science & Policy* 111 (2020): 7.

Farnsworth, E. Allan. *An introduction to the legal system of the United States*. Oxford University Press, 2010.

Frankfurt, Harry G. *Freedom of the will and the concept of a person*. Humana Press, 1988.

Friedman, Lawrence M. "Law and its language" *The George Washington Law Review* 33 (1964): 563.

Friedman, Lawrence M. "Lexitainment: Legal process as theater." *DePaul Law Review* 50 (2000): 539.

Fuller, Lon L. *The law in quest of itself.* The Lawbook Exchange, Ltd., 1999.

Gershman, Kenneth A., Jeffrey J. Sacks, and John C. Wright. "Which dogs bite? A case-control study of risk factors." *Pediatrics* 93, no. 6 (1994): 913.

Gobert, James J. "In search of the impartial jury." *Journal of Criminal Law and Criminology* 79 (1988): 269.

Gotoff, Harold. "Oratory: The art of illusion." *Harvard Studies in Classical Philology* 95 (1993): 289.

Gould, Stephen Jay. *Wonderful life: The Burgess Shale and the nature of history*. WW Norton & Company, 1989.

Grant, Peter R. "Ecology and evolution of Darwin's Finches (Princeton Science Library Edition)." In *Ecology and evolution of Darwin's finches (princeton science library edition)*. Princeton University Press, 2017.

Green, Leon. "Blindfolding the jury." *Texas Law Review* 33 (1954): 157.

Gregory, T. Ryan. "Understanding natural selection: Essential concepts and common misconceptions." *Evolution: Education and Outreach* 2, no. 2 (2009): 156–75.

Griffin, Donald R. *Animal minds: Beyond cognition to consciousness*. University of Chicago Press, 2001.

Gross, Matthias, and Linsey McGoey, eds. *Routledge international handbook of ignorance studies*. Routledge, 2015.

Gustafson, Sandra M. *Eloquence is power: oratory and performance in early America*. UNC Press Books, 2012.

Haack, Susan. *Evidence matters: Science, proof, and truth in the law*. Cambridge University Press, 2014.

Hastie, Reid, Steven Penrod, and Nancy Pennington. *Inside the jury*. The Lawbook Exchange, Ltd., 2002.

Hirshman, Elliot, and Robert A. Bjork. "The generation effect: Support for a two-factor theory." *Journal of Experimental Psychology: Learning, Memory, and Cognition* 14, no. 3 (1988): 484.

Ho, Hock Lai. *A philosophy of evidence law: Justice in the search for truth*. Oxford University Press, 2008.

Hoage, Robert J. *Perceptions of animals in American culture*. Smithsonian Press, 1989.

Hobbs, Pamela. "'Is that what we're here about?': A lawyer's use of impression management in a closing argument at trial." *Discourse & Society* 14, no. 3 (2003): 273.

Hoeken, Hans, and Mario Van Vliet. "Suspense, curiosity, and surprise: How discourse structure influences the affective and cognitive processing of a story." *Poetics* 27, no. 4 (2000): 277.

Hofstadter, Douglas. *Strange loops*. Basic Books, 2007.

Holmes, Oliver Wendell. "The path of the law." *Harvard Law Review* 110, no. 5 (1897).
Holton, Gerald James. *Science and anti-science*. Harvard University Press, 1993.
Horowitz, Alexandra. "Theory of mind in dogs? Examining method and concept." *Learning & Behavior* 39 (2011): 314.
Hyman, Neil S. "Strict liability for damage caused by animals." *Loyola Law Review* 21 (1975): 785.
Irwin, Terence. "The development of ethics: A historical and critical study." In *The philosophical forum*, vol. 42, no. 3. Blackwell Publishing Inc., 2011, pp. 269–335.
Isaacs, Nathan. "Limits of judicial discretion." *Yale Law Journal* 32 (1922): 339.
Israel, S., and B. Goldman. "Opinions: Essays on lawyering, litigation and arbitration, the placebo effect, *Chutzpah*, and related matters." (2016) (self-published).
Joyce, James. *Ulysses*. Modern Library, 1934.
Katcher, Aaron Honori, and Alan M. Beck, eds. *New perspectives on our lives with companion animals*. University of Pennsylvania Press, 1983.
Kerr, Norbert L., and Robert M. Bray. *The psychology of the courtroom: An introduction*. Academic Press, 1982.
Kosslyn, Stephen M., William L. Thompson, and Giorgio Ganis. *The case for mental imagery*. Oxford University Press, 2006.
Krauss, Daniel A. *Jury psychology: Social aspects of trial processes: Psychology in the courtroom*, Vol. 1. Routledge, 2016.
LaMay, Craig L. "Covering the notorious case: Narrative and the need for sensationalism done well." In *Institutional failures*. Routledge, 2016, pp. 167–86.
Landsman, Stephan. "A brief survey on the development of the adversary system." *Ohio State Law Journal* 44 (1983): 713.
Langevoort, Donald C., and Robert K. Rasmussen. "Skewing the results: The role of lawyers in transmitting legal rules." *Southern California Interdisciplinary Law Journal* 5 (1996): 375.
Layard, P. Richard G. *Cost-benefit analysis*. Cambridge University Press, 1994.
Leach, Amy. *Things that are: Essays*. Milkweed Editions, 2012.
Mackay, Charles. *Extraordinary popular delusions and the madness of crowds*. Simon and Schuster, 2012 (originally published in 1841).
Mahon, James Edwin. "Two definitions of lying." *International Journal of Applied Philosophy* 22, no. 2 (2008): 211–30.
Mansbridge, Jane J. *Beyond adversary democracy*. University of Chicago Press, 1983.
McClain, Emlin. "Classification of the law for lawyers." *American Law Review* 26 (1892): 223.
McDermott, Josh H. "Auditory preferences and aesthetics: Music, voices, and everyday sounds." In *Neuroscience of preference and choice*. Academic Press, 2012, pp. 227–56.
Meinesz, Alexandre. *How life began: Evolution's three geneses*. University of Chicago Press, 2019.
Melville, Herman. *Moby Dick*. Modern Library. (First published in 1851).
Michael, Helen K. "Role of natural law in early American constitutionalism: Did the founders contemplate judicial enforcement of unwritten individual rights, The." *NCL Review* 69 (1990): 421.
Midgley, Mary. *Science and poetry*. Routledge, 2013.
Miklósi, Ádám. *Dog behaviour, evolution, and cognition*. Oxford University Press, 2014.
Miller, Malcolm E., George C. Christensen, and Howard E. Evans. "Anatomy of the dog." *Academic Medicine* 40, no. 4 (1965): 400.

Minow, Martha. *Making all the difference: Inclusion, exclusion, and American law*. Cornell University Press, 1990.
Mitchell, Robert W., and Nicholas S. Thompson, eds. *Deception: Perspectives on human and nonhuman deceit*. State University of New York Press, 1986.
Morgan, Marina, and John Palmer. "Dog bites." *Bmj* 334, no. 7590 (2007): 413.
Morris, Charles. *Famous orators of the world and their best orations*. WE Scull, 1902.
Neumann, Sigmund. "The rule of the demagogue." *American Sociological Review* 3, no. 4 (1938): 487.
O'Connor, D. J. "Emergent properties." In *Old and new questions in physics, cosmology, philosophy, and theoretical biology: Essays in honor of Wolfgang Yourgrau*. Springer US, 2015, pp. 719–32.
Ong, Walter J. *Orality and literacy*. Routledge, 2013.
Ording, Philip. *99 Variations on a proof*. Princeton University Press, 2019.
Pease, Barbara, and Allan Pease. *The definitive book of body language: The hidden meaning behind people's gestures and expressions*. Bantam, 2008.
Pétard, Hector. "A contribution to the mathematical theory of big game hunting." *The American Mathematical Monthly* 45 (1938): 446.
Pinker, Steven. *The language instinct: How the mind creates language*. Penguin UK, 2003.
Potter, Mary C. "Remembering." In *Thinking: An invitation to cognitive science, Vol. 3*. (Daniel N. Osherson and Edward E. Smith, eds.). The MIT Press, 1990.
Pound, Roscoe. "Classification of law." *Harvard Law Review* 37, no. 8 (1924): 933.
Proctor, Robert N., and Londa Schiebinger. *Agnotology: The making and unmaking of ignorance*. Stanford University Press, 2008.
Queneau, Raymond. *Exercises in style*. Alma Books, 2018.
Raff, Rudolf A. *The shape of life: Genes, development, and the evolution of animal form*. University of Chicago Press, 2012.
Rawls, John. *Justice as fairness: A restatement*. Harvard University Press, 2001.
Renteln, Alison Dundes, and Alan Dundes, eds. *Folk law: Essays in the theory and practice of lex non scripta*, Vol. 1. University of Wisconsin Press, 1995.
Rhode, Deborah L. *The beauty bias: The injustice of appearance in life and law*. Oxford University Press, 2010.
Rollin, Bernard E. *The Frankenstein syndrome: Ethical and social issues in the genetic engineering of animals*. Cambridge University Press, 1995.
Saarni, C., and M. Lewis. "Deceit and illusion in human affairs." In *Lying and deception in everyday life* (Michael Lewis and Carolyn Saarni, eds.). Guilford Press, 1993.
Schlagel, Richard H. "Contextualistic realism." *Philosophy and Phenomenological Research* 41, no. 4 (1981): 437–51.
Sharp, Lesley A. *Animal ethos: The morality of human-animal encounters in experimental lab science*. University of California Press, 2018.
Sherman, Josepha. *Storytelling: An encyclopedia of mythology and folklore*. Routledge, 2015.
Shuler, Carrie M., Emilio E. DeBess, Jodi A. Lapidus, and Katrina Hedberg. "Canine and human factors related to dog bite injuries." *Journal of the American Veterinary Medical Association* 232, no. 4 (2008): 542.
Simpson, George Gaylord. *The principles of classification and a classification of mammals*, Vol. 85. American Museum of Natural History, 1945.
Siu, Ralph Gun Hoy. *The portable dragon*. MIT Press, 1971.

Smith, Edward E. "Categorization." In *Thinking: An invitation to cognitive science, Vol. 3.* (Daniel N. Osherson and Edward E. Smith, eds.), The MIT Press, 1990.
Solan, Lawrence M. "Lawyers as insincere (but truthful) actors." *Journal of the Legal Profession* 36 (2011): 487.
Solan, Lawrence M. *The language of judges*. University of Chicago Press, 2010.
Stavrianos, C., D. Tatsis, P. Stavrianou, A. Karamouzi, G. Mihail, and D. Mihailidou. "Intercanine distance as a recognition method of bite marks." *Research Journal of Biological Sciences* 6, no. 1 (2011): 25.
Sterelny, Kim. *The evolved apprentice*. MIT Press, 2012.
Stuntz, William J. "Virtues and vices of the exclusionary rule, The." *Harvard Journal of Law & Public Policy* 20 (1996): 443.
Summers, Robert S. "Formal legal truth and substantive truth in judicial fact-finding--their justified divergence in some particular cases." *Law and Philosophy* 18 (1999): 497.
Timberlake, William "Constructing animal Cognition." In *The cognitive animal: Empirical and theoretical perspectives on animal cognition* (Marc Bekoff, Colin Allen, and Gordon M. Burghardt, eds.). MIT Press, 2002, pp. 105–13.
Toulmin, Stephen E. *The uses of argument*. Cambridge University Press, 2003.
Unger, Peter. *Ignorance: A case for scepticism*. Oxford University Press, 1978.
Veblen, Thorstein. "The beginnings of ownership." *American Journal of Sociology* 4, no. 3 (1898): 352.
Vesey-FitzGerald, Brian. *The book of the dog*. Borden Publishing Company, 1948.
Walker, Lenore E., David Shapiro, Stephanie Akl, Lenore E. Walker, David Shapiro, and Stephanie Akl. "Jury selection and psychology of the trial." *Introduction to Forensic Psychology: Clinical and Social Psychological Perspectives* (2020): 337.
Wall, Tyler. "Legal terror and the police dog." *Radical Philosophy* 188, no. 2 (2014): 2.
Walsh, Froma. "Human-animal bonds I: The relational significance of companion animals." *Family Process* 48, no. 4 (2009): 462.
Walton, Douglas. *Appeal to expert opinion: Arguments from authority*. Penn State Press, 2010.
Walton, Douglas. *The place of emotion in argument*. Penn State Press, 2010.
Watts, Alan. *The way of Zen*. Vintage, 1999.
White, James Boyd. *Heracles' bow: Essays on the rhetoric and poetics of the law*. University of Wisconsin Press, 1985.
Williams, David M., and Malte C. Ebach. *Cladistics*, Vol. 88. Cambridge University Press, 2020.
Williams, Glanville. "Language and the Law-I." *LQ Review* 61 (1945): 71.
Windt, Jennifer M. *Dreaming: A conceptual framework for philosophy of mind and empirical research*. MIT Press, 2015.
Woese, Carl R. "On the evolution of cells." *Proceedings of the National Academy of Sciences* 99, no. 13 (2002): 8742.
Woodfield, Andrew. *Teleology*. Cambridge University Press, 1976.
Worringer, Wilhelm. *Abstraction and empathy: A contribution to the psychology of style*. Ivan R. Dee, 1997.
Zande, Daniel L. Vande. "Coercive power and the demise of the star chamber." *American Journal of Legal History* 50, no. 3 (2010): 326.

Index

About the Author

Dr. **Geordie Duckler** received his master's in journalism from University of Oregon in 1984, his law degree from Northwestern School of Law at Lewis and Clark College in 1987, and his doctorate in biology from UCLA in 1997. As a vertebrate paleontologist specializing in the decline of Ice Age megafauna, his dissertation and scientific publications contributed to better assessments of prehistoric animal health and comparisons with the evolution of biological stresses in endangered species. He established the first use of Harris lines as a health indicator for large mammals, and his original research on cranial and masticatory musculature of felids raised in captivity helped found baselines for predator health in zoo environments.

At the same time, as a trial attorney practicing for over thirty-eight years, Geordie has operated a nationally unique law practice engaged exclusively in the litigation and defense of animal-related disputes in state and federal courts. His diverse clientele includes pet owners, animal shelters, recreational riders, commercial farmers, ranchers, neighborhood associations, specialty breeders, equine stable owners, animal welfare activists, hunters and sportspeople, exotic owners, zoo and aquarium owners, consumers, veterinarian clients, bite and attack victims, and accused persons on animal neglect, abuse, and abandonment criminal charges. The most well-known animal law attorney in the nation, Geordie has litigated over 3,000 animal cases, including arguing over 100 jury trials. He has handled cases in thirty of the fifty states, and has argued appeals to the Oregon Court of Appeals, the Oregon Supreme Court, and the Eighth and Ninth Circuit Court of Appeals.

Geordie has also written extensively on animal law issues, including authoring ten seminal law review articles in the field throughout the 1980s and 1990s, and publishing his first book, *Juris Zoology*, in 2022. He has taught law school courses on animal law, written popular magazine articles, and presented state bar CLE programs on animal law, and has been profiled in innumerable newspapers, magazines, television shows, and radio programs about animal law issues and his cases, including in *The National Law Journal*, Court TV Radio, Geraldo, Newsweek, *The New Yorker*, *Playboy*, Bark, National Public Radio, and the BBC, and he has appeared as an expert in two National Geographic documentaries on prehistoric predators.

www.ingramcontent.com/pod-product-compliance
Ingram Content Group UK Ltd.
Pitfield, Milton Keynes, MK11 3LW, UK
UKHW020210290926
15470UKWH00001B/102

9 781666 954111